Take Down Flag & Feed Horses

Take Down Flag & Feed Horses ♘♘

Bill Everhart

University of Illinois Press

Urbana and Chicago

© 1998 by the Board of Trustees of the University of Illinois
Manufactured in the United States of America
1 2 3 4 5 C P 5 4 3 2 1

This book is printed on acid-free paper.

Library of Congress Cataloging-in-Publication Data
Everhart, William C.
Take down flag & feed horses / Bill Everhart.
p.   cm.
ISBN 0-252-02379-X (alk. paper). —
ISBN 0-252-06681-2 (pbk. : alk. paper)
1. Yellowstone National Park—Description and travel—Anecdotes.
2. Everhart, William C.—Anecdotes.   3. Park rangers—Yellowstone
National Park—Anecdotes.   I. Title.
F722.E92   1998
978.7′52—dc21   97-21146
CIP

Contents

Part 2: The Fires That Wouldn't Die, 1988

Acknowledgments

I owe my greatest debt to the Yellowstone staff members with whom I talked and traveled and socialized, notebook at the ready, during the summer I lived in the park and on subsequent visits. Most of these people appear in the book; those who do not would have had space permitted: Superintendents Bob Barbee and John Townsley, assistant superintendent Bob Haraden; assistants to the superintendent Mac Berg and Paul Schullery; information officer Joan Anzelmo; concessions management chief Buddy Surles; chief rangers Tom Hobbs and Roger Siglin; rangers Deborah Bird, Gary Brown, Tim Blank, Ted Bucknall, Terry Danforth, Duane McClure, Jerry Mernin, Dave Milhalic, Paul Miller, Dale Nuss, Jerry Phillips, and Roger Rudolph; fire cache chief Jim Sweaney; storehouse chief Ed Wolfe; seasonal rangers Jim Barker, Doug Haake, Mary Lynch, and Marianna Young; chief naturalists Al Mebane and George Robinson; naturalists Norm Bishop, Margaret Short, John Tyers, and Frank Walker; historians Tony Dean and Tim Manns; seasonal naturalist Bill Lewis; seasonal historian John Whitman; and scientists Don Despain, Rick Hutchinson, Mary Meagher, John Varley, and the Swan Lady, Ruth Shea. And I am particularly obliged to the following spouses: Bev Blank, a snowbound urbanite; Jean Mebane, sausage maker supreme; Nancy Rudolph, accomplished photographer and writer; and Elaine Townsley, a hard-pressed but gracious hostess.

Former Yellowstone employees who looked back to the good old days with much affection and a certain objectivity (and the positions they held) include Horace Albright, Park Service founding father and first civilian superintendent after the army era; superintendent Jack Anderson; chief ranger George Baggley; assistant chief rangers Scotty Chapman and George Miller; ranger Howard Chapman; chief naturalist John Good; and naturalist Stan Cantor.

Three former directors, Russ Dickenson, Gary Everhardt, and George Hartzog, former associate director Boyd Evison, and present deputy director Deny Galvin, recalling their attempts to change timeworn procedures in Yellowstone, agreed the experience was not unlike making love to a porcupine.

I owe a special debt to John Bryant, then president of the National Park Foundation, for a grant that enabled me to live for three months in Yellowstone in relative comfort.

Anyone who writes about the history of Yellowstone must acknowledge a debt to Aubrey Haines, and I do so here. I discussed the thorny matter of concessions operations with president of the Yellowstone Park Company John Amerman; Snow Lodge manager Gregg Smith; winterkeeper Dave Smith; and employees Tom Sherman and Bruce Weeter. Group leader Andy Wolfe gave me a firsthand report of how the investigation and report of his Park Service team paved the way for government acquisition of the troubled Yellowstone Park Company, a monumental accomplishment.

And, finally, I am grateful beyond words to Mary Everhart, and not only for typing all those handwritten drafts. She brought to bear a perfect literary pitch and never doubted the outcome of our enterprise. Her project was put on disk by Shirley Schainblatt.

I have written this acknowledgment only a few days from March 1, 1997, the 125th anniversary of the signing of the Yellowstone Act by President Ulysses S. Grant in 1872. It seems to me the park that is the scene of this book deserves the ultimate tribute. Yellowstone! The name itself conjures up visions of a mysterious country of spectacular contradictions. In its beginning years the park was awarded the nickname "Wonderland" after a popular story of the day, *Alice's Adventures in Wonderland*. British writer V. S. Pritchett believed some place names are "siren songs of geography," capable of pulling armchair travelers to their feet. He may have had Yellowstone in mind when he said it is also a matter "of syllables that run like a tune."

Introduction

I'd like to attribute my interest in history to a neighbor in my hometown of Gettysburg, Pennsylvania. An octogenarian who always wore a black suit and kept his small white beard neatly trimmed, William C. Storrick was a retired teacher whose book *The Battle of Gettysburg* was sold in every souvenir shop in town. Youngsters who lived nearby were of two minds about the person we called Old Man Storrick. He might, without stern rebuke, allow you to retrieve a ball accidentally kicked into his front yard — or he might not. If you were polite and careful about his rose bushes, he might unbend and chat for a moment, although a conversation was difficult because he was near to being stone deaf.

Born on a farm outside Gettysburg, he and his family had fled as the Union and Confederate armies collided there. He was then a boy of seven. Most all his friends and neighbors, myself included, heard him tell of this experience and of being present at the dedication of the Soldiers' National Cemetery a few months later, described by a contemporary in the foreword to Storrick's book: "He recalls going to Gettysburg on November 19, standing with his hand clasped in his father's, watching a doorway from which the President of the United States was shortly to appear. He shook hands with Lincoln, was awed by his great height, and listened eagerly to his plain and simple address."

There is no excuse, except youth, that Storrick's account of these momentous events didn't have the impact on me it should have had. But his experience was not unique. Other town residents had been driven from their homes by the battle and heard Lincoln speak. Their recollections often appeared in the *Gettysburg Times*. The battlefield, surrounding the town, was familiar ground. After farmers plowed in the spring it was possible to walk the furrows and pick up the conical lead bullets used by both sides. On the seventy-fifth anniversary of the battle, in 1938, more than a thousand veterans, Union and Confederate, were housed in a large tent camp and participated in the ceremonies, mostly in wheelchairs. I remember walking along the boardwalks and listening to their stories. (The *Times* marveled at their consumption of hard liquor.) Growing up in Gettysburg, one of my teachers remarked, was a constant history lesson.

At Gettysburg College I majored in English, attracted by exceptional teachers, and minored in sports, playing a little basketball and setting a new college record in the hundred-yard dash. It's possible my priorities were the other way around. I entered college in September 1939, the month World War II began. During my freshman year, Holland and Belgium fell to the German blitzkrieg, the British army barely escaped capture at Dunkirk, and the Battle of Britain followed swiftly. Those were troubling times to concentrate on studies, and when the Japanese bombed Pearl Harbor the studies didn't seem important or relevant. The next year, I enlisted, received infantry basic training, and sailed from New York in a giant convoy that extended from horizon to horizon.

My division, the 78th, landed at Bournemouth, England, in October 1944. On a weekend pass I experienced London during the blackout, one of the largest cities in the world without a light showing. We traveled through France in "Forty and Eights," tiny boxcars used in World War I to carry forty soldiers and eight horses. We ate Thanksgiving dinner standing in freezing rain in a Belgian orchard bivouac we called "Camp Mud." German V-1 buzz bombs targeted for London roared directly overhead, trailing long streamers of sparks. Aachen, Germany, capital of Charlemagne's empire, was unrecognizable as a city. Our transport trucks followed a single roadway bulldozed through endless piles of rubble, depositing us in the combat zone. Trudging through the knee-deep snow of the Ardennes Forest, we occupied the foxholes of a worn-out division. A few days later, December 16, the Battle of the Bulge began. On March 1, 1945, during a disputed crossing of the Roer, the last river before the Rhine, I suffered a badly damaged knee and was flown back to England, to an American field hospital in Herefordshire.

Beginning an extended convalescence just as spring arrived in the English countryside, I wrote home for my favorite college text: Hall and Albion's *History of England.* Each morning after I was able to hobble about I carried my book and a folding camp stool through grass greener than I'd ever seen before, through a patch of yellow buttercups to a hedge frequented by finches. I was grateful to be alive, and that gave me a sense of purpose I'd lacked in college. Reflecting upon the things I'd seen, and that I'd fought in the greatest of all wars, I promised myself that once I got stateside I'd do something serious about history.

After completing a master's degree in history at Penn State, I was accepted as a doctoral candidate at the University of Pennsylvania. The head of the history department, Roy Franklin Nichols, winner of a Pulitzer Prize for his Civil War treatise *The Disruption of American Democracy*, was the most provocative of lecturers. His two-semester course, "The Civil War and Reconstruction," was the most popular in the graduate school. Flashing a wicked smile under a dense brown moustache, he announced that the origins of the American Civil War were traceable to the invasion of England by the Romans in 55 B.C., and there we began.

Nichols was an accomplished mimic and something of a ham actor, a scholar who gleaned much of his evidence from other than the standard sources. At the end of the first semester we were in Kansas with John Brown, years away from the outbreak of the Civil War. The second semester ended with the surrender of Robert E. Lee at Appomattox Court House and a half-hearted apology, "We didn't get to Reconstruction this year, either." The class stood as one and applauded. If I didn't learn anything about Reconstruction from Nichols, I learned something else I have never forgotten: The secret of history is in the power of the story.

By chance, I encountered Fred Tilberg in Gettysburg while home for a weekend visit during my first year at the University of Pennsylvania. Fred and I knew each other casually, as people do in small towns. His wife had been my high school biology teacher, his brother dean of students at the college, and Fred, always seen in his green Park Service uniform, was the battlefield historian. He knew I was a graduate student, and after we talked a while he offered me a summer job as a ranger historian.

My duty station was Little Round Top, that craggy, boulder-strewn eminence on the extreme left of the Union line, scene of so much smoke and fury and slaughter on the second day of the battle. I enjoyed being a park interpreter. (Early on, the Park Service decided to use the term *interpretation* instead of education to eliminate any suggestion of formal instruction.) I liked talking to interested—and interesting—people at a place where history had happened. I soon found I had a lot to learn, for the Civil War is a dauntingly large canvas. On my first day on the job I got into deep water talking with a well-informed man about the confusing route that Gen. James Longstreet had followed bringing his troops into battle. Unexpectedly, he asked where Stonewall Jackson had been wounded. At Chancellorsville, I told him. "No, no," he said impatiently. "I mean where in the body?"

Near the end of my second year at Philadelphia, Fred lost his assistant to the Korean War, and I was offered the job. At the time I fully intended to finish the Ph.D. and teach on the college level but thought a year or two with the Park Service might be good experience. Besides, I needed to put a little money aside. I was nearing thirty and didn't even own a car. The day I informed Professor Nichols of my decision he was surprisingly charitable, considering I had only the orals and dissertation ahead. But it wasn't his nature to resist a parting quip. "Too bad about Everhart," he told a seminar class in my presence. "Going to Gettysburg to dig up buttons and bayonets."

I was warmly welcomed by the staff at Gettysburg National Military Park. The mood was congenial and the pace unhurried. Our offices and a dreadful old museum were located far from the battlefield on the second floor of the town's post office. The museum attracted little public attention. Freeman Tilden, a perceptive observer of Park Service interpretation, may have had one like it in mind when he told several of us one day that he sympathized with people who were leery of history museums. It's unsettling, he said, to come upon a letter from Lord Nelson to Lady Hamilton stored between a clarinet and a stuffed eagle.

Fred was an old-fashioned individual, trimly built and orderly to a fault, even in conversation, every fact carefully arranged. Once when he was on a ladder in the museum, hanging a newly acquired painting, I unwisely asked him a question. He came down the ladder, laid the picture and hammer and nails on the relief map, thought for a bit, answered in the affirmative, and climbed back up the ladder with his paraphernalia. He threatened to make the battle hard going for me, but I had no intention of memorizing the names of all Union and Confederate regimental commanders and the location of three thousand monuments in the park. Instead, I spent as much time as possible with the superintendent, Walter Coleman.

About the only thing Walter and Fred had in common was a Ph.D. in history. Walter was as liberal as Fred was conservative, a balding, comfortably padded, ruddy-faced raconteur with a raffish sense of humor and a dislike of physical exercise. He discovered in me that rare find, a good listener, for his inexhaustible store of Civil War anecdotes, both comical and moving. He introduced me to Bruce Catton's first book, *Mr. Lincoln's Army*. We agreed that Catton, a journalist, wrote our kind of history, with a style so vivid the muskets exploded off the pages. My talks to visitors were flavored with vignettes borrowed from Walter and Bruce Catton.

The first winter at Gettysburg, a time of year when visitors are few, Walter assigned me to write a history of Harpers Ferry. Located where the Potomac and Shenandoah rivers opened a passageway through the Blue

Ridge Mountains, raided by John Brown, and coveted by both sides during the Civil War, the partially deserted old town had recently been designated a national monument by Congress. Gettysburg being the closest Park Service operation, Walter was in charge. It was an important opportunity for a new employee, because the study helped set the boundaries for the land acquisition program.

I'd just finished a year at Gettysburg when the Park Service offered me a new post at Vicksburg, Mississippi. There I stepped up to Fred's level and ran my own interpretive program. I regretted leaving Gettysburg, however. I'd grown fond of Fred and Walter, and I wondered where I would find such likable and out of the ordinary people again. The answer turned out to be everywhere I went in the Park Service.

Walter retired during the civil rights movement of the 1960s, choosing to teach for a while in a small North Carolina college. No one was surprised when he was arrested and jailed for leading a band of his students in a protest demonstration. Fred was working on his monumental history of the Gettysburg campaign before I arrived. He was still writing away after he retired and could be found at his desk in the library every day until failing health intervened. "Fred took too many notes," said a colleague.

I'd learned a great deal from my year at Gettysburg, leading tours of the magnificent old cyclorama painting of Pickett's Charge, hollering the high points in noisy school buses, and helping visitors to better understand the war that determined all citizens would be free and the Union indivisible. "The chief aim of interpretation," Tilden concluded, "is not instruction but provocation." If you would charm and inform, you must delight in sharing what you know. Rather than pronouncing truths gleaned from authorities, you would do better to convey your personal opinions, whatever they may be. To interpret is to give meaning.

ᴗ ᴗ

I joined the Park Service at an opportune time, because a long period of congressional neglect was coming to an end. Rationing of gasoline and tires during World War II had almost closed the parks. Two-thirds of the employees had been drafted or had gone into war production jobs. The explosive growth in tourist travel after the war almost swamped parks still operating on slender wartime budgets. The Korean War doomed relief. By 1953 parks were absorbing more than fifty million visitors with a staff level and the run-down facilities designed for seventeen million visitors in 1940. The grave situation provoked Bernard De Voto, the first conservationist in half a century to command a national audience, to offer a grim suggestion. "Let's close the national parks," he wrote in *Harper's Maga-zine*, since Congress and the public seemed unconcerned "so much of the priceless heritage which the Service must safeguard for the United States is beginning to go to hell."

Substantial staff and budget increases soon provided opportunities for advancement. In my first six years I received six different assignments. After Gettysburg and a year at Vicksburg, I was chosen for a management intern program in the Washington office. A year later I joined the Atlantic and Gulf Coast seashore survey as the project historian, then moved to Philadelphia to supervise the historians and curators preparing to restore and refurnish Independence Hall. There followed what I considered the luckiest break of all, a transfer to that noble city, San Francisco, to participate in the national survey of historic sites and buildings. Those years made me wonder what else the Park Service had in store for me. I wasn't to be disappointed.

I hadn't expected park work to be so adventurous. At the beginning of the seashore survey I'd asked the survey chief for guidelines to help me identify national seashore possibilities. A veteran of many investigations, he smiled and said, "You'll know one when you see it." Some months later I dived into the surf off Cumberland Island from a Coast Guard patrol boat and swam ashore, my sneakers tied around my neck. By the time the patrol boat picked me up ten hours later, after I had hiked miles of beaches and explored the live oak forests and salt marshes of the largest of Georgia's Golden Isles, I knew what my boss meant.

It will not come as a surprise that I soon decided that a career in the Park Service was more to my liking than a university professorship. Its duties were more diverse, and their results more tangible. Out of our seashore survey came seven national seashores, including Cumberland Island. One of the satisfactions of Park Service enterprises is seeing things get done that will bring delight to your grandchildren's grandchildren.

In those early assignments I learned something about my colleagues that ran counter to prevailing views of government employees. Park work has always attracted the unconstrained, who enjoy freedom and challenge. I wouldn't call them eccentrics, but in my time they possessed something of the unpredictability and dash attributed to left-handed pitchers, taxi drivers, and the Gabor sisters, the kind of people Charles Kuralt would have enjoyed. They added a distinctive flavor to an organization that gave them a certain amount of running room. The Park Service, I concluded, is an organization in which if a name is mentioned a story is bound to follow.

Take for example the first director, Steve Mather, a descendant of a Mayflower Puritan, *New York Sun* reporter, high-powered salesman for Twenty Mule Team Borax (a brand name he invented), millionaire businessman, and lover of national parks. Unhappy with conditions in Yosemite, where he had camped with his family, he wrote a complaint letter to the secretary of the interior and received a famous reply: "Dear Steve, If you don't like the way the national parks are being run, come on down to Washington and run them yourself." His freewheeling style and enormous success in publicizing the parks made him a national figure, "Steve Mather of the National Parks." He once gave reluctant approval for the Great Northern Railway to put up a sawmill during construction of the Many Glacier Hotel. He let the Great Northern have one extension, but when it requested another, after the hotel was already taking in tourists, he called in the trail crew and personally lit the fuse of the first of a dozen dynamite charges that blew the sawmill to kingdom come.

Toward the end of my second year in San Francisco I received a telephone call from George Hartzog, the highly regarded superintendent of the Gateway Arch project in St. Louis, offering me a job that I almost made the mistake of turning down. By then Mary and I (we married during my stay in Washington) had fallen in love with San Francisco, read Herb Caen's column in the *Chronicle* over coffee every morning, dined frequently on cold Dungeness crab picked up at Fisherman's Wharf for a dollar each, and caught the Kingston Trio at the Purple Onion on weekends. George, a formidable salesman, urged me not to miss the opportunity of a lifetime. If I stayed much longer in San Francisco, he warned, I'd lose my edge and vegetate "with the rest of the lotus eaters."

Now almost as venerated as Mather, George is worthy of a diversion. He grew up poor in rural South Carolina, where he, his first cousin, and the teacher's son constituted the first grade of a one-room school. His family was impoverished by the Great Depression, and the odd jobs he took to help out were a way of life in his teenaged years. Working as a secretary in a law office, he read law at night, passed the South Carolina bar examination, and may be one of the few practicing attorneys who never attended law school. An army officer during World War II, he went to Washington after his discharge to seek employment and received a bid from the Park Service. His first assignment, writing a law enforcement manual, brought him into contact with many chief rangers. They impressed him as individualistic, self-reliant men, "bound to a common code," and he began to think of the Park Service as a career.

I had met George in Washington and marked him as a comer. He was then assistant chief of concessions management, and his courtly southern charm only partly concealed an impatience to get on with the job. His later transfer to the position of assistant superintendent of Rocky Mountain National Park was a surprise. Those in the organization who diligently studied such moves, about nine-tenths of the work force, surmised that acquiring field experience was a part of George's career strategy and that sooner or later he would return to Washington and a much higher position.

The chance to be involved in the building of the St. Louis memorial to westward expansion was too attractive to turn down. I also looked forward to working for a man known to be prodigiously gifted. Before accepting the offer, however, I made a few telephone calls to persons who knew George. He had a furious work ethic and exceedingly high standards, I was told. One who hadn't handled a task George had assigned him particularly well described the grilling he received. "As the questioning began I could hear the saw biting into the floor around me."

Architect Eero Saarinen's incomparable stainless steel arch had won an international competition for the design of the Jefferson National Expansion Memorial. Congress grumbled for a decade before providing funds to build the "giant wicket," with the city of St. Louis providing one dollar for each three federal dollars. In 1959, after more senior Park Service administrators declined the honor, Hartzog was selected to head the devilishly complicated project. It required him to gain the cooperation of some thirty federal, state, and municipal entities and supervise construction of an arch of a scale never before contemplated and of a material never previously used for that purpose.

My job, greatly aided by an avid staff of historians, was to research and plan a museum that would tell the story of the exploration and settlement of the West in a space under the Arch as large as a football field with exhibits as compelling and provocative as the Arch itself, or nearly so. George and I made frequent trips to the Saarinen office outside Detroit. Eero was inspiring, approachable, and open to suggestions about anything other than matters of design—and on those he was like a block of granite. He once ended a heated argument caused when George objected to a late design change that would delay construction and increase costs by saying, "George, I can be difficult." Recognizing a fellow genius, but one of a different order, George yielded.

I was fascinated by the Saarinen model room, which contained a half-dozen cardboard models of the Arch, each eight feet tall and of a different configuration so slight as to be barely noticeable. Eero and his design team were searching for a profile that would make the completed arch, 630 feet high, appear to be "springing up" out of the ground rather than "squatting down," in Eero's phrase. The talk in the office was of good design and how to achieve it, not only in structures but also in graphics, landscaping, and interior furnishings. Next to the Arch models was one of the Dulles airport terminal, then under construction. It was a new world to me.

George knew how to get the best out of people, and he pushed you to the limit. In retrospect I don't think anyone else in the Park Service could have handled that contentious and complicated enterprise as well. He had a bias for bold action, making decisions almost instinctively while the rest of us were trying to puzzle them out. Quite familiar with the rules of good management, he knew they didn't apply to him. He had a low threshold for underachievers, and if you didn't come early and stay late he assumed you didn't like your job. We developed a friendship in St. Louis that has deepened and strengthened over the years, as is often the case between two people of differing abilities and personalities.

With our research program for the museum nearing completion, we began thinking about exhibit design. George and I had reservations about the quality of Park Service museums. A dozen or so were being built every year, as budget increases continued, but the more you saw of them the more skeptical you became. Being done in haste, all were beginning to look alike. Casting around for a solution, George and I hit upon the idea of having Saarinen design the exhibits based on our museum plan. Intrigued with the idea, Eero called in Charles Eames to help prepare a proposal. It seemed almost too good to be true, a collaboration between one of America's first-rank architects and the brilliant designer of furniture, films, and exhibitions for the Smithsonian and for world expositions.

The two were able to set aside several days from their busy schedules to work up the presentation. I was invited to attend as their "curator of history." Mostly, I was an enthralled spectator. I expected to hear original ideas and wasn't disappointed. Part of it, I decided, was an intelligent approach to thinking. Talking of the Lewis and Clark expedition, Charles said that he would like to somehow convey the scene in the White House when Thomas Jefferson first unrolled maps of the known portion of the West and said to his private secretary, Meriwether Lewis, "This is what I want you to do." Not bad, I thought, filing the idea away.

But the proposal Saarinen made to director Connie Wirth was flatly rejected. The Park Service already had the best exhibit designers in the country, Wirth declared. His pronouncement may have marked the low point of my Park Service career. One of the faults of bureaucracy is that when faced with criticism or change it tends to circle the wagons. George and I understood Connie's loyalty to his employees, but we believed his confidence in their products misplaced. We resolved that if we were ever in a position to do so we would change the way the Park Service approached museum design.

A couple of years later, Secretary of the Interior Stewart Udall named George Hartzog to succeed Wirth, who was retiring. "There was," Udall said, "a twinge of anguish among the old guard" when the decision was announced, "but I wanted more dynamism." There was also a lot of throat-clearing among more senior Park Service officials who were positioned, as they thought, to be considered. On the whole, yet with a little anxiety, employees welcomed Udall's choice, feeling that although Connie had done an excellent job it was time for a younger man to take a fresh look at the way the organization functioned. George did just that. To an agency with a reverence for the old and a selected acceptance of the new, he brought all that machinery for disturbing the status quo. Under him, the Park Service became less predictable and more responsive.

Udall and Hartzog were the same age, forty-three, and both were small-town lawyers. They quickly formed an effective partnership. Surely things have rarely gone so right for the Park Service as they did during the Udall-Hartzog years. Udall, whose name deserves to be linked to that other great interior secretary, Harold Ickes, was an eloquent spokesman for environmental sanity. Wallace Stegner, who served as chair of the interior department's Advisory Board on National Parks, was greatly impressed by Hartzog's knowledge of how things get done in Washington and his skill in maneuvering legislation through the Congress. "George Hartzog proved himself one of the toughest, savviest, and most effective bureau chiefs who ever operated in that political alligator-hole," he wrote. During Hartzog's term as director, from 1964 to 1972, sixty-eight new parks were added to the system, the largest expansion in history. "Ranger," John McPhee's profile of George in the September 11, 1971, *New Yorker* demonstrated that the massive machinery of the federal government will yield to pressure from a fearless and powerful personality.

Soon after George was sworn in as director, we were sitting in his big corner office on the third floor of Interior. It was after-hours, and we may have been relaxing with something tall and cool from his private pantry. He was discussing his plans for some new faces on the "Hall of Heroes," as the corridor containing his directorate was commonly referred to in the parks, with sarcasm intended. On his desk was a copy of "Road to the Future." After St. Louis I was assigned to the task force that had prepared this long-range plan for the Park Service. Studying the plan, George said he'd detected my fine hand in the section recommending that production of all museum exhibits, films, and publications be placed under a single head. Reminding me of the pledge we'd made in St. Louis, he said, "Here's our chance," and he offered me the position of assistant director for interpretation.

The next few years were the busiest of my life, reorganizing a large and complex staff, recruiting new talent, traveling to the parks with what we called our "dog and pony show" to prepare the field for new products, and constructing a design center to house the operation—a great idea first advanced by Vince Gleason. In 1970 we opened the doors of the new facility on a high bluff overlooking the Shenandoah River, adjacent to the Mather Training Center at Harpers Ferry. Housing nearly a hundred editors and a hundred editors and cartographers, graphic designers and curators, and film producers and photographers, the Harpers Ferry Center appeared on the cover of January 1971 *American Institute of Architects Journal*, along with an article titled "Our Park Service Serves Architecture Well."

By painting the building ourselves we saved enough money to purchase furniture of a style seldom seen in a federal building. There were no clocks on the wall, no dress code, and the mood was relaxed, a community of craftsmen in pursuit of excellence. "It was touch and go," an agency publication would note later of our early years, "as new films, exhibits, and publications sent shock waves of surprise and some outrage through the Service's conservative ranks. Hartzog's support and a shower of awards from professional organizations gradually warmed the climate." In 1990 the Harpers Ferry Center celebrated its twentieth anniversary. During the ceremonies I was again reminded that at times the Park Service seems more like a tribal clan than a federal agency. Beside the entrance to the building, a stainless steel plaque was unveiled bearing my name.

∪ ∪

I retired in 1977, the day I was eligible. (Reluctantly, I'd left the Harpers Ferry Center and served two directors as a special assistant for policy.) It wasn't an easy decision, but after twenty-seven years there were other things I wanted to try. An offer from Clemson University to serve as a visiting professor for an academic year, beginning in 1978, fit in with another project I wanted to undertake. I believed Park Service people were worthy of a book.

I hadn't figured out how to go about it until John Townsley, superintendent of Yellowstone, dropped by my office a few months before I retired. We knew each other well, our paths having crossed frequently, and he wanted to know about my plans. I told him of the book idea and that I might want to concentrate on one park, maybe live there for a summer.

A staunch Yellowstone advocate, John urged me to consider Yellowstone. "Let me think it over," I said, seeing no reason to tell him it was my first choice. His offer of an apartment in park headquarters—at the going rate—was the clincher. "Mix with the staff," John advised. "Get to know them and see Yellowstone through their eyes. Eventually you'll hear all the old stories. You'll know the place is beginning to rub off on you when you begin making up your own."

You will encounter in these pages some of the extravagant Yellowstone legends that are related whenever people who have worked there get together. So many tales, so little documentation. I was first introduced to this enduring custom by Howard Stricklin during a training course for supervisors we were attending in Washington. He seemed a modest, approachable guy, for a ranger. I don't mean to speak dismissively of rangers. I'd been in the Service only a short time and knew little about them when I met Howard. A lanky man with angular features and a broad grin, he proceeded at an easygoing pace and was incapable of rancor.

One day, after listening to some less than lively lectures on how to be a good supervisor, we retired to the piano bar of the old Roger Smith Hotel on Pennsylvania Avenue. Howard had been a ranger for twenty years, mostly in the West, and felt obliged to explain the verities of the Park Service to a comparative newcomer. The organization, he said, had a decided tilt to the West, where the great national parks were located. The little battlefields and birthplaces of the East were like poor relations, in the family but seldom discussed. "Can you imagine naturalists or historians trying to run a park like Yellowstone? Rangers did for a long time, still could. That's why superintendents and regional directors came from the ranger ranks." It was done with cheerful good humor, what westerners called "stuffin' the dudes," and I took no offense. After all, my superintendent and regional director were both historians.

Admittedly, rangers have given the Park Service some of its best stories, and before Howard was through I must have heard most of them. He favored an early Yellowstone ranger by the name of Harry Trischman, one of your basic ranger immortals. Harry's forte was physical strength and stamina. According to Howard, he once skied from park headquarters at Mammoth to the south entrance, almost a hundred miles, nonstop, on a dare. Another time he took two rangers, probably fresh out of college, on a punishing backcountry patrol. The first night out, they complained the blankets in the patrol cabin were dirty. "Boys," said Harry, "sleep in these blankets tonight and tomorrow you'll smell like rangers."

Howard realized that he'd lost me when I began humming along with the piano halfway through still another Trischman escapade. Trying to convince me I had much to learn from rangers, he said, "You'll never get anywhere in this outfit 'til you've slept in a snowdrift with somebody like Harry Trischman."

"Howard," I said, sobered by the thought. "The price is too high."

In the way such things often happen, I later worked for Howard when he was put in charge of the task force that produced "Road to the Future." It was a young, feisty group, and part of his job was to bring civility to the proceedings. Howard never lost his temper, even when strong opinions were indelicately expressed, but developed a serious grimace when it seemed likely that crockery was about to be broken. As a deserved reward for the success of the product we produced, George let him choose his next assignment. Howard had always wanted to be superintendent of Grand Canyon, and the position happened to be open. He filled it capably until he retired, a good man with untiring patience and, behind those untroubled eyes, a firm resolve.

∪ ∪

Preparing for the Yellowstone summer, I found that two books were particularly valuable. A West Point graduate assigned to the Corps of Engineers, Hiram M. Chittenden first came to Yellowstone to supervise road construction in 1891, returning at the turn of the century to build the figure eight, Grand Loop road system much as it is today. His love for the park and its history is expressed in *Yellowstone National Park*, admirably written and first published in 1895. After many editions over more than a century it is still in print. Another engineer and historian, Aubrey Haines, whose degree is in forestry, first came to Yellowstone as a park ranger, saw service with the Corps of Engineers in World War II, returned to Yellowstone as assistant park engineer, and later became the park's first historian. His knowledge of Yellowstone's history is unsurpassed, and his *The Yellowstone Story*, in two volumes, published in 1977, is indispensable.

The details of my summer in Yellowstone (it began with a snowmobile tour of the park in January) are the substance of the first part of this book. I talked and traveled with so many people that summer, and my notebooks were so crammed, that I seriously doubted I could fit all the material into one book. There was little time to explore the park, although I managed a hike almost every day. Yellowstone isn't a walking park the way Grand Teton is. The trails, laid out during the military era for horse patrols, lack destinations and bridges. Aside from the grizzlies, who give pause to rangers and hikers and make Yellowstone a different kind of park, they are ideal for wilderness travelers. "I don't have to see a grizzly to have a grizzly experience," veteran Yellowstone ranger Ken Ashley remarked. "When I go out on a trail in Yellowstone I'm having a grizzly experience because just the fact that they're out there makes me more alert and more conscious of what's going on around me." After the terrible mauling of Marianna Young in early June (chapter 7), I walked more in wide-open meadows and less in deep forest.

In late August I drove back to Reston and almost immediately to Clemson. My students there reminded me how young young can be. With only a semi-troubled conscience, so many of them placed the fortunes of the Tiger football team above academic considerations. Yet with few exceptions they were attentive and receptive. I tried hard to make the subjects interesting, kept my door open all day, and scored some successes. It was an agreeable and worthwhile year, yet nothing occurred that would have suggested I made a mistake in choosing the Park Service over an academic teaching career.

Returning to Reston in the early summer of 1979, I was at last able to begin digesting my notes from the previous summer, start thinking about the structure of the book, and begin deciding which personalities and events would make the cut. I was reminded of Howard Stricklin's sermon on the importance of rangers, who began to shoulder their way in right from the beginning. I also discovered that more information was needed from a number of people and that my physical description of some individuals and locales was weak. To obtain this information I returned to Yellowstone in August 1979 for a month, then settled down to the activity that can be so engrossing and so provoking. Soon I was diverted by what I will call attractive interruptions. The Greeks would have mentioned sirens.

An old Park Service friend, Dan Davis, appointed director of the highly regarded Arizona-Sonora Desert Museum in Tucson after his retirement, made me an offer I couldn't turn down. For a good part of the next two years I was in Tucson, helping to prepare a master plan for the museum and endeavoring to apply one of Freeman Tilden's rules of interpretation to the museum sign program: "Interpretation is revelation based upon information." Dan found a guest house on an estate in the foothills of the Santa Catalinas high above the city, where Mary and I spent two glorious winters.

The next temptation arrived in a letter from Fred Praeger, for whom I had written a book on the Park Service as a part of the Praeger Publisher series on federal agencies in 1972. It had sold well, Fred said. Would I update it for his newly established Westview Press? Telling my conscience that the job would involve a quick cut-and-paste job, taking only a couple of months at least, I accepted. But when I read the book again after ten years, I was embarrassed.

In the late summer of 1971 I had completed the first few chapters of the book when George Hartzog decided it had to be ready for distribution on March 1, 1972, the hundredth anniversary of the establishment of Yellowstone, with a ceremonial dinner in Washington scheduled. Praeger agreed to deliver the book by that date if I submitted the manuscript by November 1, giving me ten weeks to write the remaining ten chapters. I made the deadline, but I promised Praeger that the new edition would be a totally different book more worthy of the organization.

I returned to the Yellowstone book after a longer interval than planned, this time to write a memoir rather than an organizational history. I found the transition difficult. The historical method drilled into me in graduate school, and the years composing memorandums in the lifeless style mandated for government correspondence, were habits hard to overcome. I was encouraged one day on my afternoon walk around the lakes of Reston, listening to an interview with the fine Canadian writer Farley Mowatt. Responding to praise of his latest book, Mowatt said, "You should have seen the first fifteen drafts."

I had scratched out almost that many before completing one that suited me, and it happened to be the year of the Yellowstone fires. A detailed account of the fires, my visit to the park the following summer to witness the impact and talk with staff members about their ordeal, and a report on the present status of the Park Service, constitute Part Two of this book.

The completed manuscript profited immensely from reviews by two veterans of the Harpers Ferry Center. The singularly talented Vince Gleason, chief of the division of publications, propelled his program into the front rank of government publications, breaking the armlock of the Government Printing Office along the way. His associate, Bob Grogg, a less volcanic although no less practiced editor, made important suggestions, including the title. Whole chapters vanished, others were tightened, and my tendency to resort to the vernacular curbed. Their unrestrained enthusiasm for the manuscript did wonders for my confidence.

The publishers to whom it was entrusted did acknowledge that it possessed literary merit, beginning with the house of Knopf. "I found it lively, entertaining and well written," the editor commented. All were of a mind, however, that the book-buying public was considerably more interested in parks than in park people. A typical comment was, "We found it to be fascinating reading; the story is well told, but we cannot see a large enough market there to support our publication of the work." To this letter the editor added a heartfelt postscript, "As a lover of national parks and the heritage they represent, and as one who has enormous respect for the men and women of the park service, I'd like to add my personal wishes for the success of your work."

On an otherwise unpromising day in February 1996 I opened a letter from Judith McCulloh, executive editor at the University of Illinois Press, which began, "Your manuscript arrived with the day-after-holiday deluge of mail. I'm just now getting to it, a little after eight in the evening. Although I'm only up to page ten of the main story, I have to tell you I've been enjoying it tremendously, admiring your easy style, appreciating the political balancing acts, and laughing out loud."

If your response is even distantly similar I will have succeeded in conveying my fondness and admiration for the people of the Park Service to whom this book is respectfully dedicated.

Part 1

A Summer in Yellowstone, 1978

1

The Beauty of the Curve

The twenty-sixth superintendent of Yellowstone National Park was giving me a little lecture before sending me off on a snowmobile. "If your machine breaks down and there isn't much daylight left, pick a tree that will keep you out of the wind. Lay in a supply of firewood to last the night. Without a fire your snowsuit is so well insulated you're not likely to freeze. More likely you'll come out of it with a story worth telling."

John Townsley was fixing breakfast for me in the kitchen of his residence in Mammoth village, the park headquarters a few miles inside the north boundary. It was a Monday morning in January 1978, and neither the dawn nor John's wife, Elaine, had yet made an appearance. I was drinking coffee at a round table by the window, peppering John with questions. He was peeling potatoes at the work station in the middle of the large and brightly lit room. After he finished slicing two biggish potatoes for hash browns, he deliberated a moment and peeled another.

John's fame as a camp cook was equaled by his reputation as a trencherman. It's rumored he majored in baked goods at college. When he had a panful of bacon sizzling nicely, he asked how many eggs I wanted him to fry up. "The usual," I said gamely. He took a double handful from the refrigerator and tipped an alarming amount of bacon grease into a big black skillet. Averting my eyes, I took another swallow of coffee and watched the snow slanting against the window. The mercury on the thermometer outside stood at ten degrees below zero.

I had planned to begin my residence in May, until he called in early January to say, "If you want to see an entirely different Yellowstone, come now. I have a snowmobile for you." He had met me in the Bozeman airport the night before, greeting me with the gentleness of a large man. It was his size you noticed first, several inches over six feet, with a heavy frame and a low center of gravity. At fifty, he carried his weight well and was still tireless on skis or a horse. He had a high pink dome, a fringe of sandy hair, and watchful blue eyes that could look at you with absolute neutrality. He's a man who keeps his own counsel.

John was old Park Service, born and raised in Yosemite, where his father was chief ranger. We had encountered one another in various places over nearly twenty years. The last time we had breakfast together, he was superintendent of Mount Rainier. Back in 1964, finishing an assignment in the Washington office, he had sold me the bicycle he'd used to commute to the interior building from northern Virginia. It was a lunker, a three-speed, upright Rudge built in Tottingham outside London. By dropping the seat to the last notch I could barely touch my toes to the ground.

Park superintendents, you will come to understand, have their reasons. The good ones put their own spin on directives that come down from region and Washington. John knew I had serious doubts about the appropriateness of snowmobile use in Yellowstone. He was out to make a convert, and yet the more he talked the more intrigued I became with the idea of a leisurely circuit of the park in winter. Privately, I considered the possibility of my becoming a snowmobile enthusiast remote.

Over breakfast John gave me a few words of caution and reminded me of a tragic accident that had occurred a few years earlier. A Yellowstone assistant superintendent led a snowmobile party over the Beartooth Highway, the approach road to the park from the northeast, which climbs endless switchbacks through a glacier-carved landscape, topping out at eleven thousand feet. A storm rolled in unexpectedly, pinning the group down. By the time a rescue team had broken through the drifts, one man was dead of exposure.

My itinerary would be much safer. All snowmobiles are restricted to the road system in Yellowstone. Machines enter from all sides of the park, and rangers are on patrol constantly. Still, Yellowstone is a big place. The weather can be unpredictable, and it is possible to tumble off your machine if you take a turn too fast, although a snowmobile trip is not a prayerful undertaking.

I never did need any of the contents of a bag John laid out in his mudroom behind the kitchen, where the Townsleys removed their cold weather paraphernalia and hung it up to dry. The "possibles sack"—a carryover term from the fur trade era—contained a box of dry rations, powdered soup, waterproof matches in a tarragon Spice Islands bottle, a knife with the maximum number of attachments, a flashlight with extra batteries, and extra socks and gloves. John needled me by saying he would have included a fan belt and spare parts, except he knew I wasn't good with my hands. I can take a slam like that now. I used to think the deficiency a character defect.

I listened patiently to his words of advice, even making entries in my notebook to show my zeal. Nevertheless, I meant to proceed cautiously and steer clear of situations that would require coaxing a fire from a handful of moss and twigs or devising a splint from a tree limb for a broken leg. This being my first adventure on a snow machine, and having overheard Mary tell a friend on the telephone that I was getting a little long in the tooth for such bravado, I resolved to take things slow and easy.

We went down the outside back stairs to John's green patrol car. My snowmobile was on a trailer hitched behind. John didn't need his head-lights, but he turned on the wipers to keep the windshield free of falling snow as we edged down the line of employee houses. Firewood on the back porches was racked up with mathematical precision. Tall circles of wire protected serviceberry bushes and shrubs from bands of foraging elk. The clouds were low and ominous, and deep snow lay everywhere. In January, Mammoth looks like a village in Alaska.

On hard-packed snow we drove by concessioner facilities boarded against the weather. At the edge of the village the terrace formations of Mammoth Hot Springs, one of the most beautiful and colorful attractions of the park, were almost entirely hidden by clouds of steam. Beyond the formations the road climbed the long slope of Terrace Mountain. The parking lot at the entrance to Terrace Drive was the end of the line for automobiles. Winter travel to the interior of the park is limited to over-the-snow vehicles.

John went about inching my machine off the trailer. I examined it care-fully. Long, slender, and low, black with lavender stripes, it was a top-of-the line Arctic Cat Panther, the model used by the rangers. I tried the bench seat of padded vinyl, looking through the slanted windscreen, not quite certain what I was letting myself in for. Driving a snowmobile seemed more pleasurable back in Reston. Now I was beginning to have doubts. Old Faithful, where I would spend the first night, was fifty miles down the road.

Actually, I could have made it to the South Pole in the outfit John gave me. He had taken one look at my boots, which had served me well in Alaska, and called them galoshes. To be honest, they did look puny compared to the sturdy leather ones he gave me. I was grateful for them and for the rest of the gear he provided: felt liners and innersoles for the boots, high wool socks, elbow-length leather gauntlets over wool mittens, a knitted head-warmer, a crash helmet, and the indispensable oversuit with multiple zippers, so well padded, John advised, that I would be uncomfort-ably warm if I wore a sweater underneath.

The starting sequence for a snowmobile is simple enough. Turn the ignition key, yank the plastic ring attached to the starter rope, and fiddle with the choke toggle. Give the motor gas by twisting the rubber grip on the handlebar. I practiced a few times and then traced a few wobbly circles that passed muster but, from the look on John's face, not by much. Riding my son Rob's motorbike had helped. The two machines have a lot in common. His more recent attempt to teach me about computers was less successful.

The snow continued at a disturbing rate by my standards. "Just a sprinkle," John said as we fastened the duffel bag on the wire rack behind the seat. "It's nothing serious." He wouldn't think it cause for concern until it piled so deep we couldn't find the snowmobile. "You'll make it to Old Faithful in three"—he looked me over, summing up my chances—"four hours." Nodding to indicate I heard the final instructions and racing the motor to show how quickly I'd learned the drill, I guided my Arctic Cat Panther out of the parking lot and chugged bravely southward at all of ten miles an hour.

I poked along through the Hoodoos, great jumbled blocks of light-colored travertine that had tumbled down from Terrace Mountain, causing the road builders to take evasive action. I drove into a tight, rocky canyon, followed it upward past Rustic Falls, enveloped in a sheath of hanging ice, and broke out of the Golden Gate into Swan Lake Flat. The terrain features were almost obscured by low, drifting clouds and the driving snow. For miles I drove through lodgepole forests, the branches of the pines bending under their snow load. Feeling more confident, I picked up the pace, but I had already discovered that a snowmobile is a disagreeable device for sight-seeing.

The cumbersome helmet doesn't permit quick glances to the side. Not that you have much time to look around. You need to focus constantly on the track ahead. The two front skis of a snowmobile soon produce a washboard surface and a bumpy ride. Yellowstone's roads are groomed by an improbable machine invented for the purpose. It cuts off the tops of the ridges and fills in the depressions. You try to reduce jolting by keeping your runners in the path worn by previous machines. It isn't easy to do, for the road is crisscrossed with random cuts, and the groove is hard to follow. When you slip out of it, the runners begin to buck like skis chattering over frozen ruts. The motor noise is as obnoxious as your neighbor's power mower on a Sunday morning, and there is no escaping the foul exhaust fumes created by the fuel combination of one pint motor oil to four gallons of gasoline.

Unable to catch more than a glimpse of the roadside scenery from inside my life support system, I cut the motor and drifted to a stop. Much of Yellowstone's snow comes from intermittent showers, and as I took off my helmet the squall through which I'd been driving began to break up. In a few moments the sun appeared, just clear of the mountains, shining on a scene of dazzling perfection. The golds and browns of summer were buried under a mantle of surgical whiteness. Yet, looking about, I discovered colors in this winter world. The tree trunks were black, and the branches green under their white icing. A few red leaves still clung to the topmost twig of a tall bush. Most beautiful of all was the subtle blue of the shadows on the snow. If I had brought a camera I wouldn't have known where to point it first.

To the left of the road there was no break in the solid ranks of the great evergreen forest. Off in the distance to the right, against patches of brilliant blue sky, I could see the snowy peaks of the Gallatins. In the meadow beside me, rocks and sagebrush were covered with a gleaming ice. It was as though I had been suddenly transported into a universe of unassailable purity.

The silence was broken by the screaming cry of a raven somewhere in the trees. A winter-white weasel, called ermine, thin as a hacksaw blade and with a flash of black at the tip of the tail, scuttled along the crest of a snowbank in electric, quick spurts. Catching sight of me, he whipped under the snow, popping out ten feet farther on. Erect and motionless, he inspected me and stood his ground.

Driving on a bit, I stopped where a concrete bridge spanned a frozen stream for a look at the Norris soldier station, a venerable log cabin built by the army in 1908. The roof supported an accumulated snow load that flowed gracefully down over the eaves, forming a hanging cornice. The author of *The Outermost House*, Henry Beston, may have had such a scene in mind when he observed, "The secret of snow is the beauty of the curve."

Looking at the reflection of the sun in a thousand brilliant snow crystals, I began to feel a twinge of affection for my Arctic Cat Panther. Contrary to my expectation, it was giving me reasons to rejoice. I understood a little better why former superintendent Jack Anderson had worked so hard to open Yellowstone to snowmobiles. "For a long, long time the rangers had the park to themselves all winter," Jack said. "It was time to give the public a chance."

When I called him at his retirement home in Oregon, he said that the first time he came through Yellowstone on a snowmobile he decided it was an experience other people should have. "I didn't think snowmobiles would be more of an intrusion than five thousand automobiles every day in summer, and I authorized their use on a trial basis. I had one reservation. Would the noise disturb the wildlife? After the naturalists found snowmobiles had no observable effect on the animals, I was convinced." Newspaper stories about the "Winter Wonderland" had an exuberant quality.

Merchants were elated, anticipating the rewards of year-round tourism. Conservationists, who intensely disliked snowmobiles, wanted them out of Yellowstone. Wisely, Jack consulted with his boss in Washington, George Hartzog. Other Park Service directors have been canny politicians. George was uncanny, a virtuoso bureaucrat exquisitely aware that everything in Washington has a political spin. Some of us believe the Park Service hasn't had a more effective leader. I once asked him how it was that the man he selected for the most prestigious field position had been superintendent of a Civil War battlefield only two years before. "Jack Anderson was a natural," George said. "I could always trust his instincts."

As well liked as anyone in the organization, Jack was large, even-tempered, and uncomplicated, a navy pilot in Hawaii at the time of Pearl Harbor. He was considering a military career after the war until the superintendent of Sequoia talked him into applying for a ranger job. Secretary of the Interior Rogers Morton had enjoyed Jack's company on a fly-fishing expedition in the park. "Why don't we invite Rogers to review your snowmobile operation?" George suggested to Jack.

"The two of us went around alone and had a marvelous time," Jack recalled. "The weather was ideal, and the elk and buffalo seemed to be obeying hand signals. A couple of bald eagles posed for us in Hayden Valley. Morton talked to everybody he encountered and asked a lot of questions. Back in Mammoth, sitting in front of my fireplace, he put his feet up and said, 'Jack, I couldn't have enjoyed myself more. We weren't doing the park or the wildlife any harm. I only wish I'd brought my family.' " Soon afterward he approved a policy authorizing snowmobile use in the parks at the discretion of the superintendents. I asked John Townsley what the reaction would be if he attempted to limit snowmobile use. "West Yellowstone would take hostages," he said.

At Madison Junction, an immense bonfire was sending flames high in the air in front of a three-sided shelter. Drivers from snowmobiles parked along the road had taken off their helmets and balaclavas and zipped down their snowsuits. Jim Barker, the ranger on duty, was talking to a youngish couple obviously thrilled by what they'd seen on the way in from West Yellowstone. A genial and comfortably built young seasonal ranger, Jim was a veteran of six winters in Yellowstone. He took heart from people who were enchanted by the experience and tried to do some missionary work with those in love with snowmobiles and primarily interested in racking up the miles. "You'll notice a lot of drivers are into their machines," he said when I explained my mission.

When they get cranked up they see no point in stopping to look around. Watching them whiz by a herd of elk without even taking a good look leads me to believe their interest is casual at best. Talking to some of them about their reaction to Yellowstone is like asking Mario Andretti how he liked the view at Indianapolis. Driving up from Old Faithful this morning I saw two machines parked at Black Sand Basin. One of the drivers was setting up a tripod. I stopped and asked the other one how things were going, and he said, "Can you believe it? I'm traveling with a guy who doesn't do anything but putter around taking pictures."

Relatively few drivers stray off the roads. What irks the rangers are those who gain a cheap thrill by "side-hilling" the steep roadside slopes. I asked Jim whether he was tempted to employ the Sedlack solution is such cases. He laughed and said, "Every time." Glacier ranger Art Sedlack became a hero of sorts when he killed a snowmobile. Either the park was experiencing more violations than usual or perhaps Sedlack became temporarily unbalanced by the sight of a snowmobile making lazy circles in the snow.

Judge Roy Bean would have applauded Sedlack's brand of justice. He took out his pistol and fired a slug into the vitals of the offending snowmobile. Park officials spoke regretfully of Sedlack's "unfortunate lapse." Interviewed by a reporter, the chief ranger avoided any mention of legal implications. Instead, he placed the incident in a more philosophical context, saying, "Man's age-old animosity toward the machine may have overcome Ranger Sedlack for the moment." Jim said that a notice was posted in the ranger office at Mammoth: "Snowmobiles must never be shot. They should be live-trapped." The Montana Wilderness Association now gives an annual Arthur E. Sedlack award for the most outrageous act in defense of wilderness.

The majority of the people with whom I spoke at the bonfire during the course of an hour or so were overwhelmed by the scenery, more so than summer visitors. Some were unimpressed, including the leader of a caravan of a dozen machines that roared up just as Jim and I agreed that it was time to do something about lunch. The drivers were wearing matched black helmets and crimson snowsuits with black stripes. A small trailer fastened behind one of the machines was unpacked, and my hunger was intensified by the smell of hot dogs blistering over the coals.

The driver in charge, sporting an impenetrable beard, was either out of sorts or a chronic grouch. Hearing that Yellowstone's roads were smooth and fast, he'd talked his club into transporting their machines by truck seven hundred miles from Saskatchewan. "It was a waste of money," he growled at me when I said howdy. On a run the day before to the east entrance, he and his cohorts were slowed by stretches of washboarding and drifts in the mountain passes. I thought him inconsiderate, even perverse, although with complainers so much is in the tone. Jim rescued me, saying loudly for effect that if we're going to reach Old Faithful for lunch, down that slow and bumpy road, we'd better saddle up.

Old Faithful village had already received a hundred and fifty inches of snow. Old Faithful Inn was like a huge Swiss chalet, the ground floor nearly hidden by drifts, the slanted roof and window gables white against the brown, shingled walls. A man using a red lumberjack shirt as an outer garment and carrying the longest saw I'd ever seen came around the corner of the inn. Seeing Jim wave, he angled toward us along a trail that had been kicked through the snow pack.

"Meet Dave Smith," Jim said. "He's a winterkeeper." Since the first big hotels were built in Yellowstone, winterkeepers, or caretakers, have been employed to keep the roofs clear of heavy snow loads. In the old days the lonely life attracted salty characters who preferred solitude. Bill Scales, for example, had refused to open the lobby of the Lake Hotel to Theodore Roosevelt and his party when they camped in the park for two weeks in the spring of 1903. Asked to account for his ungracious behavior, Scales said the honor of meeting the president of the United States wasn't worth cleaning up the mess his crowd would make.

A slim, wiry man with tranquil green eyes above a full, brown beard, Dave said he'd wanted to try living off by himself for a while, and when he heard of the winterkeeper jobs he kept applying until he was hired. Although his post was at Lake, he was replacing the winterkeeper at Old Faithful for a few days. He was twenty-eight, and it was his fifth year in Yellowstone. I asked him about the duty.

For a person of my temperament it's perfect. It taxes the muscles and relaxes the mind. I don't have to make tough decisions, and I don't get hassled. It's like a game. The snow comes down, I figure a way to remove it. The snow comes down again. On slanted roofs you fasten a wire at the ridge line, letting it hang down over the roof to the ground. You walk it along, keeping it tight, sliding it under the snow like a knife under a piece of pie. On a flat roof you use a shovel three feet wide, if the snow isn't frozen. If it is, you saw it into sections as wide as the shovel and push them off. I use this two-handed saw to cut off the cornices. The gables that break up the slanted roof of Old Faithful Inn made the winterkeepers earn their pay. The old ones, a cagey bunch, developed an elaborate system of ramps and runways to bypass them. The Park Service ruined that setup when it made the concessioner install outside fire escapes. I'm not complaining. Counting everything I do at Lake, it couldn't amount to twenty hours a week. On days when the sky is blue and the sun is bright I wouldn't trade places with anyone.

I asked if he followed any kind of routine, and he said that the lack of structure was the best part of his job. "If the weather looks promising when I wake up, I may ski down to Fishing Bridge before breakfast and watch the sun come up. Then I might pick up the shovel or the saw for a couple of hours, if I get the urge. Stormy days I say to myself, 'I'm not going out in that!' Since I'm a fair hand in the kitchen I might do a special dish, bake a chocolate cake. Then I'll lay in a supply of firewood and read all day. I have quite a good library. There aren't any bad days for a winterkeeper."

The Snow Lodge is the only hotel open in winter in the interior of Yellowstone, the kind of small and unpretentious yet comfortable hotel you can't find at a ski resort. A two-story building with a flat roof, it sits in a line of concession buildings behind Old Faithful Inn. Several pairs of skis were standing in a snowbank outside the entrance as Jim and I arrived. A snow coach was loading passengers for the return trip to West Yellowstone. Painted bright yellow and seating ten passengers, with side windows and a roof hatch, it looks better than it rides.

In the lobby, several high-backed rockers in front of a Defiant wood stove held ski jackets, hats, and mittens. The room had a high ceiling, an upright piano in one corner, and a tall young woman in a Nordic sweater behind the counter. I have never received a more cheery welcome at a commercial establishment; she and the maids and waitresses seemed to be having as much fun as the guests. The meals were a pleasant surprise, and the service came from the heart. All of the employees had the outdoor look. "Skiing by the geysers is the ultimate," one said. "It's why I work here."

I carried my duffel bag down the first-floor wing to a room at the end of a corridor that held a faint memory of cigarettes and beer. If the view through the double windows had been framed with tinsel and holly it would have made a great Christmas card. When Jim and I walked into the snug little dining room, it was nearly two o'clock. A waitress hurried over with a greeting that was like a friendly dig in the ribs. She had a spray of blond bangs and an easygoing freshness. Nothing, you felt, could dampen her spirits. "You guys look hungry," she said, busily straightening our table setting and flicking away imaginary crumbs. "I've got chili that will make you roll in the snow." We both ordered the chili. Anything else would have been missing the point.

After lunch Jim went back on patrol. Postponing an exploration of the geyser basin until I had more daylight, I took the trail to the visitor center. I wanted to meet the Old Faithful district naturalist, Margaret Short, about whom I'd heard good things. Her office was shoehorned into an oddly shaped corner meant for storage. At the time the center was constructed for the 1972 centennial, Jack Anderson had decreed there would be no office space. He said he had discovered naturalists drinking coffee in their offices once too often. He wanted them out talking to visitors.

Maggie, as her friends call her, was a gentle, serious woman, so slender as to appear fragile, with brown eyes and straight, brown hair touching the shoulders of her uniform jacket. It's second nature in the organization to pick up a person's career history. I could have reeled off the previous assignments of all of my associates and many others I knew only by reputation. I asked Maggie for a biographical sketch.

She had come out of college with a history major and an archaeology minor, worked in a publishing house for a year, and "just happened" to take a Civil Service examination because the Park Service appealed to her. Selected for her high grades, she was sent to the Albright Training Center at Grand Canyon, a facility that provides a thoroughgoing introduction to all phases of Park Service operations. She remembered that her class developed a strong bond, and she kept in touch with members scattered all over the country. "The quality of the training and the dedication of the staff sold me on the Park Service. I had difficulty rappeling down the rock faces, but I managed."

In her time, Albright graduates received urban assignments, a Hartzog decree based on the reasonable premise that people working in the parks are so removed from city stress that they need to appreciate the environments from which most visitors come. Maggie drew New York City, where the Park Service administers Federal Hall, the birthplace of Theodore Roosevelt, Gateway National Recreation Area, Castle Clinton, the Statue of Liberty, and Ellis Island. Long before her one-year tour ended, she considered resigning:

> I was demoralized by New York City the first week. I have so much sympathy for people who put up with that kind of tension. I shared a horrid little efficiency with a fellow trainee in a depressed neighborhood of Brooklyn, all we could afford on our salaries. I was held up in the subway on Palm Sunday by two teenagers armed with knives. When one girl from our class came out of a delicatessen, a man came up pointing a gun. He told her to hand over her purse or he'd blow her head off. She was so weary of it all she said, "I don't have any money. Leave me alone." And she walked away.
>
> From there I transferred to Mesa Verde, in southwest Colorado. Can

you imagine the contrast? I sometimes think I should have stayed at Mesa Verde. The park has everything an archaeologist could wish for, and the country is magnificent. But a promotion came along. I moved to Colorado National Monument, then here. For five years I've never locked my front door. I've lived where there are no neon signs or air pollution or fast food restaurants or television. No wonder Park Service people are provincial. We live in another world.

I asked about the disadvantages. She smiled and said, "It's no place for a movie buff." Once a month she would drive her snowmobile to West Yellowstone, where she kept her car. It would take a half hour to dig it out of the snow and a couple of hours to drive to Bozeman. If someone had occupied her space by the time she returned, it meant another stint with the shovel. The summers were "unbelievably hectic." All of the park's more than two million visitors that year would come through Old Faithful, most of them in three months. With the help of a couple of dozen seasonal naturalists, she manages.

Fluent in Spanish, she had a park planning assignment in Costa Rica and hoped for more. "For the things I want to do with my life, Yellowstone is a good place for me now. I like the dignity of what I do. It's such a great opportunity to be helpful to people, most of whom have a genuine respect for the park." Yet she noted that it was a downer when a man had asked her, "Can I drive my snowmobile up the boardwalk to Old Faithful!" She shook her head, then smiled. She had been in the park business long enough to appreciate quandaries.

Maggie's colleagues were protective of her, perhaps because of her frail appearance. She would have none of it, however, and made it a point to pull her own weight. One of her friends told me of being in her office one day when the fire alarm sounded. Maggie, a member of the Old Faithful fire brigade, immediately took off at a dead run. Soon the fire engine went clanging by, Maggie sitting next to the driver and holding on to her Stetson with both hands.

A year after we talked, the kind-spirited Margaret Short resigned and entered a seminary in California to prepare for a new career of service. With others of similar beliefs she had been holding fellowship meetings and after prayerful deliberation made her decision. "I feel there is a greater need for me elsewhere," she told a friend. "God has work for all of us in these times."

∪ ∪

A gale buffeted the Snow Lodge Monday night. Between volleys I could hear the whispering sound of snow brushing against the windows. By Tuesday morning the storm had left a foot of snow behind. Craig Pass to the south was closed indefinitely, giving me an excuse to stay longer at Old Faithful. Jim Barker came by after breakfast and invited me to join him on patrol. The sky had cleared, but the chilly rays of the morning sun were not yet strong enough to warm the frigid air. We made slow progress at first until other machines helped pack down the roads. New snow under the glittering sun made the settings even more stunning. We stopped often, and each time I was reluctant to move on. I retain vivid impressions from those two days of patrolling in weather that was close to perfect.

On the way to West Yellowstone that first morning we watched a pair of trumpeter swans in the middle of the Madison River. Facing upstream, they paddled just enough to keep stationary against the slow current, tipping to feed on bottom vegetation. On our return they were standing on a shelf of ice projecting from the near bank, industriously preening their feathers, their jet black beaks the only touch of contrasting color. These great white birds can attain a wingspan of eight feet, and we watched one spread its wings to shake off moisture. The glossy feathers seemed to glow in the bright sunlight.

Just down the road, several cow elk were resting at the edge of the woods, one lying down with only her head and neck above the snow. Not ten yards from us, they wouldn't expend energy by moving away, yet all heads were turned in our direction. "Look who's joining the party," Jim said softly, and the tableau came to life. That arch opportunist, the coyote, looking like a dirty gray dog, trotted down the road. Veering over close to the elk, he tucked his tail down in a truce signal, his sharp eyes missing nothing.

Another mile and Jim stopped to check the condition of an elk he called "Old Seventy-Six," seven points on one side of his mighty rack of antlers and six on the other. The ribs of the gaunt bull were almost as easily counted. He was browsing on pine needles, a bad sign. It seems unjust that snowmobiles are less a threat to elk than skiers. Elk become accustomed to noisy machines that stay on predictable paths, but a skier moving silently through the woods will startle the animals and set them running, forcing them to draw upon precious reserves. "It's agony to see elk laboring through deep snow," Jim said. "In a tough winter like this one, so many elk are near the edge. Anything that makes them burn away their energy can take them over. Exhaustion can be terminal. Ten percent of the herd, mostly the old and the young, won't survive."

∪ ∪

At daylight on Wednesday morning the thermometer hanging next to the Snow Lodge entrance registered twenty-eight degrees below zero. Peering at the scale with me was one of the hotel waitresses, late for the breakfast shift and wearing a couple of thick sweaters, a ski mask, and furry boots. We talked for a little, breathing smoke at one another, and agreed the air was so still we ought to be able to hear the snowmobiles starting up in West Yellowstone. When I told her I was off to catch an eruption of Old Faithful, she advised me that the quiet days can be deceptive. Visitors often will be unaware of the cold until the telltale white spot appears. I went back to my room and put on a ski mask.

I tramped down the street past empty and shuttered buildings, a post office, the biggest of all the Hamilton general stores in the park supplied with rustic gables over its three entrances, and a service station open to supply the snowmobile traffic. Turning off the street, I headed for the geyser basin. The rich, thick snow piled everywhere softened the effect of the buildings, concealing the asphalt of the sprawling east and west parking lots that covered much of the open space.

Off to my left were Old Faithful Inn, another Hamilton store, another service station, and the visitor center. To the right were a cafeteria and Old Faithful Lodge, with cabin units spread about in haphazard rows. The air was so cold that I expected it to crackle as I moved along briskly, my boots squeaking on the hard-packed path. Behind me, pines covering the long, high ridge were encrusted with snow. Invigorated by the brightening of the sky in the East and with sunrise only moments away, I took such a deep gulp of air that I shocked my lungs.

Emerging from the band of trees that screened the village, I entered the serene world of the Upper Geyser Basin. Completely surrounded by forests, containing the world's largest collection of active geysers, it resembled a vast sculpture garden. Drifting spray freezing on blades of grass and limbs of dead trees had formed extravagant ice displays. The rising sun gave the entire valley a dazzling beauty. Columns of steam rose from hot pools and geyser cones into the calm air. The ghostly white trees cast shadows from a low sun that gave only an illusion of warmth.

I stepped up on the long, curving boardwalk in front of Old Faithful geyser, picked out a front seat in the double row of benches, and brushed away the deep snow from the wooden slats. Immediately in front was the mound of the geyser, bare of snow, a plume of steam hanging motionless above the vent. In the stillness, sounds from the village carried clearly. A cheery voice called out a greeting. Someone was knocking together a pair of rubber-soled boots. Waiting, I was aware of the intense cold that numbed my cheeks.

I was grateful again to John Townsley for persuading me to see what he called the "other face of Yellowstone." The hundreds of spectators lining the boardwalk in the summer make an eruption of Old Faithful a public spectacle. They chatter away, fiddling with their camera equipment, anxious for the show to begin so they can get on with seeing the rest of Yellowstone. On this exquisitely clear and bracing January morning, in its own good time, hissing like a steam locomotive, Old Faithful geyser performed magnificently for an audience of one.

∪ ∪

The trip on Thursday from Old Faithful to Lake, a distance of forty miles, was relatively uneventful. Snowflakes that would soon become a snowstorm were drifting down as I climbed steadily for five miles out of Old Faithful, the road a narrow, white corridor through an unbroken forest. I had kind thoughts for my Arctic Cat Panther as it climbed smoothly over the Continental Divide twice in a few miles. The racketing roar was reassuring. From a point above West Thumb junction, I was able to glimpse the frozen surface of Yellowstone Lake.

Traveling the final twenty-mile leg around the northern portion of the lake, I was buffeted by the winds that blew off it. In the unprotected stretches all trace of the road had vanished. Where it had been cut into the slope of the hill, drifting snow had about restored the original slope. I drove between red-topped poles installed to guide snowplow crews in the spring. At Bridge Bay, the Lake Hotel was visible on a low bluff above the shore.

Lake village, near the junction of the Grand Loop and the east entrance road to Cody, is the smallest of the five developed areas of the park. To me, it's the most attractive, with a standout old hotel on the lake, a modern hospital, a general store that looks like a frontier fort, one of the oldest ranger stations, a handsome lodge, and some of Yellowstone's newest and oldest cabins. Begun in 1889, the hotel is a yesterday kind of place. Painstakingly restored almost a century later, it is reminiscent of the grand vacation hotels of the nineteenth century. A 1905 guidebook caught its special charm—and the distractions of the horse and buggy days: "Guests at Lake Hotel found a serenity absent elsewhere in Wonderland. . . . Whether one walked the lakeshore or merely sat and watched the backdrop of wooded hills and rugged peaks, the mood was one of restfulness. What a blessing after four days of stage-coach travel—of sun, wind, dust and mosquitoes!"

The Lake ranger station, also on the lakeshore, is a large log octagon structure with cabin attached. It was put up in 1923, a "triumph of woodland architecture," the octagon serving as an experimental community room for the first educational programs. Adorned with elk antlers and bison skulls, it must have been a Yellowstone Chautauqua, a room where visitors could get information and listen to lectures. The structure was in need of fresh paint, and the deteriorating logs and sagging sills suggested that more extensive repairs might be needed. Long ago, the octagon was partitioned into office space and the great stone fireplace, open on four sides to present a campfire effect, was covered over. I soon learned that its occupants thought it an undesirable residence with about as much usable space as a small apartment.

In the mudroom, I was reading a forceful notice warning visitors to remove boots and snowsuits before seeking entry when Nancy Rudolph opened the door and said, "How does a hot cup of tea sound?" A slender woman with short, straight hair and a quick, friendly smile, she seemed to be a person of warmth and intelligence who had things she intended to get done. John had spoken of Nancy's spunk. I gathered that Nancy's husband Roger, the district ranger, was larkey and addicted to irreverence.

Nancy led me through an area whose shelves resembled a grocery store. In late October, she told me, she and Roger had treated themselves to a three-day, last-time-out binge in Bozeman. She paused and added, "A binge in Bozeman? What a hope!" They loaded their van with staples, including twenty dozen eggs and a hundred pounds of flour. "Baking is essential." They brought back enough meat and vegetables to fill a restaurant-sized freezer, an ample supply of beer and wine, toilet paper to last the Rudolphs and their guests twenty weeks, and much, much more.

Few of Yellowstone's employees have previously experienced the extreme isolation and the long, harsh winters. Not many people have. Some families adjust to the rigors and relish the experience. Others are ground down. The largest number, after two or three years, are ready for a transfer. One veteran told me, "This is what the military calls a hardship post. If people come here with hang-ups, they won't get any better. The social life is minimal, the amenities few, the weather grim for so long. A simple thing like getting your car fixed, with Livingston fifty miles away, is a major logistical problem." Living in a closed and remote community beside the people you work with every day can be rewarding, or tedious, or drive you to distraction. As Nancy told me,

> I really believe I'm a rare case, but it helps to have a good, solid, loner streak, and you need hobbies. Mine are photography and the dark room, sewing, and writing—which I'm sure you will agree is the natural outlet for a loner. Roger and I enjoy the life, so far. We get along ridiculously

well. He's a good remedy for boredom. Winters supply a welcome re-lief. Roger's summers are frantic. He works all hours. If there's a serious accident or somebody lost, I may not see him for a while. I operate the Rudolph grill and motel. Just a lot of our friends drop by to visit us. We love to see them, but they don't realize they are part of an almost con-tinuous procession. Every March we can't stand the sight of another snowflake. By September we can hardly wait for the roads to close.

Roger's first words to me were: "Those goddamned, paper-pushing bas-tards in Mammoth." He was sitting at a table in the dining room, files and pieces of loose paper scattered in all directions. I gathered that a new set of guidelines had been received from headquarters, meant to ensure the sea-sonal ranger work force was an equitable mix of males and females, whites, blacks, and Latinos, and the experienced and the inexperienced.

When I observed to Roger, for openers, that he didn't appear beaten down by the bureaucracy, he gave me a grin that was pure mischief. Ap-proaching thirty, of medium height and compactly built, he was loosely wound and had dark, curly hair and high-voltage energy. The youngest of the district rangers, Roger is of the next generation, waiting his turn for promotion and not too patiently. "He isn't the type who stores up winter nuts," Townsley noted when briefing me on the people I would be meet-ing. "Roger has a different trajectory." John may have been thinking of the more measured pace of Roger's colleagues. "You need a few bright-eyed, busy-tailed guys like Roger on your team. He and Nancy have put it together in a tough living situation as well as anyone. Maybe it's because they're Californians."

The Park Service has a high tolerance for nonconformists. Otherwise, Roger wouldn't have been allowed in. Pushing the papers helter-skelter into his briefcase, he told me the story. He grew up in the Los Angeles area, "mostly on the beach," and managed to graduate from San Jose State despite head-shakings from faculty members who doubted he would settle down enough to earn his degree. In no hurry to make something out of himself, he took a job at Squaw Valley. "I'd always loved the mountain country and skiing. I enjoyed every day at Squaw Valley. I thought I'd stay forever."

A friend told him of a Civil Service entrance examination being given for park rangers. Considering the idea "halfway appealing," he passed with a borderline score. Not wishing to hide his true colors, he showed up for the interview in dirty jeans, cowboy boots, and a T-shirt bearing a mes-sage guaranteed to offend. Showing the cheek that became his trademark, he told the Park Service representative, "I'm the best you'll get." The ranger was Fred Johnson, an old Yellowstone hand known to have cut a few touches himself. Fred must have liked what he saw. Roger was accepted. He told his friend, "The Park Service must be hiring bums this year."

After orientation at the Grand Canyon training center, he drew Channel Islands, then a national monument and now a national park, where visitors were rare and the barking of sea lions continuous. He learned to handle boats but didn't lose his preference for mountains. Two years later he was selected to receive intensive training in law enforcement and sent to Yosemite.

In a widely publicized incident the year before, a crowd of several hundred young people seeking a confrontation successfully fought off an attempt of mounted rangers to disperse them. With the help of a hundred police officers from neighboring jurisdictions, and at a cost of many injuries and arrests, order was finally restored. The Yosemite rangers lacked the requisite training and equipment and the ideology to deal with the first riot in Park Service history. " 'Til then we were the friendly rangers," said one, "who when we saw an infraction, pointed at the error, and talked with the violator." Since the Yosemite incident, law enforcement has become a major function.

Roger found the duty in Yosemite Valley aggravating. Only seven miles long and less than a mile wide, it receives more visitors than the whole of Yellowstone. It had become a haven for vagrants from Los Angeles and San Francisco. He was bedeviled by hooligans who supported their bizarre life-style robbing campsites and clouting cars. "I like the end result of law enforcement," Roger said, "that is, finding ways to get visitors of whatever inclination to accept reasonable restrictions on their behavior, once they come through the entrance station. What I didn't care for in Yosemite was taking bottles away from winos and wrestling in the woods with psychos. When I took down their names and asked where they lived, they'd point to their heads and say, 'In here.' "

Meanwhile, Yosemite's high country was developing problems of its own. Hikers were pounding the trails to dust. When the superintendent put together a team to design a wilderness management plan, he rewarded Roger by giving him a place. Roger spent a year doing, as he said, what John Muir did—experiencing "a great expanding time, probably the most maturing of my life. You can't roam those mountains and not be changed." He almost turned down the Yellowstone offer, but his marriage to Nancy had induced him to get serious about his career.

He was telling me about his district, that it was not much smaller than all of Yosemite, when he glanced out the window and noted there was barely enough daylight remaining to do some jogging. We suited up and drove our machines a few hundred yards to the Lake Hotel. On the lake side, the three large porticoes, three stories high, each supported by four columns of the Ionic order, transform an unpretentious frame structure nearly a city block long into a handsome resort hotel. Roger unlocked a door in the rear, and we clumped up the carpeted incline.

Windows partially planked against the snow allowed only a dim light to filter into the spacious lobby. We piled our outer clothing on a wooden counter, and Roger briefed me on the course: follow the corridor to the far end of the building, mount the stairs, return on the second floor, and continue through four floors, repeating the pattern on the way down. I waved him on, preferring to confine my exertions to one level and at my own pace, especially at an elevation of seventy-seven-hundred feet. Shedding my boots, I padded up and down a gloomy hallway and through the sunroom, with its ancient wicker chairs, writing tables, and couches, most of them draped for the winter. There was an intriguing set of pictures of the little steamer *Zillah*, transported in sections from the Great Lakes in 1889. Carrying hotel guests from West Thumb to the Lake Hotel before the road was built, it was a rakish vessel with two decks, the lower enclosed and the upper protected by a canvas awning.

In the cold, dank air, I sat for a short time on the steps by the entrance leading to the second floor, wiping off the sweat with a towel Nancy had supplied. As Roger was doing the same, he said that he always kept in shape and enjoyed physical challenges. At the end of last summer he was talking with several ranger friends about the exploits of the old-timers. They decided to put one of their own on the books, attempting a forced march from the south entrance around the southern end of Yellowstone Lake and up the eastern shore, a distance of fifty-two miles.

They nearly made it. Starting at dawn, they reached a patrol cabin on Yellowstone Lake, eight miles from their destination, late that night. There they decided to pack it in. The night was dark, and they had run short of flashlight batteries. Months later I was leafing through the logbook at the Park Point cabin and came upon this entry for September 10, 1977. "Roger Rudolph, Bill Foreman, Allan Schmierer and Roger Siglin in for the night. Hiked 44 miles today from Heart Lake trailhead. Had hoped to reach Ten Mile Post but fatigue and lack of good lights stopped us."

On our way back to the station we stopped for a view that made you forget the cold. The surface of Yellowstone Lake was a featureless whiteness. In all directions pines descended to the shore of the lake in solid ranks. To the south and east, an irregular line of peaks dominated the skyline. A red and orange sunset was causing their snowy summits to glow like burning coals.

Nancy served a delicious roast beef dinner that evening, to which I contributed a particularly brainless pleasantry. I complimented her on managing a salad so far from a supermarket, not realizing I was consuming the precious product of her sprout garden. Later, someone sent me an article about Nancy and Roger from the April 6, 1978, *San Francisco Examiner*, entitled "Living the Good Life in Yellowstone." The winter hardships were bearable with one exception, Nancy told the reporter. She missed salad greens. Terribly. On rare occasions, "Some benevolent person will come in from the outside and bring us a head of lettuce. They make our Christmas list." I'd brought a six-pack of Coors, not in short supply, and I didn't hear a word at Christmas.

The shirt Nancy wore at dinner didn't cover several blue-pink dimples and welts on her arms. She had been mauled by a grizzly only a few months earlier. She spoke of it matter-of-factly, saying it was about what you would expect from a grizzly under the circumstances. Out on a trail not far from the station, looking for picture possibilities, she heard a growl. The bear was on her before she could think. She knew the drill well. If a tree is handy, climb it. Don't run; a grizzly is faster than a horse over a short distance. Stand your ground; a bear will often false charge. Drop anything you are carrying; it might divert attention. If seized, play dead. That's a lot to remember when your time comes.

Instinctively, she tried to fight back then went limp, and the grizzly dropped her. She figured that the episode may have lasted a dozen seconds. Help and medical assistance at the Lake Hospital were close at hand. Her wounds, although painful, were not grave, and the scars should not be permanent. Because the chance of it happening again were about the same as getting hit by lightning the second time, she was not about to change her routine.

The bathroom I was using was her darkroom, and I asked to see some of her photographs. They were of professional quality, and she'd sold a number. Roger got out the projector and ran a film Nancy made that had been bought by a Florida television station, an engaging portrayal of the children of Mammoth. Their elementary school is in the residential area, where coyotes steal the cats and yammer through the night. Their homes look down on the steep canyon of the Gardner River. On the other side of the valley, the craggy flanks of Mount Everts rise a thousand feet above Mammoth. Walking to school, the children chattered, played, and invented games, casually detouring an occasional elk, seemingly unawed by the grandeur of their surroundings. Viewing Nancy's film, you suspect it will have a lasting impression.

Sipping jug wine after dinner we talked shop. The subject of mail service came up. It was the third winter at Lake for the Rudolphs. The first two winters mail was delivered only when someone from Mammoth happened to be in Lake on business. The year before my visit, after they had received no mail in the three weeks preceding Christmas, Roger stormed into headquarters and blistered the walls. Since then Mammoth staffers have taken turns providing a regular mail service to the interior stations.

"It gets them away from their desks and reminds them what we have to put up with," Nancy observed. "Lake isn't the job they're angling for, not with this relic of a building as a residence. Families with school-age children are not considered—although Townsley might do it. He'd do anything, since he believes suffering in the line of duty is good for you." They thought John to be a throwback to the days when the army administered the park and the commanding officer expected his orders to be obeyed. John would sooner plant palm trees on the parade ground in Mammoth than give consensus-building a try in his staff meetings—or so I was led to believe.

The climate for mavericks, I judged, was less than favorable in Yellowstone. Roger had come up against procedures fixed unalterably by long practice. He thought that he should follow the advice his father gave him: "Before they come for you with a box and cover you up, you ought to try working for yourself once." He wasn't sold on the Park Service adherence to tradition. "There's a lot wrong with the old boy system, and this park has some old boys who can't get it up in the morning. What bugs me about Townsley is that every time his pulse beats it's sending out Park Service vibes." Roger shook his head, tossing off his wine. "I don't understand that kind of attitude," understanding it all too well.

Roger reserved the right to flaunt tradition, but he took his work seriously. By anybody's standards, including Townsley's, he was a genuine commodity. He ran a superior operation and didn't tolerate lackluster performance. "My district is competitive, even if you plug in the confusion factor," he told me, "and I'll try new ways if I think they have a chance." He was also on the lookout for diversions, thumbing his nose at the rule that rangers do not take annual leave during the travel season. Every August he would drive the van a thousand miles to Manhattan Beach, ten miles south of Santa Monica, for the annual volleyball tournament. He waited until Nancy had gone to bed to tell me about an event in which volleyball seemed but a minor part of the festivities. "A couple of my old California buddies keep a place for me on their team," he said, relishing the memory. "Mostly, we kick back in the sun, drink a lot of beer, watch the action, and talk about things that have no connection to what we do the rest of the year. Nancy tells me I should grow up. I guess it's about time."

Friday morning at breakfast we further depleted the Rudolph egg supply, drank many cups of Nancy's special blend of tea, and watched the comings and goings at a bird feeder sitting on a mound of snow just outside the dining room window. Chunky mountain chickadees, tiny bundles of energy with black caps and white eye stripes would sit for a moment, fluffing out their feathers to trap warm air next to the skin. Red-breasted nuthatches were joined by a hairy woodpecker, then all scattered when a pine marten came bounding out from the trees. Not so large as a house cat, with a foxy face and handsome, yellow-brown fur similar to a Russian sable, the marten is a fearless predator seldom seen. It was my first, and I was thrilled.

Nancy apologized for the feeder, saying that her only excuse was that it helped her morale more than it hurt the birds. Rangers rebuke summer visitors for feeding wildlife. Winters, they put up feeders to please their wives, and maybe themselves. The marten worked away at a hunk of suet tied to a blue china bowl. Changing tactics, he gripped the rim with his sharp little teeth and backed down the slope, dragging bowl and suet. "I'll look for it in the spring," Nancy said. "By then he'll have a full set."

The Canyon district naturalist, Frank Walker, came in while we were watching the marten carry off his prize. A capable, unassuming man then in his early thirties with a bristly mustache, he regards the world with reserved amusement through horn-rimmed glasses. Called into active service as an army officer during his first tour at Yellowstone, he had assignments both as a ranger and naturalist. He said that John Townsley felt I might need a baby-sitter on the last leg of my trip back to Mammoth. Mmmm, I thought to myself. We pulled on our snowsuits and boots and gathered up gloves and helmets. I said goodbye to Nancy and Roger, who had welcomed me with all the islander's hospitality for a shipwrecked sailor. I asked myself once again, How does the Park Service attract such people?

The Rudolphs were in Yellowstone one more winter, during which time Nancy hitched a ride on a snow coach and made it to the hospital in time to have their first baby. A few weeks before the event she wrote to say that she would walk out rather than ride a snowmobile. "Slow as it is, the snow coach is the only way I'll travel out. No snowmobile for me. I'd rather have a home birth."

∪ ∪

A few minutes out of Lake village, Frank detoured to Fishing Bridge, which spans the Yellowstone River a half mile below its exit from Yellowstone Lake. Taking refuge behind the massive log pilings, we braced ourselves against bursts of wind that cut like a sickle, either carrying new snow or rearranging the old. A pair of black-necked Canada geese were beating their way down river. If they were honking their insistent music, the sound was carried away by the wind. An island below the bridge was barely visible, its trees no more than dark smudges. I asked Frank for a weather prediction, and he said, "Whatever they're having in Siberia."

In blizzardlike conditions we entered Hayden Valley, losing the protection of the trees. Although Frank was close ahead, I could just barely see his signal to halt. Like apparitions fading in and out of view, three buffalo were approaching through the driving snow, snorting steam. Crossing the road no more than ten yards in front, they suddenly swung about and faced us, completely filling the roadway. The animals were about ten feet long and higher at the hump than my head, their faces white masks of frozen snow. They were a fearsome sight. Frank leaned forward, mesmerized. Mindful that my machine was not equipped with a reverse gear, I asked him what we should do if they headed our way. "Let them," he answered. In a minute or two, their curiosity satisfied, they moved off into the meadow, swinging their heads from side to side to push away the snow and reach the stubble beneath.

We turned off the Grand Loop a couple of miles from Canyon junction, crossing the Yellowstone River on Chittenden Bridge and driving along the south rim of the Grand Canyon of the Yellowstone. Other famous canyons of the world are deeper and wider. None, in the judgment of an early explorer, "unite more potently the two major requisites of majesty and beauty." The snow had slackened noticeably by the time we reached the parking lot, where space had been plowed out for snowmobiles. A pathway between shoulder high banks of snow led to Artist Point, the classic viewpoint of the vast silent gorge immortalized by the artist Thomas Moran.

Yellowstone's Grand Canyon is preeminently a canyon of colors. The prevailing tint is yellow, with shadings of pink and white and orange. Moran conceded that any attempt to catch this palette was "beyond the reach of human art." The steep, bare walls of volcanic rock are broken by crenelated ledges that provide nesting places for osprey. The river, green as aquamarine and seemingly hard as stone, curves out of sight around great buttresses that thrust out from the canyon wall. We watched two ravens riding an updraft a thousand feet below.

A mile from us the river surged through a wide notch and, partly hidden by a hanging curtain of ice, made its free-fall from a height twice that of Niagara. The turmoil at the Lower Falls could be judged by the clearly heard thunder. Snow that had collected on rocks and pinnacles and on the few trees dotting the precipitous slopes added a vivid contrast to the gorgeous hues of the canyon. I thought we were seeing it under the best possible conditions. Frank said the view from any point at any time is sublime. His aesthetic scale didn't register anything higher.

We stopped for lunch in the residential area of Canyon village at the home of the district ranger, Tim Blank. A well-spoken man with clean-cut features, he would not have looked out of place wearing a three-piece suit in a business office. His wife Bev, dark-haired and gracious, served an elegant lunch. She was not a complainer, yet it was evident in our conversation that for someone who delights in concerts and museums and good food, the six winters snowbound at Canyon had been dispiriting. Every few weeks she and Tim would ride his snowmobile out to their car and escape to Bozeman. "We have to," she said.

Tim said he'd received word from Townsley that Frank and I were to return to Mammoth by way of Dunraven Pass instead of the less hazardous route across the middle of the park to Norris. I considered the itinerary change a bad omen. Winter storms get in their best licks at Dunraven Pass, high on the shoulder of Mount Washburn. This section of the Grand Loop had been closed to snowmobiles for several days by the storm that stranded me at Old Faithful. In some places, Tim said, we might have to make several runs to break through the drifts. We were to carry a radio and check with him hourly. "Just a normal precaution," he said. "With luck you'll make it."

It was an irrational hope for an ill-advised venture. By Townsley's code, risking life and limb strengthens character. To hell with John Townsley and his cockeyed scheme, I told Tim. He smiled for the first time, cracked a joke about not having a St. Bernard on his search and rescue team, and told a Townsley story. John and his chief ranger were making a winter inspection tour of the interior stations. The day they were scheduled to come into Canyon over Dunraven Pass, a howler of a storm blew in. A sensible person would have bagged the trip, but the reputation of a Yellowstone superintendent is not diminished by a display of true grit. According to Tim, John and his chief ranger came down off the mountain pushing so much snow ahead of their machines that only their helmets were visible. "I wouldn't put John up there with Hannibal and the elephants," Tim said, smiling for the second time, "but he did display a certain amount of grim determination."

I let Frank talk me into driving a few miles up Mount Washburn. It was barely passable for snowmobiles, and maybe for elephants too, but Frank wanted to show me his favorite view of the Yellowstone caldera. This thousand-square-mile crater, the product of a gigantic volcanic explosion twenty-five hundred times more powerful than the one at Mount St. Helens, produced the park's steam and hot water phenomena. At the overlook, Frank and I made a serious tactical mistake. We steered our machines off the road into deep snow that hadn't been touched by the plows all winter.

The visibility was poor. In the foreground we could just see the upper wall of the canyon, with its reddish and yellow streaks. Frank's account of the most significant geologic happening in Yellowstone's history would have been more meaningful if Flat Mountain, to the south of Yellowstone Lake, marking the most distant boundary of the caldera, had been more than a shadowy form. And while he talked our machines were sinking into the soft snow. When we attempted to drive them out they wouldn't budge. We had overlooked a basic rule of snowmobiling. Before stopping your machine in loose snow, make a circle and keep repeating it until you have packed down an escape route.

I figured there was no help for it but to abandon the machines and walk back to Canyon. Frank looked at the terrain for a while and said the trick would be to put gravity to work. The path back to the road sloped slightly downhill. If we could turn the machines around, we might be able to drive them down the track we made coming in. That was a large if, for the Arctic Cat Panther must weigh several hundred pounds. Lifting and shoving, and stopping frequently to gasp for breath, we somehow managed to move the rear of the machine, at one inch per lift, through a hundred and eighty degrees. With Frank pushing, I guided the machine down the gradual incline to the road.

Exhausted, and dripping wet under our snowsuits, we sat on the rescued machine and considered our options. I said to Frank, "Sanity demands that we double up on this machine and let Tim retrieve the other one. How does that sound to you?" He turned the proposal over in his mind and said, "So we get back to Mammoth and tell Townsley that we didn't know better than to drive a snowmobile off the road into deep snow. How does that grab you?" Glumly, we stood up and spit on our gloves.

ʊ ʊ

The Townsleys lived in the big stone residence built by the army for the post commander. It had four large bedrooms on the second floor where I was assigned and a hallway not much smaller than the main corridor of the interior building. Unpacking my duffel bag, I glimpsed a dark shape move out from under the bed and sidle in my direction. I froze and might have done something foolish if Frank hadn't mentioned that John's daughter Gail kept a pet skunk in the house.

I could hear a cheerful blend of conversation and laughter downstairs as

I showered and changed into clean clothes. A few old friends were among the staff members and spouses the Townsleys had invited in for drinks. Park communities are notably convivial, in part because culturally bleak corners of the world need festive occasions. Before the party broke up, John asked me to comment on my tour, noting that I'd started out a "halfway skeptic" of snowmobile use in Yellowstone.

I said it may have been the most memorable of all my visits to the park. From the first time I stopped my machine and looked about I began hating it less and less. You couldn't experience the glory of Yellowstone in winter and not feel grateful to the snowmobile. I said that I had ended up a three-quarters convert because the machine does have some detestable qualities. In the discussion that followed I received some good-natured ribbing from a spirited minority for supporting the snowmobile camp. I was a little chagrined to be defending the establishment for a change.

After the guests departed, Elaine and John and I sat down to dinner, candles lighting the spacious dining room. When you were entertained by the Townsleys, you were made to feel that the pleasure was theirs. Tall, trim, and competent, Elaine excelled as a hostess. She had a lot of practice, for dignitaries arrive in Yellowstone regularly during the summer. The hospitality they receive is not without an ulterior motive, however. Yellowstone cannot have too many champions. "Friends of the service" have strengthened the parks mightily. Alfred A. Knopf may have been recruited in this dining room, John and I agreed.

The year was 1946. Receiving word that Knopf was planning a visit to Yellowstone, the director alerted the superintendent, who gave him the royal treatment. Knopf dated his long love affair with the parks to this experience. Five years later, in 1951, he published *The National Parks* by Freeman Tilden, now in a third edition. On his visits, the urbane dean of American publishers always carried a case of wine in the trunk of his car should there be any trouble with the local water. Park Service people found him a charming and candid companion, and he often called them a "separate and wonderful breed." In a tape he made for the Park Service archives he spoke of the "dividends" he received from his travels in the parks. "I regarded the National Park Service as far and away the finest government bureau that I ever had anything to do with. The men in my day were not time clock-punchers. I don't think you'll find that kind of spirit very widespread in the land today. I always felt happy with park people. I got to know most of the superintendents, many of the rangers, and always felt a great lightening of the spirit and clearing of the air when my car crossed the border into a national park."

Elaine said they had entertained some notable friends of the service in rustic quarters. In response to my comment that the superintendent's residence was palatial, she laughed and said, "It's a reward. This is our twenty-seventh house." She met John in Yosemite, having come up from Fresno to work summers for the concessioner while going to school, a tradition in her family. Eventually she managed the dining room at Camp Curry. John recalled the first time he saw her skiing at Badger Pass, "graceful and good-looking." They were married in the Yosemite chapel and moved to Fort Collins for his last year at Colorado State.

Not wishing to show John any preference because of his father, the Park Service almost didn't hire him. Legend attached to Forest Townsley of Yosemite. He was born on the Nebraska frontier not long after Yellowstone was established and had only a third-grade education. "He was a man," John said "who had a great sense of looking and seeing and learning." He taught himself taxidermy and then mounted specimens in Yosemite's first museum. He led rescue teams on hazardous missions in the high country and was a fearless law enforcement officer. The director sent him to reorganize ranger forces in other parks. A natural leader, he was regarded by his contemporaries as the chief ranger of the Park Service.

John had to wait several years, making do with snow survey work in the winter at Yosemite and odd jobs with the concessioner in the summer. In 1955 he received a ranger appointment at Hawaii Volcanoes. He thought he knew a great deal about rangering until an old Portuguese veteran took an interest in him. "I thought I could shoe a horse before I met Tony," John said. "He'd learned the trade in the army, and he was a precisionist when it came to shaping a hoof and working shoes for it."

After a couple of years he moved to Yosemite, then to Oregon Caves as an administrative assistant, and to Washington for management training. Attracting attention, he stayed on, always hoping to get back to the parks. Instead, "It was George Hartzog's pleasure that I consider taking on the task of organizing the parks of New York City into a single administrative group."

New York City would have been his last choice, he said. "And yet Elaine and I consider it one of our great experiences." It gave him a different perspective. "In Yosemite, when a car with an Illinois plate stopped and the driver asked, 'What can we see here in two hours?' I felt like answering, 'Why didn't you buy a postcard in Merced and save some gas?' After five years in New York I would have said to the driver, 'Pull over and let's talk about what you could do in that time and what you could get from it.'"

I liked John, but then I'd never worked for him. He was a reserved and complicated man who kept most of his staff at arm's length. He and I had always been on good terms although we were not close friends. His true friends, I believe, were those with whom he rangered early in his career. His standards were high, and no one was more dedicated to Yellowstone.

After dinner John and I adjourned to the living room. I sat on a green sofa drawn up in front of the fireplace. John stretched out with a pillow on the floor. Photographs and paintings of park scenes surrounded us. You could tell the Townsleys appreciated fine things; their furniture might have been handed down, and everything had a reason for being there. I thought the fire was doing nicely, but John began to fuss with the logs, which were giving off a bit of smoke. He thought they should be doing better. We went out on the front porch to get a couple more armfuls of wood and froze our fingers in the process.

A Yellowstone superintendent is responsible for the most popular scenic preserve in the country and for a resort complex that can accommodate nine thousand people. A superintendent contemplating policies that would benefit wildlife but restrict visitor use would be forcefully reminded by the governor of Wyoming and the state's congressional delegation that Yellowstone is a mainstay of the Wyoming tourist industry. My experience has been that whatever he or she decides, large numbers of people will complain that there should be more of this and less of that.

I asked John what it takes to be superintendent of Yellowstone, and he said, "The ability to endure dilemmas." Take fishing: "No matter what excuses we manufacture, it's a form of hunting. How can we justify killing trout, but not elk? We'd rather the subject never came up." Fly-fishermen, the most refined branch of the species, will insist that because the largest part of their time is spent not catching fish, their memory banks contain many more images of glorious days along mountain streams than of trout they have landed. Still, as John remarked, the single purpose of an angler is to catch fish, many of which are fried in a light dusting of flour or corn meal. Alluding to the fact that fishermen constitute a powerful and possibly invincible political faction, John said, with exquisite tact:

> The ambiguity of our position is due to the delicacy of our situation. As a policy analyst in Washington, I did some speech writing for director Connie Wirth. Less diplomatic in those days, I introduced the concept of a catch-and-release fishing policy in a speech Connie was making to a camping association. He as much as ran me out of his office. Now, when I speak to fishing groups, I say that nothing would give me greater joy than to teach my grandchildren how to fish in a Yellowstone stream. I mention also that the matter of fishing in a national park needs to be reexamined and that a catch-and-release policy for the whole park may not be far off. In an offhand way I suggest the time may come when fishing will

not be permitted. It's time to begin a public dialogue, just as we've done on other touchy issues that have taken decades to work through before gaining public acceptance. These are long roads.

There are novel perceptions of what constitutes appropriate use of the parks, John and I agreed. Evel Knievel applied for permission to jump a motorcycle across the Grand Canyon. A doggedly persistent patriot wanted to festoon the Statue of Liberty with a giant red, white, and blue sash in honor of the 1976 Bicentennial. Maintaining an unencouraging reserve, Park Service officials call such propositions "nonconforming uses" and reject most out of hand. A resort to reason doesn't work. Both sides believe theirs is the reasonable one. There is a parallel with the notable utterance of Oliver Wendell Holmes about law, that its life has not been logic but experience.

We remembered how Les Arnberger, the highly respected Yosemite superintendent, triggered a major dispute a few years back by permitting hang gliding on a trial basis from Glacier Point above Yosemite Valley. Scolded by conservationists, Director Gary Everhardt and Assistant Secretary Nat Reed agreed to take a look. Because I was an assistant to the director for policy, I went along to Yosemite to see what the policy on hang gliding was going to be.

I'd met Gary when he was Jack Anderson's assistant superintendent. By training an engineer and by instinct a canny negotiator seldom outflanked, Gary had a gift for winning friends. Yet he didn't do much better than break even the night he picked me up at the Mammoth Hotel and introduced me to the folks at the Blue Goose in Gardiner. Sauntering down the long bar, calling some of the regulars by name, giving one and all his trademark greeting, "How you doing?" Gary warmed up the crowd only a few degrees. No one else in the organization could have done that well. The customers at the Blue Goose put federal employees down there with the pond scum.

Nat Reed was a rarity, a wealthy Republican with a deep concern for conservation. Traditionally, an assistant secretary stays out of agency operations. Not so Nat Reed, who poked his nose, a distinguishing feature, into anything that caught his fancy. Calling you into his office, he would unfold from behind his desk to his full spare height, looking down on you like a predatory great blue heron surveying a promising pond. Ignoring ordinary channels, he issued terse orders on tiny note cards. Truth to tell, after his departure we missed him, his well-cut suits that gave the place tone, and his "Nat-O-Grams." Above all, he loved the parks and did many fine things for them.

Only a John Muir could do justice to the panoramic view from Glacier Point. "Words die away on the tongue," someone said—or should have. Straight down is the length and breadth of Yosemite Valley. Directly across, the entire drop of Yosemite Falls is visible, tumbling down sheer canyon walls. Above and beyond are the exposed granite contours and thinly forested slopes of the immense High Sierra range stretching away in all directions. Off to the right and only three miles distant, the summit of mighty Half Dome appears to be at eye level, although it is really two thousand feet higher.

Early on a bright summer morning, Nat, Gary, and I watched a pilot make preparations for the launch. Wearing a hard hat that came down to his eyebrows, he shrugged into a well-worn harness and a padded tunic attached by straps to a D-ring. Yelling "Clear!" he trotted down the incline toward the rim, holding the control bar waist high, until the V-shaped glider caught the air and lifted him into space. One by one, five more pilots repeated the procedure. Like a swarm of large and richly decorated butterflies chasing each other in slow and graceful sweeps, they skimmed down to a landing in a meadow three thousand feet below. I thought it an exquisitely beautiful sight and a tribute to the courage and skill of the pilots.

Later, with the pilots sitting around us on the rocks, a spokesman argued their case. "We are responsible people, not daredevils," he began, "and we love and respect Yosemite." Barely twenty, slender as a sprinter and wearing a blue and white jogging suit, he spoke with both conviction and poise. He was fired up about hang gliding, and he made a lot of sense:

> Veteran pilots log all their flights. A senior pilot grades us and marks our logs. Only those who achieve a four rating are eligible to apply for the slots at Glacier Point. A maximum of six flights are allowed daily, and they must be completed before eight in the morning to avoid drawing crowds. We feel that what we do is compatible with park principles. You encourage use of canoes because they make no noise and leave no mark. Neither do we. You built a ski area down the road at Badger Pass and built lifts, a lodge, and a parking lot. We have no such requirements. We see no difference between climbers scaling the face of El Capitan and hang gliders taking off from Glacier Point. Don't turn us down just because we are proposing something new. What we do is what people have dreamed of doing for a long time, soaring unassisted. Launching from Glacier Point is the ultimate.

Gary had met with representatives of the major conservation organizations before going to Yosemite. They called hang gliding a "carnival stunt" and promised an all-out campaign against it. Listening to the harangue,

I was again persuaded that if they were less preachy and possessed just a smidgen of humor they would do better. They were suspicious of things that work in practice but not in theory.

Both Gary and Nat had viewed the hang gliding experiment with misgivings. It didn't seem appropriate. They were also aware that Les Arngerger, whose judgment they trusted, hadn't made his decision in haste. So they went to Yosemite pretty well siding with the conservationists—and were won over by the candor and eloquence of the hang glider spokesman and the grace of his sport. The morning flights still continue. "I knew that guy was going to be hard to deny," Gary said to me on the airplane back to Washington. "He had the look."

John and I swapped stories long after Elaine had said good night. We had decided to turn in, and he was spreading ashes over the hot coals in the fireplace when I brought up something Bev Blank had said that troubled me. I'd told her that the lunch she served would have stacked up well with some of Washington's better restaurants. She smiled and said she didn't get many chances to practice during the snowmobile season.

John seemed to be making a project out of extinguishing the fire, or maybe he was formulating a reply. According to a member of his staff, he inherited his work ethic from a tough taskmaster, his father. "Chief Townsley demanded an honest day's work from his rangers, at the minimum. The day John left to join the marines, an old ranger dropped by to give him a piece of advice. 'When the sergeant tells you to clean the urinals, ram it up to your elbow.' Some of us think the advice was unnecessary."

As John was dusting off his hands I observed that a wife confined to a cabin for six long winters was getting the short end of the stick from the Park Service. I also didn't think that spending his days patrolling on a snowmobile was much of a growth opportunity for a district ranger. My audacity earned me a long stare from those flinty blue eyes. Once again it occurred to me that working for John Townsley, a man of not always forgivable contradictions, could have its down side.

Patiently, he explained that he'd been trying to work a transfer for Tim Blank, "a good man, in a quiet way, who hasn't caught the lightning yet." There were too many other district rangers in the Service competing for every vacancy. Paying your dues as a ranger, he said, is like taking required courses in school. You are satisfied at the time that it's a total waste of time, and yet you almost always pick up something that's valuable to you later.

One winter while I was waiting for a permanent appointment I worked on the Yosemite road crew. Our job was to sand the five miles of road between Chinquapin and Badger Pass ski area. The rule was that you had to get three loads of sand on the road before the traffic started. We shoveled three tons of sand up into the truck, went out and scattered it by hand, and came back for another load. After a half-dozen trips I had some thoughts about the value of a college education.

I took every job that came along and was getting really discouraged when an old ranger for whom I had the greatest respect said, "Well, right now, you think it's not working out, but some day the sum of all these experiences will give you some reference points that you couldn't have gotten if you had moved right into a permanent ranger job."

Bev has had all she wants of cabin life, and yet some day she may remember it differently. Looking back at my own career, the best of all experiences Elaine and I have had was the first year we were married, the summer after I finished at Colorado State. We had the special privilege of living at Buck Camp in the far south of Yosemite. This was new to Elaine, putting all our groceries on the back of a mule and heading down the trail.

I'll never forget the look of the cabin the day we rode up. The shutters were gone, and the windows were out, and you knew darned well you'd had a bear. He had distributed the flour and other stuff and torn up the mattresses. The martens living in the attic had left their sign up and down the walls. The crudest kind of mucking out was in order.

Well, little things are the ones we recall. There was a beautiful big patch of delphinium growing in the side meadow in front of the cabin. We had a water tank fixed to the wood stove to make hot water with a shower head out on the porch. There wasn't any curtain, of course, and you could stand here taking a shower late of an evening with the sun setting over the red firs and watch dozens of hummingbirds feeding on the delphinium, the most magnificent display of hummingbirds I've every seen.

Our old mule was named Gilbert, and Gilbert, having suffered a number of trials around Yosemite, had little use for me. He'd kick the hell out of me any time he could. But he just had the greatest love for Elaine. Frequently in the evenings we would see Gilbert standing in the delphinium patch watching the hummingbirds, with his head cocked over and one ear down. While our experience at Buck Camp may not be pertinent to what Bev and Tim are putting up with now, it's one of the things you build a life out of.

2

Fort Yellowstone

At dusk on a May evening four months later, driving an orange Volkswagen bug crammed with enough clothes and books to last the summer, I approached Gardiner, Yellowstone's north entrance. It had taken four days to drive the two thousand miles from Reston, Virginia. The thermometer stayed in the low seventies, and spring was at its old business of remaking the world. A fresh breeze flowed in the sun roof, and a million red-winged blackbirds assembled along the roadsides to display their scarlet and yellow epaulets.

Passing a couple of modest motels and a single line of cottages, I dipped down for the bridge over the Yellowstone River and climbed into the humdrum, changeless hamlet of six hundred souls and no amenities. Beside the K Bar Cafe a buckboard sporting a new coat of black and green paint was chained to a pole flying an American flag. Next door, the Two Bit Saloon advertised raft trips down Yankee Jim Canyon, the swiftest part of the Yellowstone River. I turned left on Park Street, the main drag. All of the stores and bars are on the north side. The street is the park boundary.

Whenever I drive from Mammoth down to Gardiner and catch sight of the false-fronted buildings on Park Street at the edge of the grassy flat, I see in my mind's eye the cluster of unpainted look-alikes facing Boot Hill, where Shane rode into town one night to settle his score with the hired killer dressed in black, Little Joe watching the action from beneath the swinging doors.

By the time I checked in at the Wilson Motel, a neat and comfortable lodging place, and had a quick shower, I was thinking mainly of a cold beer. Two venerable saloons stand shoulder to shoulder on Park Street. Unless appearances are deceiving, they were serving soldiers during Teddy Roosevelt's visit. The bird above the entrance to the Blue Goose is a middling likeness, sitting on a base of flickering blue lights. The builder used brick and water-washed stones from the river, logs, and planks. I first thought the color scheme of the Ranger Tavern—two sickly shades of green—was a tribute to Yellowstone rangers. Nothing I've heard inside the establishment would confirm that theory.

A ranger I know has devoted considerable time to "after-hours mingling" in Gardiner. He lives in the neighborhood, a laid-back guy who would probably have a miner's cabin or a geodesic dome with a couple of llamas tethered outside. He gave me a rundown on the Gardiner bar scene. Either the Ranger Tavern or the Blue Goose would be a hell of a place to raise a posse. The former, he said, draws "construction workers, rednecks, and would-be cowboys." Patrons of the latter include "drifters not in search of long-term employment and descendants of old Gardiner families with poaching in their blood."

Inevitably, with the mention of poaching, came a story. "This one happens to be true," he told me. A Gardiner man who wasn't too smart and was on everyone's short list of suspected poachers had killed an elk near a trailhead in the park. Unable to lift the animal into his van, he asked a passing hiker for help. The hiker then flagged down a ranger patrol car, and the poacher was arrested and fined. Sometime later the park was hiring truck drivers, and he applied. The personnel officer who interviewed him, no smarter than he, gave him a job. Celebrating his good fortune in a Gardiner bar, the man was heard to say, "I wonder how many elk you can load on a dump truck?"

The inside of the Blue Goose was dim and noisy, a long bar down the left side and a couple of game machines—"Deluxe Space Invaders" and "Draw Poker"—lighting up the right. Under a mounted elk head decorated with a red hunting cap, two men in woolen shirts were shooting pool. Only elitists ask for a glass when ordering beer at the Blue Goose. Locals drink Miller and Bud from long-necked bottles, and the pool sharks toss their empties into a green plastic garbage can.

Before he got to me, Larry the bartender finished telling the man on the next stool how he happened to leave his service station job somewhere in Oklahoma. The town fathers had passed ordinances that cramped his life-style: "No junk cars on your property, no dogs running loose, no loud music after ten at night, that kind of bullshit." My neighbor, who had a beard that reached to his belly button, said, "I'm for shooting all the politicians." Larry had a better idea: "If you line them up, I'll run em down with my pickup."

Listening to similar raps against people and beliefs I feel good about, I was again made aware that although Gardiner is a gateway to a renowned park, its citizens could care less what kind of an image the town projects. Lacking a drugstore or a bank or a doctor, it's a rough community to sell, and no one is trying all that hard. The Blue Goose's customers disparage the Park Service for the same reasons Alaskans detest the Sierra Club. Gardiner doesn't care for the people who live up on the government reservation, and so far as I can determine there hasn't been a flicker of cooperation between the two communities.

Remembering the warning of my ranger friend, "Nobody eats dinner here twice," I filled up on Coors and cashews and was ready for breakfast when I walked into the Town Cafe at six o'clock the next morning. I noticed that the flashing arrow above the doorway, a Gardiner landmark, had several bulbs on the blink. A leggy waitress with rings on most of her fingers and no pretensions served me eggs soft-scrambled to such perfection that I told her to kiss the cook. I ate like an orphan and sent her back for more toast. Because I would be doing my own cooking for several months, I made the most of a good meal and solicitous service.

I walked down Park Street in the bright beginnings of a new day. In the grass on the other side, a chin-high picket fence of metal was topped by a pipe to prevent wildlife from getting hung up. Between sips of ferociously strong carry-out coffee, I regarded the panorama of northern Yellowstone, so pleasing I half expected a sign with a Thoreau quote.

Half a mile wide, the meadow bordering the town is as flat as a table. Above low and treeless foothills green forests rise ever higher. Hidden from sight, the village of Mammoth occupies a bench high on the slope of Sepulcher Mountain. To the left and right, Mount Everts and Electric Peak command the skyline. In all that landscape of wondrous freshness nothing stirred. I was conscious of an upward surge of the spirit prompted by stunning scenery, the sun warming my shoulders, and the silence of a spring morning in the Rocky Mountains.

It took a while to check out of the Wilson, a homey establishment. Guests who do business without passing the time of day are considered uncivil. The man at the desk had a tanned and freckled face and a pair of honest old eyes. I asked about Jardine, the ghost town that lingers on at the end of a dirt road four miles east of Gardiner. Years ago prospectors scratched out gold at the diggings there. No one knows or dares ask what the few dozen residents do who live in the mobile homes mounted on cinder blocks and frame houses that tilt every which way.

Jardine was mostly quiet now, he said. Must have been two, three years since a nosy tourist returned from a walking tour of the town, looking in all the windows, and found his car covered with graffiti like a New York subway car. I laughed appreciatively, for there was probably a grain of truth to the story. I'd be willing to bet he was born and raised in Gardiner or Jardine and maybe a little poaching in his past, too, but little is certain in life.

I entered the park through the massive memorial arch built by the army and named for Theodore Roosevelt. It was placed opposite the old train station so tourists would be impressed as they transferred to carriages for the drive to Mammoth. Stone towers fifty feet high support the arch, on which is inscribed a lofty phrase from the Yellowstone enabling act: "For the Benefit and Enjoyment of the People."

Stopping to inspect the entrance sign, done in Yellowstone's signature colors of yellow on red, I noticed a pronghorn standing in the meadow, looking like a creature from the grasslands of Africa. I cut the motor and took a long look. He was a beauty, the color of dried grass, with striking patterns of white on the front and a large patch on the rump. Graceful black horns were slightly curved. He watched me with wide-set eyes, his muscles bunched and tense. The sound of the motor when I turned the key startled him into bounding flight.

Smaller than a deer, the pronghorn is born to run, his ancestors having invested in speed and keen eyesight for protection. If a race could be arranged to determine the swiftest land animal, the pronghorn would trail only the cheetah in the early going. Then he would move into the lead, cruising easily at forty miles an hour and capable of bursts of up to sixty. Needing large amounts of oxygen, he speeds along with mouth wide open, gulping in as much air as he can.

The north entrance road gains elevation steadily as it winds up the Gardner River gorge. (Both the town and the river were named for an early fur trapper, Johnson Gardner, but a mapmaker misled by Jim Bridger's Virginia drawl gave the town an extra vowel.) The road crosses over the river and back again, passing under the deeply gullied face of Mount Everts, a wall so abrupt it seems climbable only on a dare. Halfway to Mammoth the stream loops through a flat meadow, and the road turns from the river and sweeps up the slope of Terrace Mountain. Four miles directly ahead is Bunsen Peak, the forested cone of an extinct volcano named for the inventor of the laboratory burner, who also dabbled in volcanoes. Running between a campground and the residential area, the highway tops the last rise and makes a sharp left turn. Without warning it widens and acquires a grass median and concrete curbs, becoming a boulevard that divides the village.

Mammoth occupies a terrace of twenty-odd acres facing the hot springs formation. I've always liked the look of the place. The buildings on the south side of the boulevard have the vaguely institutional look of a military post. Those to the north, the concession facilities, suggest an old resort. There have been few additions to the village in the last half century.

The largest of the concession buildings, the hotel, has a curious shape: a four-story, unadorned, rectangular box, actually a wing added to the original hotel in 1914 and somehow spared when the old building was torn down. All of the space between the hotel and a ridge behind is filled with tidy little cabins. The restaurant next door is a gem, painted in pastel colors and with floor-to-ceiling windows. The entrance steps to the general store are flanked by bear-proof garbage cans, and the Chevron service station may have pumped gas for the single-seater Ford receiving the first automobile permit to enter the park on July 31, 1915.

Before the Park Service took over, the numerous lodge, restaurant, and transportation companies were virtually unregulated. Their pitchmen engaged in murderous competition. "They lurked at the railroad stations and attacked the tourists stepping down from the trains with the most objectionable kind of amusement-park barker's routine," reported the biographer of Steve Mather. "Greenhorns usually found themselves wrapped up and delivered before they had got their legs untangled. What they had been delivered to was a surprise and shock. . . . The kitchens . . . would have raised the gorge of a black ant."

Mather soon realized the parks were no place for the free enterprise system. He dismissed small-bore and rapacious operators and forced the reliable ones to merge until each park had one franchise holder supplying all services. The Mather solution survives. A park concession is a monopoly controlled by the government, not unlike a public utility. The Park Service sets the rules and approves the rates, protecting the concessioner from competition while looking out for the public interest. The arrangement sounds a lot better than it works.

∪ ∪

South of the boulevard are the buildings of Old Fort Yellowstone, the former quarters, offices, warehouses, and stables now serving as park headquarters. I turned into officers' row, a long line of attractive and substantial buildings with red roofs shaded by pines and cottonwoods. The first several, including the superintendent's residence, are stone. The remainder, painted brown and richly supplied with chimneys, are double quarters housing two families.

Officers' row fronts on the old parade ground. Here the Corps of Engineers transformed several dusty acres, hauling in six inches of top soil, dressing it with manure from the stables, constructing irrigation ditches, and producing a lawn that the Gardiner newspaper called "truly remarkable." Streets and concrete sidewalks were laid out, and the settlement was supplied with electricity from a power plant on the Gardner River.

The Fort Yellowstone day began at sunrise with the sounding of reveille by the bugler on Capitol Hill and the raising of the parade ground flag. A travel writer staying in the old Mammoth Hotel at the turn of the century was awakened by the racket. He saw a troop of cavalry dressed in white coveralls and riding white mounts file onto the parade ground and heard the officers' shouted orders as their horses moved through the drill formations. He thought it an impressive sight, military maneuvers on the greensward before the stately buildings along officers' row, and high mountain ridges on all sides.

Fort Yellowstone was a four-troop post, sixty cavalrymen to a troop. In the line behind officers' row are four former troop barracks and a post exchange. In the third line are four former stables, two built of stone. Quarried from the hills overlooking the Gardner River, the stone buildings have weathered to the same tan color as the outcroppings on Mount Everts. In a less formal pattern to the south are a variety of buildings, including the chapel, the last to be built and the loveliest. The three dozen buildings are on the National Register of Historic Places, and all are in use.

The fort doesn't bear the slightest resemblance to the barricaded forts of movie westerns. One of the best preserved of the army's frontier posts, it has retained most of its buildings in their original appearance and location and has adapted well to its present uses. Conveying to visitors a sense of strength and security, it seems to be keeping the modern world out and the traditions secure. The solid, functional structures have no doubt influenced what is called the "Yellowstone way." The army had good cause to be proud of its model post.

In the years after the Civil War, cavalry troops operating out of frontier forts protected wagon trains heading for Oregon and California. Considering itself the guardian of the West, the army had coveted Yellowstone from the time the park was established in 1872. High-ranking officers made no secret of their resentment when Congress placed the park under the administration of the secretary of the interior. Interior was then a catchall department responsible for the pension and patent offices, generally referred to as the "Great Miscellany."

As much as anything, feeble guidance and marginal support from Congress was the cause of Yellowstone's unpromising beginnings. Expecting the park to be self-supporting, Congress initially provided no appropriations. The first superintendent served without pay or staff. The enabling legislation contained no code of laws or legal authority to enforce regulations. Even if a poacher were caught red-handed, the only penalty was eviction from the park.

In 1875 the secretary of war organized a military expedition to inspect conditions in the park after receiving troubling reports that "Wonderland" was being destroyed. Signs of poaching were everywhere. Hide hunters had slaughtered four thousand elk the winter before, a member of the party reported. "Their carcasses and branching antlers can be seen on every hillside and in every valley."

Passing through Yellowstone a few weeks later, Capt. William Ludlow, a resourceful and perceptive officer of the Corps of Engineers, proved to be a romantic at heart when he described the geyser basins. "Nature, abandoning for the time all thoughts of utility, seems to have been amusing herself in this far-off and long-hidden corner of the world by devoting some of her grandest and most mysterious powers to the production of forms of majesty and beauty such as any man may not hope to rival."

Ludlow's enjoyment was dampened by the "hopeless and unrestrained barbarity" of vandals who defaced geyser formations, hacking away specimens for souvenirs. In the nick of time he fended off two women "with tucked-up skirts and rubber shoes, armed, one with an axe, the other with a spade," about to bring their weapons down on the cone of Castle Geyser. In 1882 Lt. Gen. Phil Sheridan toured the park with a caravan of three hundred horses and pack mules. In his report to the secretary of war he asked permission to protect Yellowstone from its enemies. "If authorized to do so," wrote the former commander of Union cavalry, "I can keep sufficient troops in the Park to accomplish this object."

Responding to public criticism, Congress provided funds for a police force. The ten assistant superintendents, who owed their appointments to political favoritism, were so grossly incompetent that they were generally referred to as "rabbit catchers." "A couple of cowboys could put the whole brigade to flight with blank cartridges," said one visitor. Poachers continued to operate almost within sight of park headquarters. A hotel company stored a ton of elk meat in its ice house and served trout killed by explosives.

The park needed strong leadership. Instead it received a rascally superintendent, Robert E. Carpenter. "He went upon the theory," observed one historian, "that the park was created as an instrument of profit to those who were shrewd enough to grasp the opportunity." Leaving Yellowstone during the winter season, he lobbied members of Congress to change the park boundaries, thereby opening valuable land on which he and his cronies had secretly filed claims. The clumsy attempt failed, but the publicity further eroded public confidence in the management of Yellowstone.

What to do about Yellowstone was the subject of a debate in Congress in the summer of 1886. A House select committee back from an inspection trip thought the park should be offered to the state of Wyoming. Those of like mind recommended it be returned to the public domain or sold to the highest bidder. A majority defended the park, but opponents were able to strike Yellowstone funding from the appropriation bill, effectively ending civilian administration.

On the evening of August 17, 1886, Troop M, First U.S. Cavalry, Capt. Moses Harris commanding, marched into Mammoth Hot Springs. Tents were thrown up, parties sent off to replace the assistant superintendents, and the civilian superintendent relieved of his duties. Regulations were posted prohibiting hunting, netting, and selling trout; defacing natural features; and running loose stock through the geyser basins. Hangers-on with no means of support—except poaching—were evicted.

Military administration, initially thought to be a temporary measure, continued for more than thirty years because it worked so well. Assuming the arrangement was permanent after a few years, the army constructed a showplace installation and named it Fort Yellowstone. The most imposing structures were put up by masons from Scotland, who brought their own water boys.

In 1889, at the age of twenty-three, the future balladeer of British imperialism, Rudyard Kipling, financed his first trip to the United States by writing travel accounts for his Indian newspaper, the *Allahabad Pioneer*. At Fort Yellowstone he received a lesson about the difference between American and British soldiers. To the brash young reporter with the fierce black mustache the troopers on duty in the park lacked the polish and snap of the British regulars back in India. By chance he talked to a Scot who had served a hitch under the Queen in England, "and the 'go-fever' being in his bones, had drifted to America, there to serve under Uncle Sam." Yes, he told Kipling, the discipline was more relaxed. "But don't you forget, Sir, that it's taught me how to trust myself, and my shooting irons. I don't want fifty orders to move me across the Park, and catch a poacher."

Kipling was as critical of the horses as of the soldiers, and said so to a young officer he met at Mammoth Hot Springs, most likely a recent West Point graduate. From a meager salary he had to provide his own subsistence, uniforms, arms, and horses. "He began to talk of his troops as I have heard his brethren in India talk," Kipling wrote. "Such a troop, built up carefully and watched lovingly, 'not a man that I would wish to exchange and I believe, not a man that would wish to leave on his own account. We're different, I believe, from the English. Your officers value the horses, we set store on the men. We train them more than we do the horses.'"

More civilians viewed Fort Yellowstone than any other installation except West Point. The fort brightened the image of the military, but the army repaid in full. It supplied competence and incorruptibility at a time when those virtues were most needed. Many proud old regiments, including a portion of Custer's Seventh Cavalry, were stationed at Fort Yellowstone. Traditionally, West Point's best students went into the Corps of Engineers. Those seeking adventure chose the cavalry. Of the eleven officers who commanded the post, six became generals and five were decorated for valor. There is a photograph of a guard mount ceremony on the parade ground in 1910. The officer of the day taking the salute is 2d Lt. Jonathan M. Wainwright. In a more solemn ceremony thirty-five years later, "Skinny" Wainwright and Douglas MacArthur, standing side by side on the deck of the battleship *Missouri* in Tokyo harbor, accepted the surrender of the armed forces of Japan.

Two events a year apart persuaded the military to withdraw. The National Park Service was established in 1916, and one of its first priorities was creating a professional corps of rangers to protect the parks. Then, after the United States entered World War I in 1917, the army agreed to turn Yellowstone over to the new agency.

Before Troops D and C of the Eleventh Cavalry formed up on the parade ground for the last time, troopers interested in park work were allowed to resign. They became the nucleus of Yellowstone's first ranger force. A photograph of the park's finest, taken soon afterward, shows thirty capable-looking men on horseback wearing the new ranger uniform: broad-brimmed Stetson, forest green Norfolk jacket, dress shirt and dark tie, and green trousers fitting into leather riding boots. Sunlight reflects from collar ornaments and the nickel-plated badge over the left breast pocket. Except for the disappearance of the high cavalry boots, a casualty of World War II, there have been few changes in the uniform.

∪ ∪

I stopped at the administration building to see John Townsley. Large enough to have quartered 120 soldiers, it's a big, squarish, stone structure, providing office space for the superintendent and the ranger, naturalist, research, and administrative divisions. The push bar on the yellow entrance door has made the same disagreeable clang for twenty years. In the superintendent's reception room, a pleasantly formal space with striking wildlife photographs, John's secretary explained he had been called to Washington unexpectedly, but Mac Berg, his administrative assistant, was expecting me. To be John's right-hand man, you'd need to be the equivalent of a utility fielder—useful, dependable, busy—and that's the way Mac struck me. He was a calm man with a serious mustache and apparently never walked more than fairly fast.

John's hostility to administrative routine was common knowledge. "For paperwork," a staff member told me, "he has the attention span of a hummingbird." He couldn't operate without the support of a person like Mac, a former ranger who wanted to be a superintendent. Untroubled by long hours, and a bachelor, he was getting valuable experience and considered himself lucky. He told me of the remarkable improvement in the restaurant at Chico Hot Springs, a rustic lodge thirty miles north of Mammoth where local characters tie their horses out front. We made a date for dinner. He offered helpful instructions about housekeeping matters, gave me the key to my apartment, and I went back to my car.

I drove down the boulevard and took the service road through the maintenance area. The first building on the left, a big stone structure, was the fire cache, the fancy name used in all parks for the place, even if it's no bigger than a broom closet, for storing fire-fighting equipment. A red fire engine, brightly polished although not of recent vintage, was parked at the ready in an open bay. Beyond, signs hanging from long, low buildings, also former stables, identified the blacksmith shop, the electrical shop, the paint shop, the equipment repair shop, and the grounds maintenance shop. Across the road were dozens of trucks, graders, oilers, rollers, and the big Snow Blast rigs for the winter drifts. Next to them was a Thiokol over-the-snow machine, a small cab positioned above widely spaced caterpillar treads. Smaller versions of this maintenance facility are seen in all of the developed areas.

Someone, with a feeling for the work of the Corps of Engineers, had salvaged an old horse-drawn Austin Grant grader and placed it on the grass at the end of the motor pool. Compared to modern equipment it looked like a toy, with rusting iron wheels and a complicated set of gears for adjusting a blade so small I marveled that the original Grand Loop was built with such puny equipment.

The apartment building functioned somewhat like a motel, housing park bachelors, couples, and people from the regional office and design and construction center who may be sent to Yellowstone on extended stays. Set back in a grove of pines and shaped like the letter *H*, with a high-pitched roof, wooden shutters on the double windows, and exposed timbers at either end, it suggests a mountain chalet. I found apartment M on the second floor of the north wing, and it provided for all my needs in a room measuring twelve by twenty feet, plus a closet and bathroom. The walls were so thick that I heard nothing from the other occupants, nor from the inmates of the jail across the street, although I often fell asleep listening to the quavering yelp of the coyotes and was awakened by ravens clattering away in the trees outside my windows.

The layout was so compact you couldn't take two steps in any direction without barking your shins. The sleeping space at one end had frilly white curtains at the windows, a padded easy chair, and a double bed boasting a reading light and a headboard compartment for storing books. The kitchen alcove at the other end held an electric stove, a sink, and cupboards. The refrigerator was against the wall in the middle, opposite a circular dining table provided with two straight-back chairs. The walls were bare, and the furniture of the indestructible variety; and the radiator hammered me awake every morning at the stroke of six. I was indescribably grateful to John Townsley for making it available.

Mac Berg had instructed me to draw kitchen supplies and bedding from the storehouse, a weathered frame structure with a porch full of a dozen or more electric stoves and refrigerators that had seen hard use. Ed Wolfe favored me with an expressionless stare when I pushed open the door. Immediately I was back in the supply room of Company I, 311th Infantry, 78th Division in wartime Camp Pickett, Virginia. My supply sergeant there was a tall, laconic man, and he too guarded his treasures against all entreaties. The orders Ed received from the superintendent's office, to give me whatever I asked, made him more gloomy than usual, or suspicious, or both.

I was properly patient and respectful. Early on I mentioned I'd worked with Gary Everhardt, obviously one of Ed's favorite people. I commented on a clipping pinned to the wall telling how Ed had taken a nine-pound brown from the Gardner, and he began to warm up. He took me downstairs, and I had my pick of the cutlery, such as it was. He even insisted that I take a couple of extra blankets, of the scratchy army surplus variety. But there had been a run on sheets, he said, and he could spare me only one until the laundry truck came next week. Game, set, and match to Mr. Wolfe.

I was ready for exercise by the time I finished unpacking and putting things away. Changing into jogging clothes, I started for the overlook above the Mammoth Hot Springs, about two miles distant. Loping through the parade ground, I could see aspen on the lower slopes of the mountains, their leaves a lighter green than the dark forests above. As the road tilted upward, I slowed down accordingly.

The Mammoth Hot Springs formation is one of the largest of its kind in the world. The terraces are constantly changing. Blue Spring, Cleopatra, Angel, vividly alive in the 1930s, are now gray and lifeless because hot water seeps were blocked and new outlets appeared elsewhere. Minerva Terrace has been likened to Carlsbad Cavern turned inside out. The water descends a stairway of pools, the overflow trickling down scalloped walls tinted by algae. Enough colors are present to fill a Crayola box. In the hottest run-off channels, white and yellow bacteria create brilliant contrasts. In the cooler water, oranges and greens and browns predominate.

From my vantage point on the upper terrace drive I could trace the westward course of the Yellowstone River to the point where it exited the park at Gardiner. On the far side of the river, the land rises sharply, broken by rocky plateaus and forested ridges. Stretching across the northeast horizon, the Absarokas were still mantled in snow. Below me, Mammoth was one tiny smudge. Above this rugged and defiant landscape, containing few people and much empty space, puffy white clouds drifted slowly in a windless blue sky.

Most Yellowstone visitors do not stray from the roadsides or the popular features. One reason for this, I am persuaded, is the perception that Yellowstone is an unquiet land populated with animals of unpredictable tendencies. Fear of the grizzly is endemic. A supervisory ranger I know said that although he had no qualms about patrolling the backcountry, he wouldn't take his wife and children. I also think of the man who came over to me and clutched my arm one morning when I was about to enter the Mammoth restaurant for breakfast. "Maybe I'm being foolish," he said, "but my wife went out for a stroll some time ago and hasn't returned. Do you think I should call the rangers?" Just then he saw her sauntering down the sidewalk of officers' row and hurried off. He obviously felt that in Yellowstone danger of an unknown kind isn't far away.

As I jogged by the hotel on the way up to the overlook, a bus was unloading passengers. A woman stopped to gaze at the handful of buildings, the outlandish hill of hot spring deposits, and the mountains above. She turned to a companion and said, "This isn't a real town."

3

Memorial Day Weekend

For tourists, May in Yellowstone is good news and bad news. It's hard to tell if winter is mellowing into spring or spring into summer. One day will be sparkling clear under a warming sun. The next will bring a chilly drizzle or enough snow to bring out the plows again. On the average there are nineteen days with temperatures below freezing in May, six in June, two in July, four in August, and fourteen in September. The few May visitors drive tentatively and talk like pioneers.

In early March the maintenance crews begin the formidable task of plowing the 370 miles of paved roads, the distance from Washington, D.C., to Albany. In some sections a bulldozer leads the way, pulling a wedge plow. Behind, a snow blower squirts the snow off to the side in a steady stream. Equipment operators are guided by the snow stakes, red tips marking the road shoulders, green the special obstacles. In the rugged mountain country traversed by the northeast and east entrance roads, a crew may be lucky to clear a mile a day.

Residents at the district stations check the daily progress by radio. The crews generally open a single lane on their first pass, enabling rangers and winterkeepers to retrieve cars stored for the winter. Chutes are cut through the side banks in buffalo territory, allowing animals that take advantage of the easy passageway to avoid the traffic. The opening dates for some entrance roads are the result of factors other than weather. Jackson and Cody, the south and east tourist centers, have exacted a promise from the Park Service that those entrances will be opened on the same day, May 1, so that neither is put at a disadvantage. Snowmobiling is so important to West

Yellowstone that the community persuaded the Park Service to delay the opening of the west entrance for a week to extend the snowmobile season.

On Friday of my first week in the park I checked the calendar taped to my refrigerator door. No appointments were listed. The next day was the start of the Memorial Day weekend. A pilgrimage was in order. In the box on the calendar for Saturday, May 27, I wrote "Old Faithful Geyser." It's important to plan ahead.

∪ ∪

Saturday was a day of promise. Storm clouds from the previous day had been swept from the sky, and the sun, coming up strong, began working on the hard frost. As the road to Old Faithful shook clear of the narrow canyon at the cliffs of Golden Gate and entered a wide, open plain, the sight of a trumpeter swan flying low across my path was instantly exhilarating. I cut the motor and rolled down the window. The soft clattering sound of air rushing over flight quills was clearly audible. There has always been something compelling about these great white birds. In ancient times they were creatures of legend and folklore. To lift into the air they "walk on water," using their webbed feet to gain speed as they skim along. I thought the encounter a good omen, and at mile 5.5 from Mammoth I pulled into a parking area beside a Ford Pinto partially devoured by rust.

A young woman in a red warm-up suit and a green cap, ear flaps down, was scanning the ridge behind Swan Lake with field glasses. "You're in luck," she said, pointing with a woolen mitten. A hawk with a slender body and pointed wings slipped above the sagebrush, showing white underparts, and in a flash was gone. I'm not good on hawks, I told her. "That's your marsh hawk," she said, talking like a bird book. "Note the white rump and how he held his wings above the horizontal, tilting side to side." Then she relaxed and gave me the widest of smiles and said, "You don't see many marsh hawks here."

Shivering in the early morning chill, I wandered over to look at the exhibit on the geology of the Gallatin range, hoping the caption writers had made the story more gripping than usual. I've had mostly bad luck with geology exhibits and geology walks, or maybe it's because when geologists start talking about layered breccias and lubate landforms I start thinking about lunch. "These mountains, recently uplifted, are composed of the park's oldest rocks." No doubt true, and yet it was hard to be serious about Pre-Colombian metamorphic rocks on a day when the surface of Swan Lake was so unscarred that it reflected the bordering hills and trees immaculately. Learning that the Gallatins were shaped by enormous heat and pressure two billion years ago did not quicken my pulse as much as observing the way their snowy peaks showed a flawless white edge against a vivid blue sky.

When I could uncurl my frozen fingers and get the key in the ignition slot I drove to Willow Park, at mile 9.5, a deep thicket of bushes and trees hiding Obsidian Creek. A woman in a zippered sweater and dark blue slacks, her gray hair caught in an insecure knot, was looking into the brush, camera at the ready. The sticker on the front bumper of a van with Washington state license plates identified the owner as a member of the North Olympic Fire Department. The one on the rear said, "Thurson County Fair August 2–5 What a Week." The fireman was in the driver's seat, nursing a head cold. He cranked down the window and said, "Morning. Look's like it's trying to warm up. There seems to be a moose in there. My wife wants a photograph and won't leave till she gets one."

A motherly woman with a laudable sense of priorities, she put her camera aside and insisted I take a cream-filled doughnut from a box she had purchased in West Yellowstone, all the while apologizing that it was a day old. The coffee she poured from a gallon thermos into a heavy enameled cup was strong and comforting. We were eating doughnuts and drinking coffee, standing side by side, when a cow moose poked her head through an opening not a van length away, looming black and huge out of the willow scrub. The woman would have been no more shocked had an intruder sauntered into her living room.

Only a little less startled, I registered the comically long nose, the ears furled into points and standing straight out like horns, and the growth of skin and hair hanging from the throat. The luminous eyes glanced our way, giving us a brief assessment, then the huge creature, taller than our heads at the shoulder, silently backed out of sight. I discovered my mouth was still full of half-chewed doughnut. The woman was distraught that she hadn't remembered her camera. I told her anyone not blessed with the most stoic disposition would have done the same.

Elk were everywhere, with their chocolate brown necks, coffee tan bodies and white rumps. Obsidian Hill, at mile 17, was made famous by Jim Bridger. The rocky formation, topped by a few pines, was formed when a volcanic flow lost headway and hardened. The true nature of the rocks is concealed by a weathered gray patina, except where fresh breaks reveal the shining black obsidian glass. To discourage souvenir hunters, identifying signs have been removed. Hunting here one day, according to legend, Bridger sighted a magnificent elk. Taking careful aim, he fired without result and did so again and again until he realized the mountain of glass was acting as a telescope and the elk was twenty-five miles away. Sharp-edged tools made from Obsidian Hill and traded from tribe to tribe have been found in Indian sites as far distant as the Ohio Valley.

From mile 33 at Madison Junction to Old Faithful the Firehole River and Grand Loop Road are side by side much of the way. A renowned trout stream, the Firehole is also one of the most pleasing to the eye. I sat for a while on a log at a place where sunlight touching the riffles made them sparkle like silver. The sound was lovely, broken only by a strident flicker endlessly repeating his name. Pines along the far bank provided a bright green backdrop. Downstream, a mallard's chicks were practicing skimming on a bottle-green pool.

The waters of the Firehole are not like those of an ordinary cold-water mountain stream. Flowing through thermal basins and receiving run-off from geysers and hot springs, the Firehole stays in a summer mode all year. Chemical elements from the discharges act like fertilizers, enriching the food chain and enormously increasing productivity. Rainbows grow faster in the Firehole than they do in many fish hatcheries. What you have in the Firehole, someone observed, resembles a bird feeder fifteen miles long, only there are brown and rainbow trout instead of finches and grosbeaks.

Perhaps fifty spectators were assembled at the double row of benches in front of Old Faithful Geyser when I sat down next to a woman who wore a plaid woolen scarf, one end dangling to the ground, and a wool hat with a narrow brim that must have been sat upon repeatedly. She was reading a booklet with a familiar blue and white cover, "The Story of Old Faithful," and lost no time telling me the geyser doesn't perform regularly and that we could be in for a long wait.

Geysers are among the rarest of nature's wonders, Yellowstone containing more than half of the earth's supply. Their requirements greatly restrict their occurrence. Water from melting snow and rain must soak into the ground far enough to reach a volcanic heat source, at depths up to twelve thousand feet. A circuitry must exist that will conduct the hot water back to the surface, a round-trip journey taking up to five hundred years. Passing through a rhyolite bedrock, super-heated water at temperatures above 500 degrees Fahrenheit deposits geyserite, which seals the plumbing system against leaks from steam pressure. Where these conditions exist, geysers erupt as the natural outcome of water boiling in a confined space.

When you consider that Yellowstone is earthquake-prone—about five unfelt tremors are recorded daily and on rare occasions a hundred—the durability and regularity of Old Faithful is remarkable. The epicenter of the Hebgen quake in 1959, the country's fifteenth strongest, was only forty miles away. A hundred geysers with no previous record of activity began to spurt. Others became dormant. Fountain Paint Pot changed its location to a parking lot. Old Faithful was spared, displaying only a slight increase in the interval between eruptions. On Yellowstone's fiftieth anniversary, in 1922, a tranquil pool in Obsidian Creek suddenly blasted rocks and mud several hundred feet in the air. Exhausted by its contribution to the celebration, Semi-Centennial Geyser has not been heard from since.

It would seem from the records that Old Faithful has more than lived up to the name given it by the 1870 discovery expedition. Members watched nine eruptions and found the intervals varied from sixty to sixty-five minutes. Observations between 1947 and 1973 of forty-seven thousand eruptions gave a figure of 64.9 minutes. Although intervals have varied from a low of thirty-three minutes to a high of 148 minutes, the official position is that Old Faithful has never missed a performance. Carbon-14 tests of partially silicified wood in Old Faithful's cone puts the geyser's age at about three hundred years.

It was running behind schedule this morning. I jotted down comments of my neighbors. "I'm excited," a woman said to her husband, who replied, grudgingly, "It'll be better than most of what you see these days." Two jolly ladies wearing identification tags talked a blue streak, but not about Old Faithful. One said, "The bus driver told me you wouldn't come to a better place for geysers."

An apple-cheeked boy with a mouthful of widely spaced teeth and a thatch of carrot hair was being told about geysers by a father who treated him with commendable kindness. Unfortunately, patience was not one of the young marvel's virtues. Soon he contracted a case of the fidgets and began doing jumping jacks on the boardwalk behind the benches. His father asked, less indulgently, "Andy, do you want me to slap the hell out of you?"

Andy was spared richly deserved punishment when water began to splash from Old Faithful's vent. After a few false starts, a shaft of water and steam rose from the crest of the low mound as deliberately as a rocket leaving the launching pad, pausing a few moments at ever higher levels. Then, in a spectacular explosion of boiling water, hissing and roaring, the column shot skyward in one continuous surge to a height of well over a hundred feet. A tall white cloud billowed out from the main stem, sunlight glinting on the cascading droplets of water. In three or four minutes the towering jet dropped slowly down. One of the tour ladies murmured, "Lovely, just lovely." Glancing at her watch, her companion said, "Just in time for lunch." It's hard to beat a spectacle that performs dependably and at short enough intervals not to unduly delay the busy tourist.

Congress opened the way for a hotel at Old Faithful by passing a law in

1894 permitting construction of facilities one-eighth of a mile from a natural curiosity. Connected by a short walkway to the boardwalk in front of its namesake geyser, Old Faithful Inn achieves the difficult feat of standing out while fitting in. Rising improbably high in an incomparable setting, it is not what architects call a background building. There isn't a better illustration of the paradox between loving nature and making a living. Now it would be unthinkable to intrude in such a fashion on the natural scene, but environmental awareness has been a slow-dawning concept.

I stopped to look up at the steeply pitched roof. Here and there dormer windows outlined by a crossed lodgepole motif had landed in a lopsided arrangement thought to be evidence of the architect's sense of humor. Robert Reamer was turning thirty when given a free hand to design a hotel at Old Faithful, and it set the style for many of the grand old lodges that have been built in the national parks. His crew of frontier artisans, experts with axe, adze, and drawknife, fashioned a building of hand-hewn character and rustic elegance. Improbably, they began work in the fall of 1903, continued through the harsh Yellowstone winter, and finished in time for the 1904 summer season. Call it carpenter gothic. Reamer took his cues and his materials from the surrounding landscape, building for an era when people traveled more elegantly than they now do, and with trunks.

You enter through a split-log double door with a sturdy iron locking bar, grilled peephole, and coiled spring bell-ringer. The lobby is of astonishing proportions, a soaring expanse of beams and struts, the balconies supported by pillars made from tree trunks. Reamer's carpenters scoured the forests to find matching sets of curved branches for railings. The enormous free-standing fireplace of volcanic rock is actually eight fireplaces, a large one on each side and a smaller one at each corner. Tall, padded armchairs on an island of carpet near the fireplace have been occupied by generations of weary travelers who have seen all they want to see of Yellowstone until they rest.

On a fine June morning in 1904, Reamer might have stood where I was standing, admiring his just completed masterpiece, flags snapping from their poles on the elaborate roof platform, eight stories high. Forty rigs with open sides and forward-facing seats for eleven passengers would be loading under the hotel's spacious porte cochere. Loquacious drivers were mostly young cowboys supplementing marginal wages: "Society Bob" loved to dance, "Cryin' Jack" was perpetually sad-faced, and "Geyser Bob" told stories of his own invention. Women in smart white blouses and men in dark suits and straw hats took their places. And so, wrote Aubrey Haines, Yellowstone's premier historian, with a crack of the whip and shouted endearments to the horses, spaced five hundred feet apart to reduce dust, "the lumbering Yellowstone Wagons took their places in the slow moving procession—every tourist filled with a nameless exhilaration, everything especially beautiful, especially marvelous."

I'm as concerned as the next person that facilities should not be intrusive, but I believe Reamer's creation is sensitive to its site. Should we remove such lodges from the parks, as some demand, we know what would replace them in the gateway towns. Daniel Boorstin remarked that the proliferation of chain motels and fast food stands has made every place in America into any place. When you wake up in Old Faithful Inn, you know you're not in Syracuse or Sacramento. The ornamental candlesticks circling the pillars in the lobby were designed by Reamer and crafted by his artisans. Their low-wattage bulbs recall a time of lamp glow and shadows. This is a hotel of memories.

My purpose in driving to Old Faithful was not solely patriotic. Earlier in the week I received a press release put out by the superintendent's office reporting an encounter between a grizzly and an employee of the Old Faithful Lodge, Tom Sherman. It was so cryptic that I resolved to talk to Sherman and get a few more details. While jogging near Old Faithful Geyser, according to the release, he "noticed" a grizzly bear following him. "The bear advanced to his position, stood upright, and batted him twice, once in the right arm and once in the left arm." The author of the account was in a less playful mood than the bear, saying only, "Mr. Sherman quickly left the area. He suffered no serious injury and did not solicit medical attention from the Old Faithful clinic."

Having paid my respects to the inn, I walked to the other end of the geyser boardwalk and took the path to Old Faithful Lodge. Less imposing than its neighbor, it is still a fine building with many similar rustic touches. The two young women at the reservation desk glowed when I mentioned Tom Sherman's name. Following a map they supplied, I was able to identify the budget cabins ("Bring your own towel; showers nearby") and the budget shelters ("Bring your own sheets, pillow cases, pillows and towels; showers nearby"). Tom's supervisor was sitting cross-legged on a table in a supply room filled with bins of dirty linen and tables of clean sheets. "Tom's a neat guy," she said with feeling, as had the desk clerks, "Really nice."

He was pushing a two-wheel cart carrying his supplies out of cabin 140E, and it was immediately apparent why women liked him. Of medium height and slender frame, he had brown eyes and hair, grainy skin, and a calm view of life. He struck me as a person having no need to varnish his accomplishments. I'd promised his supervisor not to interview him on company time, and he brightened when I suggest we talk over lunch. First he had to change out of his "Raggedy Ann," the detested uniform shirt of the Yellowstone Park Company that is verboten in the dining areas. We ate in the coffee shop, a square of tables enclosed by a white picket fence in the lobby.

A native of Ardsley, twenty miles out of New York City, Tom was finishing his freshman year at Vassar when he heard about job possibilities in Yellowstone and signed up. Running was important to him, and he thought the trees would make the miles easier. He boarded a Greyhound bus in the New York Port Authority Terminal and after a two-and-a-half-day trip had arrived in Mammoth a week before we talked. With a hundred other college students he sat though several days of orientation, including a session on bear safety given by a park ranger. Intending to spend a lot of time on the trails, he listened carefully and asked questions. Then he went out and bought a "bear belt," with bells attached, designed to prevent unexpected confrontation.

I mentioned I'd watched Bill Rogers win a ten-mile race in Washington during the Cherry Blossom Festival in April. He said, not boastfully, that he'd finished 318th out of five thousand in the New York Marathon the year before. He had also run well in the Boston Classic before coming west and expected to be in the top 10 percent when official notification of the order of finish was mailed. I was deliberating whether to tell him that I jogged around Mammoth every morning before breakfast when the waitress brought him the largest salad on the menu and two glasses of milk, a good choice for a serious runner. Between bites of chicken, ham, and cheese, he told me how he had disobeyed one of the ranger's warnings: never run from a grizzly.

Three days earlier, he had arrived at Old Faithful, worked a full shift learning to clean cabins and make beds, and prepared to do some jogging. "I picked up my bear belt, and my roommate laughed at me. He said, 'This place is like your home town. You won't see any bears around here.' I felt foolish and stuck it back in the drawer, which was kind of interesting when you consider what happened to me later. We had just been talking about a story in *Runner's World* magazine about the wife of a Yellowstone ranger [Nancy Rudolph] who went out for a walk last year and was mauled by a grizzly."

While they talked, Tom donned his favorite white outfit of carpenter gloves, turtleneck sweater, Adidas shorts, and Brooks running shoes. In a light snowfall he took the trail that continues from the boardwalk in front of Old Faithful Geyser, crossing the Firehole River on a log bridge. A little farther on, he veered to the right on a spur trail that climbs through a lodgepole forest to an overlook. He felt the elevation as he worked through the switchbacks. A fat squirrel sitting on a log got the finger, New York-style.

By the time he reached Observation Point, it was snowing hard. He stopped to do a few hamstring stretches and for the first time since entering Yellowstone was aware of the silence. Halfway down the trail, a rustling in the bushes close behind him made him break stride and glance back over his shoulder. He said, "I can't express what I felt when I saw that grizzly catching up to me." An old bounty hunter once said that at such a moment one feels a softening of the bones. Tom stopped and faced the bear:

> I didn't panic. I was functioning well, I was thinking logically, although I said to myself, "Oh no, not me." I looked for a tree to climb, but there aren't any grabbers on a lodgepole. The ranger who warned us not to run said it's better to play dead. I wanted more control than that. The bear was only a couple of steps away, standing up on his hind feet. For some reason I crouched down and clenched my fists. The ranger told us a bear can be distracted by dropping something. I tried one of my gloves. He chewed on it and spit it out. That's when I felt it wasn't going to work out for me. I tried to disengage, standing up and taking a slow backward step. He banged me on the shoulder so fast I never saw it coming.

Tom unbuttoned his blue denim shirt, showing me red welts on his right shoulder about an inch apart where the claws had raked him. Before he could react, he received another clout on his other shoulder, "harder than the hardest punch my brother ever threw." Without conscious thought, he whirled about and ran down the trail, ran like a madman, shortcutting the switchbacks. He could hear the bear behind him.

Two men were standing on the Firehole River bridge. Tom yelled "Bear! Bear!" and ran with them toward the crowd on the boardwalk at Old Faithful. Somewhere behind him the bear broke off the chase. Tom was directed to the ranger station behind Old Faithful Inn and gave a full report. "From there I went to the employee pub. Every time I told the story somebody bought me a beer." A long telephone conversation with his father helped settle his nerves. He lay awake most of the night, thinking of what had happened, and what could have happened.

We ordered ice cream for dessert, and I asked him how he felt about running in the trees now. He took a while to answer. "It's too early to tell. That was a weird scene. Some of the guys say the bear acted a little like a turkey. That's easy to say. I knew if I guessed wrong he would do a number on me. It's funny. I've always been a pretty secure person, until this happened. I'm not sure when I'll feel like running in the woods alone. I think I'll stick to the pavement for a while."

I didn't see Tom again, but after returning to school in the fall he wrote a long letter to me. He wasn't able to get the grizzly out of his mind. He ran the trails only a half-dozen times all summer. "I took a friend along and we kept up a steady stream of high-toned chatter. And I always wore my bear belt." He couldn't stand the thought of sleeping in bear country and never used his backpack. "It bothers me that I didn't have a true hiking experience. Even near Old Faithful I was uncomfortable. I was super attentive. I'd zero in on every little noise. My clearest remembrance of Yellowstone is the paranoia I felt when I was alone, thinking of those dark pine trees."

After Tom went back to his cabin-cleaning chores I revised my plan for the day. I'd looked forward to an afternoon of exploring the Upper Geyser Basin. All such rambles are rewarding, no two alike. Mary and I once idled away a good part of my birthday in the basin. The inscription in the book she gave me that evening recalls a rousing time. "For Bill, on whose day all hell erupted—the Grand, Castle, Grotto and Old Faithful, of course."

Tom mentioned that his bear had tags in both ears and a collar around his neck, which indicated that the rangers had a file on him. I walked over to the Old Faithful ranger station on the edge of the parking lot. It's shaped like a house trailer, with a couple of pay telephones in the front and a fire truck in the garage behind. The ranger at the information desk was helping two young men find a good place to camp. Their Kelty packs and their hiking boots were unsoiled. The ranger pointed to Heart Lake on the USGS map mounted on the wall.

"It's an ideal destination," he told them. "Parts of the trail are still carrying snow, but not enough to be an obstacle. This early, you can have your pick of some beautiful campsites. Rustic Geyser on the west shore is a scaled-down version of Old Faithful, operating on a similar schedule. From Rustic it's three miles up to the fire lookout on Mount Sheridan, at an elevation of 10,308 feet." The hikers were smiling and nodding. "One more thing. Grizzlies are especially active this time of year. Be alert on the trail. Make noise when you can't see ahead. The odor of food attracts them. Rather than cooking I suggest you carry fruit and candy bars." The hikers went into a swift huddle. On second thought, they decided, it might be better to save Heart Lake for another day.

While they examined the map for a place more tranquil, the ranger led me to a cramped room in the rear. Dave Milhalic's office is barely large enough to hold a desk and a filing cabinet and an extra chair. Stacked neatly in one corner is the gear he would wear if he had time to hike to Heart

Lake. Dave gave me a warm welcome. A tall, unruffled, articulate man with blue eyes and hair on the shaggy side, he had an assured way of speaking and an evenhanded way of looking at things.

His was an unusual case. Several years earlier he had done the unthinkable, resigning from the Park Service to take a position with the Bureau of Land Management. His mustache of RAF proportions only partly hid a smile when I asked, in mock horror, what had tempted him to leave. He said that for as long as he could remember he had wanted to try Alaska. When BLM offered him a chance, he took it. His BLM superiors liked his work so well that they gave him a promotion—and transferred him to Denver.

He then decided to return to Alaska on his own and set up a boating enterprise. At the last minute, Yellowstone called, offering him the Old Faithful slot. "It was the only assignment preferable to Alaska. I've put Alaska on hold. It looks like we're going to have some great new parks there in the near future. Who knows? Maybe there will be a spot for me." There was. After the Alaska Lands Bill passed in 1980, he was appointed superintendent of the Yukon-Charley Rivers National Preserve.

The talk got around to my session with Tom Sherman. Dave pulled a folder out of the file cabinet and flipped through it. On September 13 of the year before, the Interagency Grizzly Study Team darted a female and two yearling cubs feeding at the West Yellowstone garbage dump. One of the cubs had failed to develop normally because of a large growth in its mouth. An operation to correct the difficulty was unsuccessful, and the animal was destroyed.

The other, Tom's bear, was entered on the records as Bear 27 and given the standard paraphernalia: a red plastic tag in each ear (numbers 606 and 607), a tattoo on the lower lip (F14), and a radio transmitter collar. Since coming out of hibernation he had kept the rangers busy. A week earlier he had chased a woman into her trailer in the Madison campground, fifteen miles to the north. The investigating ranger barely got back to his pickup in time after Bear 27 charged him. A few hours before scaring the bejesus out of Tom Sherman, he closely pursued a woman in the Old Faithful residential area. There may have been other encounters with visitors that were unreported.

"With the Sherman incident he's developed into a problem bear," Dave said, closing the file and resting his hands on the edge of the desk as if he expected to be called out on another Bear 27 incident momentarily. "He's a subadult but has the equipment to injure a person seriously. Or terminally. It's hard to salvage a bear once he's picked up a bad attitude. After he's found a meal somewhere, he never forgets it. He's losing his fear of humans, and he's made Old Faithful his beat." I asked him about options. He ticked them off:

> Continue to sit tight, hoping his bad habits are not yet fixed and that he might drift away. That's possible but not likely. Try to trap and re-locate him. That transfers the problem to the backcountry and puts backpackers at risk. Bears find their way back after being relocated. Close down Old Faithful—the lodge, inn, cabins, restaurants, stores, gas sta-tions, everything. I'm fairly sure the public and the Congress aren't ready to turn Yellowstone over to the bears. Or, shoot Bear 27. What it comes down to is that you don't like any of the above. Sherman is a physically quick guy who lucked out. There's a reason running from a grizzly isn't recommended. It's called "acting like dinner." We're in a box. We don't want to kill this bear. However many grizzlies we have, the population is dangerously low. But if he tears someone up tomorrow, how do we explain why we waited so long?

When I returned to the station later in the afternoon there was a note from Dave saying a trap would be set for Bear 27 that evening. He invited me to join him in the morning to check the results.

∪ ∪

Up with the ravens on Sunday, I skipped the jogging routine and break-fasted on coffee and a bagel liberally slathered with strawberry jam. I drove through a bright, cloudless morning that turned the Firehole River indigo blue and pulled up to the Old Faithful ranger station at the appointed hour of seven. Dave was waiting beside a light green patrol car that had PARK RANGER on its front and rear and a blue dome light mounted on its roof. From the look of him, he had been ready to go for hours. Brown shoes gleamed with polish, the green trousers had a sharp crease, and the green jacket was wrinkle-free. He wore the gold shield of his authority above the left pocket and a gold nameplate over the right pocket. His stiff-brimmed Stetson sat squarely on his head.

He brought me up to date as we went north on the Grand Loop. At dark the night before the trap had been baited with a slab of bacon and hauled to the far end of Fountain Freight Road. About midnight a patrol ranger found that the barricade blocking access to the road had been pulled aside and a car was parked down the road. Driving slowly, he used a bullhorn to warn the intruders that they were risking an encounter with a grizzly. Three youths came strolling down the middle of the road, unconcerned, offering no apologies. They'd heard about the trap and decided to investigate. Nothing in it yet, they told the ranger. "What he told them would have sizzled the bacon," Dave said.

The Fountain Freight Road became a dead-end spur when the Grand Loop was relocated many years ago. An orange sign on the barricade, a red-and-white-striped sawhorse, announced that "The Area Behind This Sign Is Closed Because of Bear Danger." Getting back into the car after replacing the barricade, Dave shook his head. He predicted compliance would be low and the resentment level high. By an unlucky coincidence he was closing off a stretch of the Firehole much favored by fishermen on the opening day of trout season. "Some of them would elbow a grizzly out of the way to fish this water. On a day like this you couldn't blame them."

For the first mile we passed through greening meadows and pine woods, the river a short distance off to our right. A long-tailed magpie floated by on a light breeze, the white wing patches flashing in the bright sun. Beyond clusters of intense yellow flowers I couldn't put a name to, unless they were goldenrod, I could see the glistening green head of a mallard drake feeding along the river bank. More mallards passed overhead with quick-time wing beats. Why are ducks always in such a hurry? On the other side of a dinky little bridge over the Firehole, Dave pointed to a forested hillside. Bear 16, the mother of Bear 27, was up there.

"She hasn't moved much for three days now. Probably killed an elk and is staying with the carcass, feeding when she gets hungry. The spotter plane came so close to her that when Dick Knight from the Grizzly Study Team had trouble with his antenna he put a ballpoint pen in the socket and picked up her signal. Too bad the transmitter on Bear 27 went dead some time ago."

The transmitter, weighing about three pounds, is designed to withstand hard knocks and is generally reliable. For protection, it's placed between layers of conveyer belting and encased in urethane plastic. The ends, containing two wing antennae, are bolted around the bear's neck. Knight flies a grid pattern over the park and its environs three times a week. When he picks up a signal, he drops down and tries to make a visual sighting. The area covered, more than five thousand square miles, is so large that each flight takes ten or twelve hours. Only twenty transmitters can be monitored. Because grizzlies in forested country are impossible to count, population estimates are unreliable.

Dave pulled over to the side of the road, noting the trap was around the next bend. He looked unconcerned as we walked along, hemmed in by lodgepoles. I was on the lookout for a peremptory strike by Bear 27. Up on the ridge, where Bear 16 lurked, the wind hummed in the trees. A raven on a dead branch accused us of something, convulsing his body with every croak. When we ignored his warnings, he worked his wings and prepared to fly. A thrashing in the underbrush made my heart thud. Dave didn't flinch, his nerves being that much better than mine, or maybe he recognized a red squirrel when he heard one. Not wishing to take the play away from a district ranger, I let him lead the way.

The trap sat at the edge of a clearing. As we approached, I saw that the door was still poised above the opening. "Dry hole," Dave remarked. A bear trap is a simple but effective contraption, an eight-foot section of steel culvert pipe forty-two inches in diameter mounted on a two-wheel trailer for hauling. An aromatic bait, in this case bacon, is attached to a steel cable that triggers the heavy metal door hanging in a frame above the open end of the pipe.

A wooden sign on top, DANGER BEAR TRAP, is meant to discourage the curious from fooling around with the trigger and dropping the door on their extremities. To prevent injuries—and lawsuits—the door is dropped during daylight hours. It made a horrendous clang in the quiet glade when Dave pulled the release. "That might have solved our problem," Dave said. "Then again, maybe it wouldn't." Hearing footsteps, we wheeled around. A man carrying a fly rod was walking down the road.

He was wearing a tan shirt with busy pockets on the sleeves, and an old fishing hat dripping trout flies was jammed down on his shock of white hair. "I've been looking for one of you rangers," he told Dave and began ticking off his complaints. For eight straight years he'd planned his summer vacations around the trout season on the Firehole. Lazy rangers who welcomed every chance to reduce their workload by closing off sections of the park had panicked at the sight of a bear and closed the stream with no warning. He had a friend "in Washington" well placed to deal with bureaucratic indifference.

I thought him a cross-grained, self-important blowhard, but Dave took the rebuke patiently. Not by a twitch of his mustache did he show the irritation he felt. His response was courteous and firm. The warning signs must be obeyed. Willful violators would be charged before the U.S. magistrate. He ordered the fisherman to vacate the restricted area immediately. Something in his voice caused the man to examine him more carefully. Talking a little less confidently, he informed Dave that he was withdrawing under protest and would be posting a letter yet today to his friend in Washington detailing the whole tedious rigmarole. "Do that," Dave said pleasantly.

When we got back to the barricade, there were more unhappy fishermen. They surrounded Dave in a way that said that all actions must now be explained and accounted for. On his way to the car he was intercepted by a young woman. Her children hadn't seen a single black bear. A man in the campground told her that the rangers had killed them all. Once she got started on bears there was no stopping her. Dave heard her out, and as he was getting back into the car he said something I didn't quite catch.

Before we could get underway the radio crackled, signaling an emergency in the campground at Madison Junction, six miles away. Dave gave me the background. Seventy male students from the Cody high school had begun celebrating the end of the academic year in the campground the evening before. The more they drank the more obnoxious they became. Campers protesting their behavior were cursed and threatened. Almost all packed up and moved out. It took eighteen rangers to achieve nominal control. Because the hooligans were too drunk to drive, they had been given until nine o'clock that morning to vacate the campground. When reminded of the deadline, they had said that Yellowstone didn't have enough rangers to make them go. "There's a question of whether we're on the offense or defense," Dave said.

We joined a strike force of rangers standing in the grass at the flagpole beside the campground office building. Some obviously came in a hurry, wearing whatever piece of uniform was handy, probably to keep the sides straight should hostilities begin. They were in an edgy mood, unhappy with the way the operation was being handled by the district ranger. In seclusion, he had issued no instructions. "He's considered all the options," said one, "and they've canceled each other out."

While we waited, I talked for a while with a ranger of less than average height, well put together and a biking enthusiast. In 1976 he'd taken a semester off from college and biked from California to Washington, D.C. "I wanted to do something for the Bicentennial," he said, "so I took a course called 'Appreciation of America.'" He'd been with the first contingent called to the campground. "We might as well have tried to reason with the inmates of a loony ward. Telling them to knock it off was like pouring kerosene on a fire. The worst part was watching families drive away in the middle of the night. I'm not saying a free-for-all would have solved anything, and there's no profit in beating up on juveniles, but it was our responsibility to keep order, and we blew it."

None of the rangers carried a gun nor so much as a billy club. Nevertheless, they were a sturdy bunch, ready to do whatever it would take. I did a head count. We were fourteen rangers and a retiree. "Let's do something," I heard one of our number say, "even if we have to make it up as we go." Dave's displeasure with the absence of leadership was evident. He didn't measure professional competence by the number of years of faithful service.

An hour passed, two hours. I inspected the notice board on the wall of the office. There were messages for R. Childes, W. Jessen, and L. Brennan. A sign on a stanchion in the middle of the entrance road advised "Select Campsite, Leave Something to Mark as Occupied and Return Promptly to Register Here." I walked across the road, where an ice machine and soft drink dispenser were in a roofed enclosure. I didn't have the right change for either. A jogger came by and gave me a howdy. A ranger trotted out from the trees that concealed the campground and called, "Here they come!"

A black Trans Am led the procession, its hood flamed with red and purple figures. The driver slowed his machine to a crawl as he passed, the engine rumbling and popping. He favored each of us with an insolent glare that plainly said he hated our guts and dared us to name our game. Mud-spattered Jeeps and Ford Broncos followed. The occupants seemed to me a bunch of sullen, hung-over, would-be toughs. "A bumper crop of jerks in Cody this year," one ranger remarked.

In a lull after a dozen vehicles had moved by, Dave tapped me on the shoulder. He wanted to make a swing through the trap area. Before he could start the motor, the radio sputtered again in that barely intelligible argot favored by flight controllers and taxi dispatchers. The pilot of a private airplane, fighting a balky motor, was attempting to reach the West Yellowstone airport, using the entrance road as a guide and, if need be, a landing strip. The Communication Center in Mammoth, which handles all radio communications in the park, estimated that we were two or three miles behind the airplane. Dave did a left turn that made the tires sing, and we were on the entrance road.

The west entrance road winds along the Madison River, a stream famous for its brown trout population. You can see about as many fish from Seven Mile Bridge as you can from Fishing Bridge. As we flashed over the bridge I was watching the road ahead intently. I'd never done eighty, or more, in Yellowstone. The Com Center relayed a message from the pilot. His engine had failed. He was attempting a landing on the entrance road. Dave pressed the accelerator down a notch. If the airplane crashed and caught fire, seconds could be critical. Then came the calm voice of a ranger. "I have an aircraft down four miles from the west entrance station."

Not more than a minute or two later we entered a long straight-a-way. The single-engine Cherokee Archer, white and red marking, had ended up against a tree on the right shoulder. From a distance it seemed in good shape. Up close I could see that the tree had loosened one wing, and the fuselage was dented and ripped. Two rangers were on the scene. One was helping two women and a man into his patrol car, and the other man gave Dave a quick briefing.

One woman had a bruised shoulder that required attention at the hospital. The other woman went along for company. Because the party would need transportation, the man would pick up a rental car. The ranger and Dave needed to huddle with the pilot and begin putting together an incident report. Could I keep traffic moving until more rangers arrived? "Sure," I said, "I can handle that." I'd misjudged the drawing power of an airplane with a busted wing sitting beside the highway. I soon learned why a traffic cop develops that rapid circular motion with his hand and arm. I waved the curious to keep going, keep going, and for a while it worked.

My nemesis was a skinny old geezer at the wheel of an elongated mobile home. He edged over and stopped beside the airplane. Ignoring my signals, he cranked down the window and whined, "Why can't I get out and take a picture?" That's when the nonchalance went out of my performance. "Because I don't want you to stop! Now move it!" I yelled back. The ranger who relieved me must have been watching. He had the amused expression and insincerity of the young dealing with their elders. "Nice job, sir," he said. "Mind if I take over?"

I helped the pilot haul out the baggage and stack it on the good wing. Agreeable and casually dressed in chinos and a button-down white shirt, he took the mishap better than most would take a dent in a new car. He said the landing came off well, and he thought he was home free until an oncoming vehicle refused to yield. The two couples were on a vacation trip out of Fort Collins. He'd prefer to stay around and see Yellowstone. The women might have other ideas.

I helped a ranger who was pushing a wheeled device measuring the distance from the skid marks where the plane touched down to the spot where it wedged against the tree. After a while Dave returned from some investigative work. His eyes had not been glued to the road during the high-speed chase. He had the instinct of a law enforcement officer, a part of him always watching. He'd noticed two fishermen near the bank of the Madison just as the ranger reported the landing and made a mental note to drive back and check with them.

They pointed out the trees the pilot had clipped as he glided down. Searching around, Dave found several pieces of fabric from the wing and fuselage. He enclosed each in a clear plastic envelope, along with a sketch map of where the pieces were found. "You never know what evidence will be helpful when the National Transportation Safety Board team investigates the accident," he said, delivering the envelopes to the ranger in charge of the report. If you were to ask me whether most rangers are as professionally competent as Dave Mihalic, I'd say, well, yes. He may be a good detective, but he isn't a cop. He used the siren sparingly on the run from Madison Junction, flicking it on and off. He said that drivers can do foolish things if you tailgate them with your siren blaring and they have no room to get out of your way.

The afternoon was well advanced when Dave came walking over from the patrol car. "It's the campground fiasco again. Looks like a straight replay." Only half of the Cody delegation had left the campground that morning. A hard core stood pat and continued to taunt the rangers. Now the district ranger was calling for reinforcements. "Sorry about lunch," Dave said. "At this rate we'll be lucky to get dinner."

Many of the faces were familiar as we reassembled at the flagpole. So was the lack of information. We waited a long time until the district ranger walked out of the campground office. He announced that everything was under control, sounding as if he were bucking a trend. He also said he'd been on the telephone with Roger Siglin and gave us the word from the chief ranger. A detachment of rangers would be posted at the campground for so long as the Cody campers remained there. He read off the names of the babysitters, one of whom voiced the frustration felt by all: "What a goddamned disgraceful operation."

Roger later discussed the incident with me and summed up what he told the district ranger. I'll omit the performance evaluation. The failure on the first night to single out the ringleaders and charge them with documented offenses put the rangers in a no-win position. Use of force the next day to clear the campground would have been pointless and quite possibly unsuccessful. Waiting them out was wimpy, but, as it turned out, it worked.

Driving back to Old Faithful, Dave reflected on the day's happenings:

I started out trying to outsmart a grizzly and then got into a spat with a fisherman. If you look at that line of Winnebagos ahead of us, or consider the campground hard cases and the airplane incident, you appreciate a ranger spends most of his time on people problems. The ranger setup is called the division of resource management and visitor protection. It should be called the division of resource protection and visitor management.

Yesterday I pulled down a guy who was speeding on the Old Faithful approach road. He was in a rage because he couldn't find his way out, and he said some harsh things. I gave him a courtesy warning instead of a ticket, he cooled down, and we parted amicably. I must say there are times when you consider getting into another line of work. You have to remind yourself that when you put on the green jacket and the big hat you can't allow yourself to get down on people.

Biscuit Basin meadow was lime green against the white of the sinter deposits bordering the hot springs. Two shaggy buffalo had drawn a crowd to the meadow. Cars were parked along the road helter-skelter, and picture-takers were dangerously close to the motionless animals. Dave brought them back to a safer location on the bridge over the Firehole, where they pelted him with questions about buffalo. A persistent young man still years from teenager status and with a beguilingly bad haircut asked one last question and then several more. I learned that a buffalo is a patriarch at ten, is almost never attacked by a grizzly, is a strong swimmer, and prefers shoving contests to using his horns.

Appreciative visitors have a way of refreshing the most jaded of public servants. Dave returned to the car with his batteries recharged. "The personnel cuts keep us from doing much of that," he observed as we idled along behind a home on wheels proceeding at Clydesdale speed. "Every year we have less rangers and more visitors. Instead of assigning all of my rangers to patrol duty, I wish we could spend some time with the visitors. My oldest seasonal told me the other day, 'That's what we did in the 1950s. We talked to visitors nonstop. We couldn't get away. And it was great.'"

He nodded toward the cloverleaf intersection as we took the Old Faithful exit. "It blew me away the first time I saw it. Imagine the changes a ranger like Dale Nuss has known." Dale had been around a long time. His father ran a camp for Boy Scouts here before the roads were paved. At the age of six, riding on the top of a pack mule, Dale saw Yellowstone for the first time and did a few camp chores. It was 1930, and the trees along the road were coated with dust. Every day the Grand Loop was sprinkled by water wagons. Yellowstone couldn't have had more than a couple of hundred cars a day then. "Dale can remember when the going was good," Dave said. "The cloverleaf isn't a bad symbol of how much a ranger's life has changed."

I didn't suggest that Dave have a beer with me when we stopped at Old Faithful Inn. A ranger doesn't drink in uniform. Nor was he ready to call it a day, even though it had been twelve hours since we started for the trap. There were still things that had to be done, and no nonsense about overtime pay either. He invited me to ride patrol with him again, saying switch-hitters who take notes and direct traffic are in short supply.

I made a beeline for the Bear Pit Lounge. It may not be all a bar should be—dim and quiet with wood paneling and bowls of peanuts—but it's a snug haven. Shaped like a half-circle, it has a long bar along the base and a row of tall windows forming the curved wall. The high ceiling is deco-rated with a pinecone motif. A molding above the windows contains wild-life silhouettes. The chandeliers are of hammered iron, the tables covered with leather, and the upright chairs comfortable. With the name etched in glass above the door, it lacks only Humphrey Bogart in a tuxedo to give it real class.

I ordered a Coors and from my stool at the far end of the bar surveyed the scene. Not many tables were occupied. Halfway down the bar, a man in a worn tweed jacket with leather patches on the elbows contemplated a martini. Although Miss Marple, Agatha Christie's wonderful busybody, wouldn't have been caught dead in a bar, her double wandered in, carrying a book instead of her knitting. The man with the martini ordered a refill and so did I. Light from the fading sun gave the room a cheerful appearance.

The beer was refreshing, and time had slowed to an agreeable pace. I had been in the company of an exceptional ranger, and yet few of the rangers I have known could fairly be called ordinary. Dave professed surprise when I said we'd crammed a week of patrolling into one eventful day. "Nothing unusual," he replied, perhaps a bit too heartily. "Nobody arrested. Nobody torn up by a grizzly. No lost children. Just the usual routine." Turning the images of the day over in my mind, I had only one regret. I should have told that crabby fisherman at the bear trap, "Get lost, buster. Mr. Milhalic doesn't take that kind of shit from soreheads."

I got change from the bartender and walked out to the dispenser in the lobby for more potato chips. It had been a long time since breakfast. On my return I inspected the two beautifully carved panels at each end of the bar. On one panel, three bear cubs frisk about, turning over stones and investigating a log under the watchful eyes of their mother. On the other, the cubs are attempting to climb a tree, the frazzled mother standing guard below.

The cavorting bears and Dave's mention of Dale Nuss reminded me of a session I had with Dale the day after arriving in Yellowstone. Dale was a homesteader, someone who chooses to remain in one park for an entire career, refusing all invitations to move on. Yellowstone, of course, is the place where the art has reached its highest form. Except for a brief inter-lude at Shenandoah, Dale hadn't strayed from the park since starting as a seasonal in 1947 while attending Colorado State.

"It's easy to see why Dale identifies with grizzlies," a ranger remarked to me. "They have a lot in common." I'd no doubt Dale can be an awkward cuss, an out-of-date kind of fellow with an air of take me as you find me about him. He was also proficient, unbending, and admirable. However his colleagues felt about his opinions, he said things straight, and for that they respected him. The preceding year, a new ranger, a woman, was terrified when she was assigned to "Nasty" Nuss for a project. Soon, in private, she was calling him "Nicey" Nuss. I found him to be considerate and generous, although he could keep an argument going a long time. He was in the midst of one then. A district ranger for many years, he had recently been put in charge of bear management, a post he didn't seek. He thought that Townsley was pushing him toward retirement. So did everyone else.

Dale had heavy shoulders, a crop of iron-gray hair trained forward, and a firm mouth and chin. When he laughed he showed gold fillings. I hadn't seen him for years when we bumped into each other outside the administration building. At his invitation I followed him to the ranger offices on the second floor. Several rangers in the vestibule were having a good laugh at the expense of one of their number who had crunched the front of his patrol car spinning off a strip of glare ice, "A sure ticket to Tuzigoot," Dale observed. Solely because of its quaint name, the agreeable Indian settlement site in the Verde Valley of Arizona is the supposed Siberia of the Park Service, where bunglers are sent for penance and reflection while they rediscover the virtues of picking up trash and cleaning restrooms.

Dale asked his secretary whether everything was under control. "Of course, Mr. Nuss, just like it always is," she answered, being kindhearted. The partitions of Dale's cubicle had a just-snapped-in-place look, the desk hardly used. I inspected the photographs on the walls. One showed an enormous cloud of smoke almost filling a valley under a high peak. "That was a real shocker to the boys at Cabin Creek," he said, referring to a backcountry cabin on the upper Yellowstone River, where it empties into the Southeast Arm of Yellowstone Lake:

> A hungry grizzly with cubs tore off a piece of the Cabin Creek roof and wrecked the inside. I was the district ranger at Lake, and I sent a crew down to make repairs. Before they finished, a lightning strike started a fire up-river. It smoldered for several days. They looked it over and figured it wasn't going anywhere. I took the helicopter down one morning to check progress on the cabin and was back by noon. After lunch I looked down the lake and saw this smoke over Cabin Creek. The wind had come up suddenly, and the fire was off and running. Burned the cabin to the ground. Proves you can't tell about forest fires, or grizzlies either for that matter.

I had caught Dale in a reflective mood. Talking of the Cabin Creek affair, he mentioned that of the many scrapes he'd had with grizzlies, three could have gone either way. I'm listening, I said. He leaned back in his chair, hands clasped over his head, and told me a story that had a certain comic quality, although there was no indication he saw the humor of it even after twenty years. He spoke with an economy of words and didn't heave around in his chair. Once he paused to take a can of Copenhagen snuff from his hip pocket and thumbed a pinch between his cheek and gum. I kept my head down and doodled in the margin of my notebook. It happened at the Trout Creek dump, he said, when he was releasing a grizzly from a new trap he had designed. It was positioned in the bed of a pickup truck, the opening flush with the rear edge of the truck so the bear would drop directly to the ground. Usually a released bear will run like a scalded cat. Now and again one will seek revenge. To provide against such contingencies, Dale had rigged an A-frame above the trap door. A rope through a pulley suspended from the frame allowed him to stand in the bed of the truck well out of harm's way when he raised the door. The release operation was a success, he said, but the patient came close to murdering the doctor.

> This was one mean grizzly. They don't come any meaner. He never quieted down all the way out to Trout Creek. When we were ready, I told the driver to slow down so the grizzly wouldn't be injured, and I pulled the rope. The gate went up, and the grizzly went out. He rolled over and came up running—back toward the truck. In a couple of bounds he caught up and tried to get at me, but the space between the trap and the side of the truck was too narrow, and he fell off. Next thing I knew, he caught a grip on the spare tire. You remember how the spare was mounted on the side of those old trucks, don't you?

I nodded yes, scribbling hard. Dale was in the grasp of his memory. He was back on the Trout Creek Road, the truck rocking and swaying, the claws of the grizzly scraping against the metal side of the truck. "Oh, Christ, but he was a big one," he said, banging his clasped hands on the desk for emphasis. "That bear had attached himself to the spare somehow, swinging at me with one arm and not missing by much. I was yelling at the driver to do something, when he made a sharp turn and the bear went flying. The whole deal didn't take thirty seconds, and I was still holding the rope."

The bartender at the Bear Pit interrupted my reverie by asking if I desired another of the same. Mindful of the drive ahead, I reluctantly declined. As I walked around the corner of Old Faithful Inn, I saw a coyote with an unusually big, bushy tail sleuthing along on some business of his own, close enough that I could see the light color of his eyes. I drove back to Mammoth in the last hour of daylight, the sky a lovely deepening blue, and dreamed fitfully of bears most of the night.

∪ ∪

In a drenching rain, chief naturalist Al Meban and I approached Tower Junction, the intersection where the northeast entrance road joins Grand Loop. Off to our left, under a solid bank of dark clouds, Pleasant Valley was a blur of meadows and slanting hills. It was Wednesday after the Memorial Day weekend. Our destination was the Lamar ranger station, ten miles out the entrance road. Once the site of the buffalo ranch, the complex provides instructional space and sleeping quarters for the Yellowstone Institute. Privately funded and administered, the institute offers a variety of summer courses taught by guest professors.

Al was an old friend, our paths having crossed many times. He wanted to make sure the institute facilities were in good shape for the opening session and had invited me to come along. The figure of a ranger advanced out of the mist, flagging us down. Water was running off the brim of his Stetson as he bent down to tell Al that a retired couple from Israel had lost control of their car and gone down a steep embankment. Fortunately, the vehicle was upright, but the man might have suffered a back injury. The ranger had other obligations and hoped Al could take him to the clinic at Mammoth.

The three of us managed to lift him up the slick incline and ease him into the back seat of Al's patrol car. He apologized for the fuss, insisting that his injury was of little consequence. Being agreeable, he yielded to his wife's insistence that he see a doctor. He observed that living in Israel conditions one to the unexpected.

The couple had been to Grand Teton, and they reacted to our national parks as do so many foreign visitors. Their impression of America, often, is of a country that has squandered its natural resources and rejected the kind of restrictions on land use that are common in Europe. They have difficulty reconciling this view with a park system preserving an area nearly the size of Great Britain. Our Israeli visitors spoke warmly of a national park near their home in Haifa. Looking it up in *The United Nations List of National Parks and Equivalent Reserves*, I found that Mount Carmel National Park has one full-time employee, two creatures of note—the spotted eagle and the rock dove—and occupies twenty square miles. Tiny countries adapt the national park idea to their own context.

At the Mammoth clinic an alert young doctor with a competent manner determined that the man had sustained no structural damage. He advised bed rest and aspirin for the rest of the day. Al made a reservation for the couple in the hotel across the boulevard and arranged with the service station to retrieve their rental car. He and I then adjourned to his office in the administration building. While he called Lamar to explain his tardiness, I looked out the window. There was more rain coming. And wind. Al insisted that I put my feet on his desk and look into an advance copy of a new book on Yellowstone. I protested once, to be polite and did as he suggested.

Old Yellowstone Days proved to be good reading, a collection of impressions and experiences by travelers of note who had visited the park before and just after the turn of the century. The editor, Paul Schullery, had passed six summers and parts of several winters in the park as both historian and naturalist and was well on his way to becoming a fixture before moving on to take up a writing career. Schullery included an account by Owen Wister, who wrote *The Virginian*, of his visit to Yellowstone in 1887.

Wister and his companions camped in the trees a short ride from the Upper Geyser Basin, bathed in the Firehole River, and lounged in the Fountain Hotel, predecessor of Old Faithful Inn, which he described as, "chiefly of canvas, walls and roof, and to sleep there must have made you intimately acquainted with how your neighbors were passing the night." Geyser-gazing was the favorite occupation of the guests. They were aided by a youngster who normally spoke in a deep bass voice. When excited, he tended to screech. Now he would be called a bellhop. In those days, Wister noted, there was no bell, but the boy hopped a great deal:

> We would be sitting, tilted back, reading our mail, the tourists would have ceased talking and be lounging drowsily, the boy would be at the door, motionless as a set steel trap. Suddenly the trap would spring, the boy would catapult into the door, and in his piping treble scream out: "Beehive's a-going off!" at which every tourist instantly started from his chair, and a leaping crowd gushed out of the hotel and sprinted down over the formation to catch the Beehive at it. Beehive finally quiescent, they returned slowly, sank into chairs and exhausted silence; you could have heard a mosquito. But the steel trap was again set, sprang soon, and again the silence was pierced: "There goes Old Faithful!" Up and out they flew once more, watched Old Faithful, and came back to their chairs and silence more exhausted.

I was chuckling over Wister's conclusion that the black bears were so successful cadging food from tourists that the next step for them was to take over the hotels and dismiss the management when Dave Mihalic walked into the office and said, "We shot Bear 27 this morning." He was in Mammoth for a review of the case and tracked me down, knowing I'd want to hear the details. Pulling a chair over to the desk, he propped up his feet and said, "That bear was jinxed all the way."

On Sunday evening, after dropping me at Old Faithful Inn, Dave reset the trap on the Fountain Freight Road, with no result. On Monday, the rangers and bear management people huddled. Bear 27 had not made an appearance for five days. In early June a grizzly will range widely, searching for food, and easily cover twenty miles in a day. It was possible Bear 27 had moved on. They hoped to God he had and decided to take one more chance. The trap was removed, and the area reopened.

The next day, Tuesday, an employee of the Old Faithful Inn took a stroll before breakfast. He had stopped on the boardwalk, taking in the view, when he realized he wasn't alone. A bear was standing right beside him. "Like Tom Sherman, the guy was pumped," Dave said, "Only, he didn't wait as long. He ran like hell." There was no doubt of the bear's identity— red ear tags and a radio collar.

"It was decision time. Bear 27 had no fear of humans and would continue to approach them. The only argument in his favor was that he hadn't hurt anybody, yet. But there is no such thing as a tame grizzly. Sooner or later the person he approached would do something to trigger his heritage. We had the feeling time was running out on us, and maybe luck too. We recommended the bear be destroyed. No one up the line disagreed."

At dawn, Dave and two rangers armed with rifles took position in the Old Faithful residential area. They didn't wait long. A bear edged out of the trees, then started in their direction. Dave made a positive identification. One of the rangers had a clear shot at medium range. The bullet caught the bear squarely in the left side with enough shocking power to have downed an elk. Bear 27 ran a hundred yards before he fell. Dave made certain with his pistol. The three stood there looking at the dead bear, not taking any pleasure in the deed. One said, "Too bad. It wasn't really his fault."

It is customary, in the case of grizzlies, to have an autopsy performed. This one, done at Montana State University in Bozeman, was a shocker. It helped explain why Bear 27 approached people and frequented the residential area. Popcorn was found in his stomach. Somebody had been putting out food for him.

There were a lot of angry people inside and outside the Park Service when the autopsy findings were released. A grizzly being fed by park residents! Townsley threatened legal action if the guilty party could be found. Local conservationists had formed a Save the Bears group to oppose what they believed to be the needless killing of problem bears. At a protest rally at Old Faithful that was widely publicized, they denounced the Park Service and John Townsley for what they called "needless slaughter." "I agree with them," John said when we talked about it, "except I had to make the decision on the basis of the information available, and I had to consider the safety of the public as well as the welfare of the grizzly population. I regret the loss of that bear as much as anyone, but I respect a grizzly's capacity for violence."

4

Stopping the Clocks

As much as any animal, the buffalo evokes memories of that most powerful of American dreams, the frontier. For a time in U.S. history, the West was buffalo land. Reputedly, it contained the greatest concentration of a single species ever to exist on earth. Buffalo images colored the public perception of a primitive land so filled with herds of the shaggy beasts that it was like an outdoor shooting gallery where you could plink away at the biggest targets on the continent.

Buffalo were a part of the diet and rich idiom of mountain men and American Indians. A trapper described his companion as "a big feller with hair frizzed out like an old buffler's just afore sheddin' time." He called another "brave as a buffalo in the spring," the opposite of "I run as ef a wounded buffler was raisin' my shirt with his horns." The Sioux, naming each winter after an exceptional happening, would say of a mild one, "Winter when the buffalo stood among the tipis."

A future commander of Fort Yellowstone chased and killed the first buffalo he ever saw. "This should provide fresh meat for the whole troop," he told his orderly proudly after inspecting his trophy. Recognizing the animal as a withered old loner driven from the herd, the sergeant hid a smile. "Lieutenant," he said, "there ain't nothing worth eatin' on him but the tongue."

It was October 1871, and George Anderson, fresh out of West Point, was leading his troop of cavalry from Kansas to Colorado, following the trace of an abandoned stage line through some of the best buffalo range in North America. Winding over the low hills in a double file behind its guidons, the long column was only a day out of Fort Hays when the lone bull appeared. By the time Anderson made camp that evening, buffalo in small clusters were visible in many directions.

Soon after breaking camp next morning, and for the rest of the day, Anderson saw buffalo by the thousands, dark spots on the yellow brown of the autumn prairie. On the third day an unseasonable blizzard trapped the soldiers in a small ravine on the banks of the Smoke Hill River. That night a living tide of buffalo, driven by the storm, piled up against the river barrier and thundered by the camp. "For six days we continued our way through this enormous herd," Anderson wrote, "during the last three of which it was in constant motion across our path. I am safe in calling this a single herd, and it is impossible to approximate the millions that composed it."

The buffalo pressing against Anderson's column and frequently bringing it to a halt were only a part of the Republican herd, one of four aggregations that had once numbered perhaps sixty million. The buffalo moved across the prairies as the stars move and seemed as unalterable. Fifteen years after Anderson's men threaded their way through the "countless multitudes," the buffalo had vanished, swept away as if by a deadly pestilence. Their disappearance may have been the most lamentable of all the calamities suffered by wildlife in America.

The man who did as much as anyone to awaken the nation to the wanton destruction of the buffalo, George Bird Grinnell, is all but forgotten now. A young paleontology student at Yale, he spent the summer of 1870 in the West hunting fossils with a Peabody Museum expedition. Two years in his father's New York brokerage office failed to diminish his longing for the West's wild country. He went back to live and hunt with the friendly Pawnees, returning for the next forty years almost every summer to collect scientific specimens and document Indian culture.

Grinnell was as comfortable squatting beside a cookfire of buffalo chips, eating hump ribs with his fingers, as he was dining in the White House with his close friend and fellow conservationist Theodore Roosevelt. He wrote more than twenty volumes on the buffalo Indians, ranging from technical studies to fiction. Yet, said one historian, of the millions of words written about American wildlife, "it would be difficult to find more moving prose than Grinnell's eulogy to the buffalo."

"On the floor, on either side of my fireplace, lie two buffalo skulls," Grinnell begins his tribute. "They are white and weathered, the horns cracked and bleached by the snows and frosts and the rains and heats of many winters and summers." With the easy grace of a country fiddler he carries readers into the past. "Often, late at night, when the house is quiet, I sit before the fire and muse and dream of the old days; and as I gaze at these relics of the past, they take life before my eyes. The matted brown hair again clothes the dry bone, and in the empty orbits the wild eyes gleam. Above me curves the blue arch; away on either hand stretches the yellow prairie, and scattered near and far are the dark forms of buffalo."

Then, Grinnell continues, mounted warriors charge and shout. In an instant the herd becomes a black mass sweeping over the prairie, the horsemen bringing down many fat cows. Returning on their tracks, they skin out the buffalo, rope the meat and robes on their horses, and with much laughter and banter ride away. "After them on the deserted prairie, come the wolves to tear at the carcasses. The rain and the snow wash the blood from the bones, and fade and bleach the hair. . . . So this cow and this bull of mine may have left their bones on the prairie, where I found them and picked them up to keep as mementos of the past, to dream over, and in such reverie to see again the swelling hosts which yesterday covered the plains, and today are but a dream. So the buffalo passed into history."

Capt. George Anderson took up his duties at Fort Yellowstone in 1891. The first targets of his formidable talents were the poachers. An expedition that surveyed the entire West in 1886 located fewer than six hundred buffalo, including those in Yellowstone. Taxidermists in Livingston and Bozeman were selling mounted buffalo heads for up to a thousand dollars, a huge sum in those times. Lacking legal authority to prosecute, Anderson was restricted to destroying a poacher's property and expelling him from the park. A giant of a man with red hair and a temper to match, he resorted to delaying tactics, holding a poacher in the guardhouse for weeks while deliberating whether to escort him to the east or west exit. Bills to provide the park with law enforcement powers attracted minimal support in Congress.

One spring morning in 1894, an army scout and a sergeant on ski patrol in the snowy wilderness north of Yellowstone Lake followed a set of snowshoe tracks to a cache of six buffalo heads suspended from the limb of a tree. Distant rifle shots led them to a notorious poacher absorbed in the task of skinning out five buffalo. Given a little more time, he might have wiped out the herd. On the way back to Fort Yellowstone with their prisoner, who was forced to drag the evidence on his own toboggan, the patrol met a party of journalists in the employ of George Bird Grinnell, by then editor and owner of *Field and Stream*. Grinnell used the pages of his influential weekly to draw the public into his campaigns for many good causes, including stricter game laws. His field correspondents, Emerson Hough heading the team, would later write much of *The Covered Wagon* while a nonpaying guest of the Yellowstone superintendent.

Hough's dramatic story, wired from Fort Yellowstone, caught Anderson's bitterness that he could not legally punish the poacher: "His arms and outfit will be confiscated, and I will sock him just as far and as deep into the guard-house as I know how, when I get him, and he won't get fat there either. That is all I can do under the regulations. I shall report to the Secretary of the Interior and in due course the Secretary of the Interior will order me to set the prisoner free. There is no law governing this park except the military regulation. There is no punishment that can be inflicted on this low-down fellow." The confident poacher told Hough, "I haven't arranged my plans for the future. I may go back into the Park again later, or I may not." But the several stories Hough wrote for *Field and Stream* aroused the public and produced immediate results.

A bill "to protect the birds and animals in Yellowstone National Park, and to punish crimes in said park," introduced in Congress thirteen days after the capture of the poacher, was signed into law two months later. Comprehensive and explicit, it assured legal protection of Yellowstone's wildlife. The provisions, soon extended to the other parks, are still in force. Grinnell deserved much of the credit for this law, although the infamous poacher later complained that he never received the credit he deserved for bringing law and order to Yellowstone.

Buffalo gave me a thrilling moment during my summer in Yellowstone. It happened the week after Dave Milhalic set the trap for Bear 27 and not far from that site. On a tip that a sizable herd of buffalo had been spotted in the vicinity, I was driving the Fountain Freight Road. The day was on the chilly side, prompting me to park just beyond where the road swings to the left and narrows for the old bridge over the Firehole River. As I dug out my down jacket I checked the sedge meadow off to my right. A buffalo appeared from the woods, then another and another. Buffalo were spilling into the meadow by the dozens.

For a better view I climbed on top of the car. My hands holding the binoculars seemed steady, but I couldn't say the same for my breathing. They passed directly in front of me, at times breaking into a light-footed canter, pausing occasionally for a few mouthsful of grass. From my perch I could have nearly touched two of the animals scuffling among themselves at some minor irritation.

A bull larger than my VW—males can weigh two thousand pounds—stopped a few paces away to look me over. He was shedding his heavy winter coat before the heat of summer, the new hair shading from dark brown at the shoulders to almost black on the hindquarters. The head was low to the ground, all but the tips of the inward curving horns hidden by long, matted hair. The neck rose almost vertically to the hump. Widely spaced obsidian eyes regarded me with what I took to be unthreatening interest. The billy-goat beard and fly-swatter tail made his bulk less alarming.

Calves were light in color, a faint sandy red. Until they acquire the hump, they look more like cattle. Only two or three weeks old, they flung themselves in all directions. One faked to the left and right, made a twisting leap, and landed running. Catching sight of me, he skidded to a stop, quiveringly alert, permitting me to marvel at his nimbleness.

The 1894 Lacey Act came almost too late to save Yellowstone's buffalo because high prices spurred poachers to risk arrest. In 1902 the superintendent reported an official count of twenty-three. That year the army purchased three bulls and eighteen cows from ranchers in Texas and Montana who had captured calves from passing herds. Moved to a corral in Lamar Valley, soon called the "buffalo ranch," the "tame" herd of plains bison eventually mingled with the remaining wild stock of mountain bison. Mary Meagher could observe, in the first sentence of her doctoral dissertation, "The bison of Yellowstone National Park are unique among bison herds in the United States, being descendants, in part, of the only continuously wild herd in this country."

I sat on the car roof long after the stragglers disappeared as they entered the forest on the other side of the meadow, their dark shapes blending with the shadows of the pines. Climbing down, I examined the hoof marks in the soft earth, hefting a divot that had been dislodged and reluctant to leave the scene. Buffalo can be exciting, not for what they are but for what they were. In the era of the great herds it had taken Anderson six days to thread his way through the dark sea of buffalo. My herd numbered something over a hundred and took ten minutes to cross the meadow, and yet I felt I'd witnessed a spectacle. There are sights you see in Yellowstone that almost convince you that the clocks stopped there a long while back.

∪ ∪

I first explored the Yellowstone country in the summer of 1958 while a member of the historic site survey. Assigned to San Francisco, I joined several survey historians for the purpose of documenting the route of the Lewis and Clark Expedition. From Three Forks in western Montana, where the Jefferson, Madison, and Gallatin rivers combine to form the Missouri, we advanced up the diminishing west fork, the Jefferson, to the Continental Divide. Following the Lolo Trail, the still evident track of the Nez Percé Indians who crossed the Rockies to hunt buffalo on the plains, we continued down the easy slopes of the Clearwater, the Snake, and the Columbia to the Pacific.

We traced the Missouri to its source. In the book published by the Park Service on the survey, a photograph I took shows a colleague with one foot on either side of a rivulet. Meriwether Lewis recorded in his journal that one of his men had done the same at this location "and thanked his god that he had lived to bestride the mighty & heretofore deemed endless Missouri." All of the West was once like the stretches of remote and untouched country through which we passed.

The detailed journals kept by the expedition leaders enabled us to identify their campsites. "Encamped opposit a Small Island at the mouth of a branch on the right side of the river which is at this place 80 yards wide, Swift and Stoney, here we were compelled to kill a colt for our men & Selves to eat for the want of meat & we named the South Fork Colt Killed Creek." As we read the caption of the Forest Service sign marking the site, one of our number said, "We are walking with the ghosts."

On the day the survey team assembled at Bozeman, two of us who had flown in a day early investigated a site where the expedition came close to discovering the marvels of Yellowstone. At Livingston the Yellowstone River swerves to the east and begins its long traverse of Montana. At this bend of the river, in the early afternoon of July 15, 1806, a band of eleven men in ragged buckskins and on Indian ponies, a young Indian woman with an eighteen-month-old baby on her back, and a cavalcade of fifty horses approached from the west. It was a detachment of the returning Lewis and Clark Expedition, led by Capt. William Clark.

After recrossing the Rocky Mountains, the expedition divided for the only time, Lewis scouting the country to the north of the Missouri. Clark's mission was to reconnoiter the Missouri's largest southern tributary, the Yellowstone. At the riverbend he could look south through the gap cut by the river to the snow-capped Gallatin Mountains within the present Yellowstone park. He was unaware that a short detour in that direction would have produced a startling discovery. The Mammoth Hot Springs were but fifty miles distant. Instead, Clark followed the Yellowstone River downstream, catching up with the main party on the Missouri six weeks after the separation. An exploration of the Yellowstone country worthy of the name would have to wait another sixty-four years.

For reference, our survey party carried a set of the *Original Journals of the Lewis and Clark Expedition*, edited by Ruben Thwaites, the five volumes containing at least one entry for every day of the journey. I brought a copy of Bernard DeVoto's one-volume condensation, partly because it was easy to carry and partly because I admired DeVoto. One of the finest nonfiction writers of his time, he breathed life into everything he wrote. An enemy of the lukewarm martini and a champion of conservation causes, he defended the national parks like a belligerent watchdog.

I'd met DeVoto a few years earlier when I was invited to the meetings of the secretary of the interior's Advisory Board on National Parks, then headed by publisher Alfred A. Knopf. During a coffee break DeVoto gave an amusing account of a summer spent following the trail of Lewis and Clark in preparation for *The Course of Empire.* In the widest view, DeVoto argued in a volume that won the National Book Award for history, the quest of Lewis and Clark for a direct route between the Atlantic and the Pacific was the final act in the line of exploration that had taken Columbus to the New World.

The year he tracked Lewis and Clark was 1946, the first travel season after the war, and to hear DeVoto tell it he suffered privations comparable to those endured by the Captains of Discovery. Tourist cabins were on a par with sheepherder huts, and roadside diners served food that would have turned a grizzly's stomach. But in the middle of his journey he wrote to a friend, "calling this western tour the best thing he had ever done in his life."

The year before our survey DeVoto's ashes had been scattered from an airplane near Lolo Pass. It was a spot, according to biographer Wallace Stegner, where Benny "used to sit on a rock beside the stream and make remarks about anyone who would rather be riding a goddam horse." Later, friends mounted a plaque on a boulder beside the Lochsa River, whose nearby tributary was the expedition's Colt Killed Creek. There, in a forest wilderness he loved, "tourists who probably never heard his name, but should have, can read a sentence or two about him . . . on a stream that he loved, at the side of a historic trail that he had followed from end to end with the excitement of discovery."

∪ ∪

My most treasured memento of Yellowstone is the claw of a grizzly bear. It's before me now, resting on the butcher-block surface of my writing table between an old pewter mug holding freshly sharpened Berol Mirado pencils and a wine glass holding bird feathers picked up in the course of my afternoon walks on the pathways of Reston. When in need of distraction I measure the curved length of the claw. The result is always the same, exactly four inches, a half-inch longer than my middle finger. As functional as a surgeon's scalpel, it has the look of a cordovan shoe, except that few things in nature are of a single color. A close inspection reveals narrow bands of lighter and darker brown converging at the tip. Hollow and whisper-light, it's made of keratin, the stuff of horns and hoofs, but its configuration is derived from deep time.

A grizzly claw is never "razor sharp." Mine is rounded at the tip, having been used for pick and shovel work. Digging up the succulent bulbs of the glacier lily, a grizzly will convert a meadow into a plowed field and will dismantle a pile of rocks the size of a stretch limousine to get at a marmot. The claw is still a murderous weapon. When a grizzly meets up with a porcupine, he flips it over and with a rake of his claws cuts the body free and leaves behind a pin cushion of quills, or so they say.

I spotted the claw on one of those warm summer days that show Yellowstone at its best. I was a member of a planning group preparing for the Second World Conference on National Parks, to be held in Yellowstone in 1972, the park's one-hundredth anniversary. We were meeting with representatives of the park concessioner at Old Faithful Inn, trying to anticipate problems that might come up when you are housing and feeding people from eighty-five nations. Outside, Yellowstone beckoned. Several of us decided not to return after lunch. We gave our proxies to straight-arrow colleagues, supplying a cover story should director George Hartzog call.

We were taking John Muir's advice to climb the mountains and absorb their good medicine in the hope that our bureaucratic aggravations would drop away like the leaves of autumn. We settled on a convenient trail with a gentle grade leading to the vicinity of the former Rabbit Creek garbage dump. This and the dump at Trail Creek had been recently closed and covered over, excluding garbage from the grizzly diet for the first time in eighty years. The possibility of running into a grizzly was termed ridiculous by the member who had proposed the excursion and whose identity you may have guessed. Grizzlies, I announced, were no more partial to this trail now than any other. Unknown to me, a recent spate of grizzly activity had prompted rangers to consider closing the area to hikers.

On a path quilted with pine needles we ambled along at a leisurely pace and with much conversation. As we moved from an open meadow into the shade of a thick stand of lodgepoles, a gray jay startled us with a sudden fuss. A joker yelled, "Grizzly at twelve o'clock!" With that, the talk dwindled.

About an hour from the trailhead, as we came out of the woods and caught a view of a far ridge, one of our number stopped suddenly and pointed. Off to one side of the trail, vegetation had been uprooted and the earth exposed. White bones and brown chunks of fur were strewn about. A battle to the death between two grizzlies, we deduced. The winner, no doubt, ate the choice parts of his victim. Coyotes and ravens and other scavengers had picked the carcass clean. Hikers had carried away the collectibles.

Poking around the edges of the struggle site I kicked over a clod of dirt and uncovered the claw. Before showing it to the others I held it in my hand a moment, trying to imagine how much damage it had done in this and other clashes. I was aware of a prickly feeling at the back of my neck, like a small boy feels when facing the incalculable. Often when I pick up the claw and run my fingers over the smooth surface I think of the place where the two grizzlies met and neither would yield. Occasionally, I reach for DeVoto's chronicle of the Rocky Mountain fur trade, *Beyond the Wide Missouri*, leafing to the page marked with a rusty paper clip. In a single sentence DeVoto says all that needs to be said about the myth-making traits of the grizzly bear.

By that passage we have been introduced to Capt. William Drummond Stewart, late of The King's Hussars, he of the hooked beak, Guardsman's mustache, and ramrod bearing. On one of a half-dozen trips to the Rockies, Stewart took with him the young Baltimore artist Alfred Jacob Miller, the first to paint the way of life of the mountain men. In Miller's works, Stewart is always mounted on a white horse. Hardened trappers regarded Stewart as an equal. That he had not been decorated for valor at Waterloo was of no importance, DeVoto noted. Not when a trapper would say, "Thar was old grit in him too, and a hair of the black b'ar at that." For the enjoyment of his companions Stewart sent back to England and got a suit of armor for Jim Bridger. The annual rendezvous that summer could not have seen a queerer sight.

The death of his elder brother brought Stewart the title of Sir William, nineteenth of Grandtully and seventh baronet (and master of Birnam Wood). For the walls of Murthley Castle, holding pikes and halberds, casques and jeweled daggers, gauntlets and arquebuses, Stewart brought buffalo and bighorn heads, medicine pipes and warbonnets, and the horn bows of the Nez Percé. Next to the works of Raphael, Leonardo, and Caravaggio, collected by his ancestors, Stewart hung "Roasting the Hump Rib," "Attack by the Crows," and "The Trapper's Bride," all by the eminent American stylist Alfred Jacob Miller.

We learn from DeVoto that six months after returning to England to put his inheritance in order Stewart was en route to Egypt and Constantinople. Waiting for a ship in London, he wrote to one of the great figures of the Rocky Mountain fur trade, Bill Sublette. Let my friends know "that if I am in life and health I shall be on the Susquadee [Green River] in July, '41." DeVoto thought that as Stewart made plans for a return to the Rocky Mountains his thoughts perhaps returned to his first mountain rendezvous, when the supply train from St. Louis arrived and every trapper and brave let go a volley such as Stewart hadn't heard since Waterloo and never in his life such yelling.

DeVoto allowed his own imagination free play. The reek of London's coal smoke would have reminded Stewart of a buffalo-chip fire burning at daybreak and the smell of sagebrush dampened by dew. Carts rattling on the cobblestones outside Stewart's hotel window might have recalled a Platte River crossing, his wagons mired by quicksand, the drivers shouting and cursing the mules to the far bank. Then, in DeVoto's evocative sentence, "Something moves in the willows and the Manton is cocked and Sir William stands up in his stirrups—Ephraim is there, Old Caleb, the white bear of the mountains, so terrible that to kill one is a coup as glorious as striking with your bare hand an enemy in his own tipi."

∪ ∪

If the testimony of generations of Yellowstone rangers can be relied upon, and I could take either side on that debate, a singular episode in park history took place at the Norris soldier station only a few miles up the road from the Rabbit Creek Trail. I first heard about the untimely death of the Old Faithful winterkeeper from Bob Luntey when Bob and I were stationed in the Washington office.

A former Yellowstone ranger on temporary assignment in Washington, Bob had caught the eye of the assistant director responsible for studying proposed new parks and became his administrative assistant. Every time Bob tried to get a transfer back to the field he was given a promotion or a summer interlude in Alaska. A young-hearted, even-tempered, compact bundle of energy with a winning smile, Bob seemed to have anything needed stashed away in his pack, including the makings for the best hot-buttered rum drink I've ever tasted.

We were of the same age, single and pursuing two comely young women who shared a house in Georgetown. (I married Mary the next year, Bob held out longer.) We were part of a congenial Georgetown crew that would throw a party every Saturday or take off for the ski slopes or Rehoboth Beach. With a long Washington's Birthday holiday coming up, I proposed an outing at Cape Hatteras, counting on the nearby Gulf Stream to warm the area even in February. The Outer Banks had put their spell on me, the lonely, impermanent islands and the little villages with their suitable names—Avon, Salvo, and Rodanthe. We crossed Oregon Inlet on a World

War II LST converted to ferry service. Ocracoke Island was like Samar-kand.

Dinner the first night was a burlap sack full of oysters, on the half-shell, stewed, and baked. The weather was so balmy and the stars so brilliant that we strolled the beach past the lighthouse to the Cape. Then we gathered driftwood and sat on blankets around a crackling fire on the beach in front of the Cape Hatteras Cottage Court. Stories were told, and I had fair suc-cess relating Civil War anecdotes. It may have been the one about the death of Robert E. Lee's favorite artilleryman, "the gallant Pelham," that trig-gered Bob's memory. When he said it reminded him of the time a Yellow-stone ski patrol brought the body of the winterkeeper fifty miles through the snow, he had everyone's attention.

The winterkeeper at Old Faithful lived by himself, visited only by the monthly ski patrol and in touch with Mammoth periodically when the single-line telephone was operating. The line had gone dead one winter after a blizzard, and when the ski patrol next approached Old Faithful there was no wood smoke rising from the winterkeeper's cabin, an omi-nous sign. The rangers found him dead on the cabin floor, frozen stiff. The next morning they loaded him on a makeshift toboggan and started back to Mammoth.

At Norris station, which they reached the first night, the deceased was not brought inside lest he thaw out. After dinner the poker game began, a cabin ritual. Observed one ranger evidently more sentimental than most, the Supreme Being plays no favorites. The winterkeeper had a lucky streak on the last patrol, winning almost every pot. This time he'd drawn the wrong card. Then, Bob told his hushed audience, without a word being spoken the rangers pushed the table and an extra chair over to the window. One went outside and propped the toboggan against the cabin wall so it caught the light from the window. As each game was played the rest of the evening, a hand was dealt to the empty chair of the absent friend.

Bob's recital tickled his listeners. I liked it as well as the several renditions I've heard since, although it does have a familiar ring. Still, I was saddened that Aubrey Haines, in his indispensable chronicle, *The Yellowstone Story*, elected to throw cold water on what he termed "an enduring Yellowstone legend." Not entirely to their credit, historians feel obliged to expose the most amiable of fables. Aubrey was satisfied that the legend was based on an actual but completely different event. The dead man was a soldier, he died at the Snake River station, and the date was 1904, long before rangers were in the park. Aubrey quoted from the tape of a retirement party for Harry Liek, neglecting to mention that Liek was a certified hell-raiser to whom truth had long been a stranger. As a crony tells the Liek version of the legend,

> I remember Harry tellin' about the dead soldier. Brought him from Snake River—got as far the Fountain ranger station, and the soldiers had just come back from West Yellowstone with a bottle of whiskey, so the guys got in a big poker game, played poker all night—so, Harry says, "We better let old Joe"—the dead soldier lying there—"play a hand." So they stood him up by the window, so he could watch them play poker; they played poker until ten o'clock the next day and it was on the south side of the building. The sun came out and he started to thaw out and wiggle a little bit, and Harry says, "Wait a minute Joe, I'll be right out and open her up."

Granted, Aubrey knows more about Yellowstone than any person alive, but I don't think he has the straight of this business yet. Soon after his book came out, my duties took me to the regional office in Santa Fe. A cocktail party materialized—it's what they do best in Santa Fe—and I ran into George Miller, the recently retired assistant regional director and former Yellowstone assistant chief ranger. When I told George about Aubrey's treatment of the winterkeeper story he swore an oath and went to get us another round of margaritas.

Turned out, George was in on the whole deal. He was with the ranger patrol that found the body of the winterkeeper. He remembered the card game at Norris as if it were yesterday. He gave me the names of the other rangers, the date, everything. But I kept eating those good crisp tortilla chips dipped in that fiery salsa and washing them down with margaritas. Next morning I couldn't remember any of it. I'm 91 percent sure that George wasn't putting me on. So I have a question for my good friend Aubrey Haines. Is it likely George could have made it to assistant regional director in a crack outfit like the Park Service if he was unable to tell fact from fiction whenever he started drinking margaritas? Well, maybe in Santa Fe.

5

Outsiders among the Insiders

Mary Meagher was on the way to becoming a Yellowstone legend. A recognized authority on the buffalo, she headed the park's research staff. She had to fight to get there, and she gave as good as she got. A prickly personality and a woman to boot in a work force that had been as male-dominated as a local fire department, she was almost more than Yellowstone could bear. You reached her office on the third floor of the administration building by turning left at the top of the stairs and passing through a reception area to her office in the corner. I entered cautiously on a blustery June morning. She looked at me with cool surmise, as if she were the examiner and I was a candidate for something, which I suppose I was.

She motioned me to a chair that seemed to have been fashioned from a snowshoe. The low seat made it difficult for the occupant to feel at ease or to take the initiative. Her office was, like Mary, purposeful and tidy. Bookshelves lined two walls. Reports and files and yellow boxes of camera film were stacked neatly on a table. A shelf held a silver hard hat, a black and yellow snowmobile helmet, and a smashing, broad-brimmed leather hat fit for a garden party. The mandibles of a half-dozen elk were mounted on the wall, one above another, and a well-stuffed blue pack lay beside her chair. Pinned above her desk was the Charles Addams cartoon of a satyr carrying a startled woman into the forest. Next to it was a photograph of a buffalo lying on his back in a wallow, all four legs in the air.

Mary, small and trim, studied me from behind glasses that had hexagonal rims. Her skin was fair, her eyes blue, and her hair reddish-brown, parted in the middle, and cut short. She wore khaki slacks, suede boots, small gold earrings, and her trademark sweater over turtleneck in shades of brown and red. During the course of our conversation she mentioned with glee a description of her given by a poacher she had testified against: "That short, dumpy, red-headed chick." Mary needlessly hindered her career by lashing out with scathing evaluations of so many of her colleagues. Some were people for whom I had high regard. She had a kinder, gentler side, but few experienced it.

She had first applied to the park fifteen years earlier, holding a master's degree in wildlife biology and a strong desire to do research on buffalo. Yellowstone was unimpressed, offering her a typist job—if she increased her speed. For years she was a "floater," taking whatever was available and working for a while as a museum curator. She managed to do some research, much of it on her own.

She had been a student of Starker Leopold at the University of California at Berkeley. Taking his advice, she began work on her Ph.D., continuing to work intermittently as a naturalist at Yellowstone and doing fieldwork. Her dissertation, "The Bison of Yellowstone National Park," established her credentials. Soon afterward, Dr. Mary Meagher became a Yellowstone wildlife biologist, replacing the head of the office when he transferred two years before. "At a lower grade," she pointed out:

> The reason I sound warped is that I was treated, like shabby, for so long. Things have improved, but the Park Service still isn't there yet when it comes to equal opportunities for women. Now I'm being used as an example of what women can achieve! I wasted so much time surviving. That's what I resent most.
>
> I was flying the park on a bison count some years ago and saw a poacher's shack that couldn't be seen from the ground. I reported it to the chief ranger, who all but told me I should stick to counting buffalo. He was reminding me that rangers know best. It's called the ranger blessing. Rangers don't like to take advice from biologists. But to hear it from a woman!

Scientists can be an irritant to a superintendent. They serve two masters. For this reason, and because of their personalities, Mary and John Townsley were frequently at sixes and sevens. John, a company man, was loyal to the organization, willing to forgive its faults, breathing on the coals of the old legends. The Park Service hadn't treated Mary well enough to earn her commitment. She believed that it shortchanges natural history research, hiring ten times more rangers than scientists and is fearful of alienating the traveling public. She mentioned with delight that she'd humiliated John in front of assistant secretary Nat Reed by "demolishing" a decision she considered excessively pragmatic. "A real superintendent would put the resources first and make all else give way."

I asked her what she would have John do. "I know we are mandated to balance preservation and use. In the past that's been a realistic goal. Now we must put preservation first. I can't predict whether the grizzly is going to make it or not in Yellowstone. Everything that encourages visitor use hurts the grizzly's chance to survive. Where a conflict exists between visitors and grizzlies, I'd exclude the people and remove the facilities. Of course Congress, the concessioner, and the public would have fits."

Mary remained at Yellowstone in part because field research is what she liked best. The backcountry, she remarked, "can be irresistible and glorious." She had logged uncounted hours on horseback and skis. "Not all scientists can put up with backcountry constraints, and there isn't any substitute for knowing how to work the country like the rangers. Give them their due. But the backcountry can be hazardous. I was bringing a horse in from the picket line one morning. He tripped over the wire and fell on me, gashing my head. I was grateful we had a doctor at the clinic who was good with a suture needle."

In my experience, only people who have dealt up close and personal with a grizzly have earned the right to call one a "griz." Mary told me of the time she was flying over the lower end of Astringent Creek, north of Pelican Valley, and saw a big male grizzly on an elk carcass. The pilot turned and came in low to give Mary a close look. As they roared by, he took a swipe at the airplane with one paw. "The griz," Mary said, "doesn't back off from anything."

Mary's administrative and supervisory duties gave her little time for research:

> I'm in the crisis business. I can't plan two days in advance. All Yellowstone wildlife problems pass over my desk. Scientists from around the country, media people, too, call me and talk at length. A great deal of research by outside people is being done in Yellowstone. They need to be briefed and require logistical help. I provided substantive assistance to more than a hundred and fifty researchers last year. I also spent Christmas and New Year's Day in the biology lab at Bozeman. The Park Service gets its money's worth out of me. I've about had it with administration, but I can still get excited about research. I'm not burned out on that. I have so much invested, all that data on bison mortality waiting for me. I have a need to see it through. I can't live with bagging it.

From spring until fall Mary occupied the residence of her choice, an old patrol cabin without electricity on the Blacktail Plateau seven miles from

Mammoth. Reached by an abandoned service road, it sits in open sage-brush country above a small stream lined with willows, a small barn and corral behind. Invitations to the "Meagher ranch" were prized. At gather-ings there, I'm told, the lamb stew contained meat of uncertain origin from a previous party, the bread was chewy and the wine robust, and a volume of Robert Service was known to make an appearance.

"When I get away from the office in the evening and drive out to Black-tail, into that grand chunk of Yellowstone, everything comes together. Measured against geologic time, my worries matter a lot less." A friendly fire crew reinforced the back porch with heavy timbers so that her horse could rattle the door latch at five in the morning. Mary would oblige with a generous dollop of oats. "He'll plant his front feet on the porch and watch me through the door for hours. Horses are gregarious. They need com-pany."

So, I suspect, do private people who live by their own value systems and are impatient with those who fail to measure up. Stan Cantor, former Yellowstone naturalist and keen observer of the Yellowstone scene, told me of another side of Mary Meagher:

It was the winter we trapped buffalo in dreadful weather. Mary had set up the exercise to test for brucellosis. Days of chasing those big obstinate critters takes a lot out of you. The saying is, you can herd buffalo any way they want to go. It helped that we had a congenial team of rangers and naturalists and biologists and helicopter pilots. By the time we ran out of buffalo we were ready for a party. Mary's entrance caused a significant commotion. Can you imagine her in tights and floppy ears, dressed as a Playboy Bunny? Mary is a Yellowstone original.

∪ ∪

Women have achieved high positions in the Park Service—John reported to a female regional director—yet a black face under a ranger hat in "the great Western parks" is a rare sight. A black family in the campgrounds is almost as unusual. Tony Dean, the park's single black employee, was a native of Washington, D.C. He and his friends didn't use the Washington parks when they were growing up, and he told me why. "We were turned off by the ranger uniform. In Yellowstone people respect it. I can't walk around in Mammoth without visitors stopping me to ask questions. In Washington the uniform signified authority. The black community didn't see the guy wearing it as a friend. They saw him as The Man, who is out to get you, and that made him bad news."

Tony supervised the interpretive programs in the north district. As park historian he was also in charge of the Yellowstone Archives, an extensive and valuable collection that was being moved to a new location in the basement of the visitor center the day I caught up with him before the start of the summer season. His office in the second floor of the visitor center could best be described as a splendid clutter. Fascinating scraps of Yellowstone memorabilia were everywhere. On the floor were stacks of logbooks in which soldiers at each patrol cabin made daily entries during the army era. Their sightings of wildlife helped Mary plot buffalo population patterns.

I'd met Tony in January, and he bounded out from behind his desk, beaming his pleasure at seeing me again. When he said, "Hello Bill," it came out about five words long. Turning thirty, jaunty and outgoing, Tony was instantly likable. Below average height, he had a small man's gift for being a natty dresser. His uniform was letter-perfect, except for the stacked heels of his dress shoes. Tony had style. He must have decided early in life not to settle for average.

Asked if he'd had as much trouble getting into the Park Service as Mary, he erupted into laughter. "I didn't ask them. They came to me." It happened, he said, after the rioting and burning in Washington caused by the assassination of Martin Luther King in 1968. The previous year, a "Summer-in-the-Parks" program had been initiated, providing bus transportation for children, live music and entertainers in the neighborhood parks, and a variety of recreational activities for all age groups. Almost all of the green spaces in Washington, the monuments, memorials, and many buildings—including the White House and the Kennedy Center—are administered by the Park Service. Administratively they constitute a separate region.

Trying to be more responsive to the needs of inner-city residents after the King tragedy, the national capital region decided to hire community relations specialists. Tony, then a high school teacher in Prince George's County, bordering the District on the southeast, was looking for summer employment. He was surprised when he heard of the program. Who would have expected a government agency to think of that? A friend chosen for one of the community relations jobs recommended Tony, who received a seasonal appointment. At the end of the summer he was offered a permanent position. "Basically, my job was to inform the power structure how black citizens wanted to use the green spaces of Washington and help develop programs."

He liked the work and couldn't complain of the way he was treated, yet he had reservations about the attitude of Park Service employees outside Washington. "I'd heard things said around the office that suggested to me rangers in the parks were racists. They all refused transfers to Washington. Why else but because it's a black city?" Believing his opportunities for advancement in the Washington school system were few, he "took a chance on the Park Service." At the end of the first year he received a rating of excellent and was sent to the Albright Training Center at Grand Canyon.

We were interrupted by the telephone before Tony could give his reaction to Albright. Paul Schullery, who had done much to systematize the archives, wanted Tony to run down a couple of references. Tony had several questions of his own. While they talked my thoughts went back to the time I was a management intern and a former Yellowstone ranger buttonholed me in a corridor of the interior building, telling me his dream of building a training center.

Frank Kowski was the training officer, a big man in his early forties with thinning hair slicked straight back and a forehead creased with worry lines. He was addicted to string ties with implausibly large turquoise clasps and dangling silver ornaments. A relentless ragger, he had a deep, rasping voice and affected a threatening scowl that fooled no one, for this was a warm-hearted man. I find it hard to write about Frank without resorting to clichés, a highfalutin' term that would have provoked him into a cleansing obscenity. We trainees developed an affection for Frank, and because of his diligent efforts in our behalf privately referred to him as "Mother" Kowski.

He started at Yellowstone in 1937, fresh out of Iowa State, with a degree in forestry. He and Lois were married in the chapel at Mammoth and soon thereafter departed for a summer in the backcountry. In a particularly nasty example of what passed for humor in the ranger ranks, his chums steamed the labels from all of the canned goods before loading them on the pack horses. A Coast Guard officer in the South Pacific in World War II, Frank was Yellowstone's assistant chief ranger when appointed chief of training for the Park Service in 1951. He liked to say that the selection was a reward for outstanding performance. That didn't square with colleagues in Yellowstone, who claimed he was a slow learner.

Kowski anecdotes abound. One of my favorites, he told on himself. His first year at Yellowstone, on a sparkling day in fall, he was sent out to close one of the entrance gates for the winter. About to fasten the iron barrier, he saw an unusually large herd of elk in the valley beyond. Swinging the gate open, and failing to notice that it swung shut behind him, he drove out and sat watching the elk, grateful as he often was for the satisfactions of his job. Driving back, he took one last look over his shoulder and crashed into the gate, demolishing the front of his patrol car.

He took a dim view of Washington as a training site. "Christ Almighty," he would rumble. "How can you teach people about parks in a crummy hotel?" He had the extravagant idea, which he never tired of relating, that the Park Service should build its own training center. One year Connie Wirth included it in his appropriation request. Frank's jubilation was short-lived. Congress thought it pretentious, declining to provide funds, and Frank suffered a severe heart attack. Compassion for the despairing Kowski moved Connie to squeeze enough money out of his reserves for Frank to launch a shoestring operation in Yosemite in 1957.

I'd just transferred to San Francisco, and he invited me to talk to the starting class, thirty bright and eager young trainees in full uniform behind jerry-built tables filling every inch of an attic storage room in the valley museum building. One look and I told Frank he'd better cancel the lecture on fire safety. Not to worry, he said. Can't you see the Lord is on my side? Five years later Congress was satisfied that the idea had merit, and Frank built the present handsome complex, the Albright Training Center, in the trees a mile back from the South Rim of Grand Canyon. We expected him to retire at "Kowski College," but George Hartzog, no friend of home-steaders, made him an offer he couldn't resist: superintendent of Sequoia. Frank did so well that he was rewarded with that cushiest of berths: regional director at Santa Fe.

Tony ended my woolgathering by announcing, as he hung up the tele-phone, "Paul, you are outstanding." He said that no one had ever gone to the Albright Center with lower expectations. He was determined not to be brainwashed. "Instead, I was won over. The instructors were impressive. The people from Washington and the field areas who came to talk to us were of the same quality. What impressed me most was their commitment to parks and their desire to serve people. It didn't take long for me to de-cide Tony Dean was 100 percent wrong about rangers being racist. They wanted to work in the parks, not in the big city."

Back in Washington, he was soon moved up to area supervisor, coming in contact with John Townsley, chief of operations for the national capital re-gion before he went to Yellowstone. Appointed superintendent of the home of the black orator and statesman Frederick Douglass, Tony said he felt the way a geologist would feel if put in charge of Grand Canyon. "Then John walked in one day and said he had a place for me in Yellowstone. It was so outrageous, so unexpected. Wilma and I weren't totally opposed to leaving Washington, but we weren't anxious to be the first black family in Yellowstone either. It wasn't in our game plan."

John insisted he come out to the park for a week before making up is mind. "To my surprise, I liked what I saw. I liked the idea of taking on something so entirely different, and I knew Yellowstone would look good on my record. My skin would still be black, but my blood would have a tinge of green. John was a big factor. He had helped me in so many ways in Washington. I respect him as much as anyone I know. So I said yes. Wilma and I were confident no one was going to beat us down or take away our pride in being black." In fact, the hospitality shown his family by the Mammoth community went far beyond common courtesy:

> Our neighbors wanted to do anything they could to help a black family from the city get comfortable. We didn't need everything they offered, but we appreciated their attitude. On the first day Tony and Kia Danita went to school, it seemed that all the children in Mammoth knocked on the door wanting to escort them. The comforting thing about living here is that we've discovered so many things we enjoy doing together. In Washington, after dinner, Wilma and I were busy with choir rehearsal or sorority meetings or going out with friends. Here we'll spend the evening together putting together a jigsaw puzzle. We're into cross-county skiing. I've bought outfits for everyone. The kids have lost the Saturday morning "Pink Panther" syndrome. They play outside, and we don't check on them every five minutes like we did in Washington.

Tony had only one reservation about Yellowstone and a question for me. Yellowstone was not like the rest of the country. Here his children knew nothing of racial intolerance. Would a sheltered life put them at a disadvantage later? Was it good for them to be growing up in a completely white culture? I couldn't devise an answer. Tony too was silent for a moment, then let out a whoop. "I guess the world isn't going anywhere while the Deans are in Yellowstone, and fifteen minutes with their grandmother when they see her next will put them back in the picture."

National parks are largely the domain of the white middle class. I didn't see the opinion expressed by Benjamin Hooks until after my meeting with Tony. I thought it was sentiment the Park Service needs to ponder. "For black Americans, ever so preoccupied with the consuming struggle for civil rights, jobs, and equality," wrote the executive director of the National Association for the Advancement of Colored People, "recreational pursuits such as visiting national parks and monuments often seem a luxury that are hardly worth the effort. So much of constructive involvement has been washed out of U.S. history, that few national shrines or public monuments have any reference or provide an emotional uplift for blacks. When it is remembered, also, that much of American history contains another type of pain for blacks—the pain of slavery and centuries of discrimination—one is left to marvel that blacks really bother to visit some of these monuments at all."

When I asked Tony why so few blacks visit Yellowstone, he said much the same, noting:

It doesn't speak to what urban black families consider familiar or exciting. Given a choice of vacations, my friends would opt for the Virgin Islands and the Bahamas, New York City and San Francisco, or Disney World for the children. One came back from the Caribbean and said to me, "I love that down-in-the-islands atmosphere." A Yellowstone isn't in their career plans, either. Why would they want to live in a totally white community? It sounds threatening to them.

When I tell them how much we like living here, how really exciting it is to explore the park, they say, "Oh, Tony, you're out of it. You can have the trees and wild animals." Blacks prefer the city scene. That's where their relatives and friends are. Think of it, only four girls in the Mammoth fourth grade and hardly any extracurricular activities. My coming here was a long shot. I'm glad I came. But I think it will be a long while before another black makes the same choice."

Tony was late for a meeting with Al Meban. We walked down the front steps and out on the porch of the visitor center. Looking at the mountains, he said, "John took me into the backcountry for a few days. What I saw and what I felt I can't express. In country like that you believe things will get better in life." He said, "Catch you later," and was off, dodging around the slow-moving tourists, one arm out for balance. Looking back, he waved his Stetson as he whipped around the building—a guy with a good heart and good moves.

Several months later Tony was promoted to the Albright Training Center staff. I saw him there the following May. Kowski had begun the tradition of naming each of the orientation sessions for a retired Park Service personage, and it seemed to be my turn. I was invited to attend a few classes, mix with the trainees, and give the graduation address. Tony had left word at the reception desk to be notified the moment Mary and I checked in. I started to exchange high fives, but he had me in a bear hug first. He had a way of treating you as if you were the high point of his day.

I noticed Tony's enthusiasm level had dropped a notch or two. He'd left Yellowstone with mixed feelings. The family wasn't thrilled about moving so soon, and he felt he owed John Townsley more than one year. The Washington office had leaned on him, the argument being he could make a greater contribution at Albright by serving as a role model for minority trainees. The teaching was more difficult than he expected. With less varied field experience than the other instructors, he had to do a lot more preparation. The park community had welcomed the family, but nothing could match the unrestrained warmth of Yellowstone. Tony said, "We'll always consider that year at Mammoth a special time in our lives."

The party on graduation night was a relaxed affair featuring potluck delicacies, a keg of beer, and musical interludes. The evening was winding down when song sheets were passed around. The salute to director Bill Whalen, we were told, was about to begin. The trainees, mostly technicians, had a score to settle with Whalen. In a situation more complicated than it sounds, and which will be explained shortly, many persons eligible for professional positions in the Park Service took technician jobs, hoping and expecting to achieve professional status. It didn't work out that way.

Whalen had traveled from Washington to address the trainees several weeks earlier. Director at thirty-six, having skipped most of the steps up the career ladder, Bill had promising gifts, some of which deserted him at awkward times. He once lectured the park concessioners, a contentious group, as if they were schoolboys and provoked a rebuke from the powerful head of the House Interior Committee, Mo Udall, who demanded he be fired. Bill had been more than blunt with the trainees, and they responded in kind. It is one of the attractive qualities of the young that while still on the sidelines they believe themselves capable of outplaying the varsity. I remember the feeling. Apparently Bill did not. He said he had three thousand job applications on file and encouraged the discontented to resign.

Our musical director for the graduation party, Lyndel "Meko" Meikle, historian from Grant Kohrs Ranch in Montana, was a stem-winder of a young woman with long, dark hair and flushed cheeks. Noting the performance would be recorded, she asked, "Shall we send the tape to Bill Whalen?" The response caused the floor joists to tremble. A motion for a short delay so that all singers might draw a full cup of beer to refresh their vocal cords passed easily.

The best thing about "Ode to a Feral Ranger" may have been the title, although the lyrics were saucy and the chorus poignant: "He lives on park technician pay, which is to say from day to day." It was sung to the tune of "Turkey in the Straw," an air so ancient it was evidently unfamiliar to those who joined in late and never caught up, giving the music a fugue-like quality. I cannot say too much about the improvisations—if that was the intention—of Dave Herrington, a fiddler from Big Thicket, Texas. Rhythm accompaniment was by Oscar Rodriguez, of Guadalupe Mountains, Texas, who wielded a mean set of spoons. Dissatisfied with the first take, as well she might be, Meko scrambled up on a table and called for another. "Pronounce every word so even Bill Whalen can understand it," she implored us.

Saying goodnight to the Albright director, Gene Daugherty, I asked if he really intended to send the tape to Whalen. His left eyelid dropped fractionally. "I'm honor bound," he replied. "And even if it should go astray, think of the good it has done already." I said I feared boat-rockers were becoming an endangered species in the organization. The cheeky defiance of this group was a hopeful sign. "I get that feeling from every class," Gene said.

ʊ ʊ

The next year, leading a training class on an extended hike into the canyon for the first time, Tony Dean died tragically, the result of an accidental fall from the trail. The untimely death of one so young and spirited, who had accepted the Albright assignment "for the good of the Service," was a grave loss to family and friends and to the Park Service. Hearing the sad news, I remembered an endearing habit that may have caused some conversation in Yellowstone. Unlike his colleagues, who put on their Stetsons the moment they walked out the door, Tony carried his in his hand. Wearing the big hat would have crushed his Afro, the proud badge of his blackness in an alien environment.

6

Mernin Country

The southwest quadrant of Yellowstone, larger than Rocky Mountain and Zion national parks combined, could be called "Mernin country." Here, the folklore says, district ranger Jerry Mernin kept the traditions alive. "A lot like Jerry Mernin," they would say of a promising young ranger. "Another Mernin" was used more sparingly. He was the standard by which field rangers were measured—and not only in Yellowstone.

His contemporaries saluted a man who had steadfastly refused to change his ways and saw no profit in moving from park to park in order to get ahead. Career advancement was not his trip. Neither was management. He avoided meetings by scheduling a backcountry patrol. "Jerry's gone to ground," the chief ranger would be advised. With apologies to John Le Carré, he was the ranger who refused to come in from the cold.

I had met Jerry twenty years earlier on a hiking trail. Mary and I were enjoying one of Yosemite's best-kept secrets, the High Sierra tent camps that form a great circle in Yosemite's backcountry. Located at elevations of from seven to ten thousand feet, tucked away among granite domes and sparkling mountain streams, they offer pleasant comfort and hot showers to weary hikers. For a little baksheesh the packer who brought in food supplies and clean sheets by mule train every day transported our backpacks to the next camp in the circuit, reducing our burden to a single daypack holding lunches and fishing gear. John Muir did it this way, carrying a loaf of stale bread and notebook in a cloth sack and sleeping under the stars. I doubt he could have relished the Range of Light any more than we did.

We started out one cool morning from Merced Lake camp, the sun bathing the landscape with its brightness. We were on the last leg of our trek, fifteen miles down the Merced River past Nevada and Vernal falls and into the valley at Happy Isles. Walk in any direction, Muir advised, for this is a magic place.

Not far out of camp we encountered a picture-postcard young ranger on a chestnut horse, leading a pack animal. He stopped, exchanged a few pleasantries, and rode on. Because he favored his father, who headed ranger activities in the San Francisco regional office, I recognized him immediately. Jerry Mernin senior was well over six feet tall and lean, with a crew cut and a hawk visage. They said he was "badge heavy" as a ranger, a strict constructionist on law enforcement matters, an intimidating man who took his work seriously. Both Mernins had the same deep baritone voice.

I didn't see young Jerry again until my snowmobile tour in January. Jim Barker and I were patrolling southward from Old Faithful when he waved us down. Walking toward us, he took off his helmet and put it under one arm. He spoke to Jim about something, then walked on to my machine. I noticed him size me up with one practiced glance before greeting me. I would have known that voice anywhere.

Jerry was not a desk person. I suppose he had one, although I never saw it. Some information for which I'd asked him was forwarded much, much later with a note: "I am just characteristically late with any paper work." In the manner of the subsistence hunters of John McPhee's *Coming into the Country*, he was a man of maximum practical application. He may not have been entirely of the same bent as the unrestrained types living around Eagle, Alaska, but he leaned in that direction. He didn't mind going against the grain. After brief stints at Bryce and Grand Canyon, he had been at Yellowstone since 1964, declining all chances to transfer.

As Mac Berg said of Jerry, "He's the classic ranger. When the rest of us go out with him we're going to school. If I ever get in trouble in the backcountry I hope they send Jerry to drag my ass out." "I saw him handle an ugly scrape at the Lake Hotel after the bartender cut off a couple of disagreeable customers and they began making threats," Dave Smith recalled. "Someone called Jerry. The way he walked into a situation like that and faced them down without any stalling or bluffing, that's hard to teach. He retains absolute composure." And a member of his staff remembered, "I was listening to a radio conversation between Jerry and one of our seasonals, a new guy handling a law enforcement problem in the backcountry. Jerry's instructions were clear; then he said something even more useful. 'Never forget who you are and what you represent.'"

The Snake River ranger station, headquarters for Jerry's district, looks like a summer cottage. For a government residence it has an excessive number of windows of the old-fashioned kind, divided into small panes. Maybe the rangers who built the station in the 1920s as a duplex residence and office wanted to make the long winters more cheerful. The paint on the wood siding is a faded pink. A wooden post attached to the steep, green roof holds a network of antennas. The two-story building sits behind a screen of pines a couple of hundred feet from the road and a quarter of a mile from the entrance station. Behind and out of sight are quarters for seasonals, storage sheds, snowmobiles under tarps, and a barn and corral holding the horses used for backcountry patrols.

For a day in early June, the wind had a barbed edge to it when I parked at the rear of the station and knocked on the back door. From the moment I joined Jerry and his wife Cindy in the corner dining room off the kitchen, Jerry's formidable German shepherd Ross watched my every move. Cindy, slender and with short, dark hair, used a cigarette holder and was wearing a green T-shirt trimmed in white. She had her own opinions and spoke them. She no longer wintered in Yellowstone. "Cindy just got bored beyond help," Nancy Rudolph told me. A nurse, she was working on a degree at Towson State University near her parents' home in Baltimore but spent Christmas vacations and summers in Yellowstone.

Jerry had strong, regular features, an erect bearing, and the sinewy build of a top skier, which he was, giving a hint of physical resources instantly available. His hairline had begun to recede, leaving a black forelock in the middle of his forehead. Speaking in a deliberate cadence, he held some vowels an extra beat. When in uniform he wore the Stetson low in front, a finger-length above his eyebrows. That day, he was wearing work pants over boots and a heavy blue shirt tricked out with white buttons.

We sat around the circular table in the sunny dining room until the coffee gave out and Jerry got a call from the office. After starting a fresh pot, Cindy showed me the living room, a space of agreeable proportions with a black woodstove sitting on a well-polished wood floor and a large and healthy spider plant hanging from the ceiling. A wooden spindle that once held cable had been refinished and served as a coffee table. Around it were two comfortable armchairs for Jerry and Cindy and a blue one that served as a nest for Ross. Along one side, a dozen green plants and several small artifacts were displayed on low pedestals of varying heights cut from pine logs. Records from classical to bluegrass were stacked on a bookcase next to the changer. The walls, painted a wash green, held framed paintings of cowboy scenes and original cartoons by a local artist, Rick O'Shay. I leafed through a book by Jerry's favorite author, Joe Back, whose *Horses, Hitches and Rocky Times* describes in loving detail every piece of equipment peculiar to horses.

Cindy went off on a chore, and Jerry poured more coffee. He talked a little about John Townsley, something he seldom does. They had a lot in common and became friends years earlier in Yosemite, where their fathers were well-regarded rangers. Their careers might have reflected the influence of their fathers. "As a ranger, John was as good as they come," Jerry said. "Still is. He's also an impressive speaker, exceptionally good at public relations, and totally at ease with the movers and shakers. But when he comes visiting your district you'd better have everything in good order. Patience isn't one of his virtues." He asked if I'd heard the story of John and the Yosemite packer. I had, but I wanted to hear Jerry's version.

The packers who supplied the High Sierra camps when John was a ranger there (and where Mary and I made the circuit) weren't the real thing, Jerry noted. They dressed like cowboys, but a real cowboy wouldn't have touched the job. What they liked to do best was to show off in front of an audience, preferably one containing attractive young females; they would ride their pack strings through the camps, tack rings jingling and mule shoes ringing on the rocks. Meanwhile, they were kicking up trail dust that settled over everything. John became fed up. He told the packers supplying the camp in his district that they would henceforth use the trail that led to the rear of the camp. "One of them must not have known John, or maybe he was a hardhead. He kept on riding through the camp. One day John was waiting for him in the middle of the trail. He didn't say a word. He grabbed the packer by the scruff of his neck and the seat of his pants and jerked him out of the saddle. He duck-walked him to the trail he wanted him to use and told him to use it from now on. A ranger ran into the packer later and kidded him about the incident. All the packer said was, 'The big son of a bitch meant what he said.'"

Back when Jerry learned the trade from his father, rangers did it all. They kept an eye on the concessioners, fought fires, were responsible for wildlife and forestry surveys, handled press relations, maintained trails, and did construction work. Now the superintendent of Yellowstone has specialists on his staff responsible for each of these activities. Some years earlier the Civil Service Commission ruled that the duties of a ranger did not constitute a profession, that is, one requiring college preparation. Rescuing a mountain climber or administering first aid, trapping and relocating grizzlies, monitoring backcountry use—all are important skills but not elements of an academic discipline.

Park Service response to the ruling demonstrated the bureaucratic law that all solutions beget other problems. A new occupational category was created: the technician. They would perform the less-than-professional duties of the rangers, freeing them, in theory, for supervisory and administrative and any other functions blessed by the commission. The rangers were not happy, for they would no longer be doing things that attracted them to the job in the first place. "If they aren't careful, one observed, "our job will become vestigial, what's left after the technicians take over."

The new setup satisfied no one, including the new technicians, who soon argued that they were doing rangers' work for technicians' pay. One of the few options available to rangers was to specialize in law enforcement, and some elected to do so. Others were wary, remembering the old saying that you can make a law enforcement officer out of a ranger, but you can't make a ranger out of a cop. Most rangers hold law enforcement commissions, awarded after intensive instruction at a federal law enforcement training center, but most do not regard it as their specialty. What attracted them to park work had nothing to do with carrying a gun and making arrests.

Another old saying, that you don't have law enforcement problems above five thousand feet, is no longer valid. Compared to Yosemite, Yellowstone doesn't have a serious law enforcement problem, yet its jail is put to good use. In an average year rangers will handle several hundred incidents of robbery and larceny and as many as five hundred vehicle accidents, resulting in a considerable number of appearances before the resident U.S. magistrate or in the U.S. district court in Cheyenne.

John Townsley always had the ability to take a long look down the road. He knew what he wanted to be from the time his father let him climb on a pack mule for a trip into the high country, but he had a premonition. "One of the reasons I decided to move into management was that I didn't sense the traditional ranger career would continue much longer. I have enjoyed every day I've worked for the bureau. I've had great opportunities, been privileged to work in wonderful places, and met interesting people, and to contribute, I hope, in some way." John may have been speaking for many of his colleagues when he talked of his druthers: "But given my choice I would have been a ranger in my dad's time in one of the great Western parks."

The way Jerry saw it, John wanted a district ranger to be part mountain man and part manager, eager for new challenges in other parks. Jerry disagreed:

I don't think a ranger should take a Yellowstone assignment if he isn't willing to settle in. The park is so vast it takes years before you are familiar with all of it. There's such a spectrum of values in Yellowstone. A geologist or a wildlife biologist could work here productively for an entire career. So could a ranger.

I understand why few young rangers are willing to make that kind of commitment. They want the experience of serving in Yellowstone for a few years, but for the sake of their spouses and children they want good schools and convenient shopping and medical services—and maybe some social amenities, too. When the long Yellowstone winter closes in and the routine begins to bite, they start checking the vacancies in other parks. Since promotion now depends on developing administrative skills, they head in that direction. Those who do may never season out as general-purpose rangers.

The district ranger does have a management responsibility as important as any in the park—overseeing the backcountry and the people who use it. You do that only by being a presence there, just as you are when you patrol the roads. You protect the backcountry by monitoring it and by minimizing the impact of people. For a person accustomed to grilling steaks over a charcoal broiler, naturalizing a fire ring by burying and removing every trace of the fire is a new concept.

When I'm on the trail I pay attention. It's the difference between doing a thing a hundred times the same way, not thinking about it and not pushing yourself, and getting something extra out of it each time. I enjoy the flowers and the look of the country. I notice trail conditions and look for animal signs. I prefer not to make a lot of noise, a personal prejudice, although I'm not lackadaisical about grizzlies. Not after seeing a few up close. Riding a mule on a trail one day, I came face to face with one. The mule spread his legs, gave the grizzly something between a snort and a bray, and the grizzly departed. If I see fresh grizzly scat I'm doubly alert. I've seen what they can do to people. When you trap one and he throws off the drug a little early, it can be alarming. All those teeth and all that muscle! You feel differently about a grizzly after you've run your hand through his fur.

A ranger's primary responsibility is to help people enjoy and appreciate the park. There are times, however, when caution is called for. If I'm only giving a citation to a camper who chopped up a tree for firewood or a picnic table, I try to cover all eventualities. If there's something about a car parked where it shouldn't be, I look the occupants over as I approach. I'm acting deliberately casual, but I'm taking everything in. I say, "How are you?" or, "Having some trouble?" I let them make the first move before I make mine. One of my accidental characteristics is that I don't have trouble projecting authority. Ebullience would come hard for me.

Before leaving the Snake River station I asked Jerry to show me his barn, and we walked several hundred yards to the weathered brown building with green shingles at the edge of the pine forest. It was ready for a John

Townsley inspection. The floors were swept clean, and everything was in its place, although Jerry did a little straightening. I recognized some of the paraphernalia from the Joe Back drawings. Coils of rope, wood-backed brushes, hobbles to keep horses from going back to where they were fed last, saddles, bridles, halters, feed bags, tarps, saddle blankets, and pack saddles—all neatly hung or stored away. Behind the feeding bins, the tack room was carefully insulated with wire netting to keep hungry mice out. Several nests were built tight against the screen.

I hefted one of the big leather panniers, box-shaped containers the size of a large, deep suitcase that fit on each side of a pack animal and are slung by straps fitting over the sawbuck saddle. Panniers must be loaded with care to balance the weight. Other articles are tied behind the saddle, and a water-proof canvas cover is fitted over everything. The whole must be tied down and around with a thirty-foot lash rope, and here things get damnably per-verse for those who don't know their Joe Back. In a final flourish you gather up the ends of the rope and secure the cargo snugly with a diamond hitch.

There is a routine to breaking camp in the morning. One by one, the horses are brought in and lined up. The gear is sorted and divided into piles, stowed in the panniers, and lifted onto the saddles. Watching the scene, I have experienced a helpless feeling, confident that I could never be so willfully matter-of-fact about throwing the diamond hitch, especially if I were about to experience the many moods of a horse.

Rosita was standing with several other horses when we came out of the barn. She approached Jerry immediately, pricking up her ears. Even to my untrained eye she was of handsome proportions, a sleek, dark Morgan that Jerry had gotten in trade from a ranger at Big Horn Canyon, who thought she was on the fractious side. Jerry was obsessively fond of her. "She does everything well," he said. "She's friendly, she's comfortable, she walks well, and she pickets well." Soon aware that no carrots were to be had, she lost interest and stepped away.

Resting his arms on the top rail of the fence, Jerry gave a nod that took in Rosita, the corral and barn, and everything beyond. "This is one of the reasons I stay here. In what other fantasy job would you get paid to ride a horse in such incredible country? A ranger in Yellowstone can still be what he wants to be and what a ranger should be. If it's possible anywhere, it's possible here. I'm for anything that makes a ranger diverse and keeps him from being warped into a specialist."

It's reassuring to know that despite occasional grumbles no one in Yellow-stone, not even Townsley, wanted Jerry Mernin to be anything but what he was. "He elevates our respect for what we do," Roger Rudolph told me. Jerry's choice was the one his colleagues put away in favor of the career ladder. It's possible they had occasional regrets, and maybe Jerry did too. He and John were part of a dwindling and unrepeatable generation. They regretted the constant erosion of the standards and practices taught them by their fathers. Yet something was being passed on by these two bone-deep rangers: skills, traditions, and pride in their profession.

7

A Lucky Young Lady

Around ten o'clock on the morning of June 13, 1978, a Tuesday, a young woman named Marianna Young drove through the south entrance in a dark blue Volkswagen. Twenty-one years old and a former student at Ohio State University, she was working that summer as a waitress at the Signal Mountain Lodge in Grand Teton. She had lived in the area for a couple of years, working summers in the park and wintering in Jackson.

An experienced hiker, she was looking forward to a peaceful day on the trail after the hubbub of the restaurant. Her destination was Heart Lake, reached by an eight-mile trail that passes through prime grizzly country. The weather report broadcast from the Com Center called for a mostly sunny day in the seventies with a chance of late-afternoon showers changing to snow in higher elevations. Turning into the trailhead just north of Lewis Lake, Marianna found the grassy parking circle nearly full of vans and cars. Amid general excitement, about twenty-five members of a church group were getting into their packs. Bad luck she thought, not much chance of getting away from the crowd.

Hoping to outdistance the group, she parked her car quickly and made for the trail. Five feet three and a half inches tall with blonde hair and blue eyes behind large glasses, she was wearing a red "Jackson Surplus" T-shirt, blue daypack, hiking boots, and the lucky blue shorts she'd used on an Outward Bound trip in Colorado. She had been trying to lose weight, believing she looked "a little chunky."

A sign at the registration box warned hikers of bear danger. "Grizzlies and black bears are present throughout the park. Whether they avoid you or defend themselves against you may depend on your behavior." A short way down the trail she passed another sign: DO NOT HIKE ALONE. For the first mile she walked at a brisk pace over mostly level ground through fringes of pine and open meadows. The forest closed in, the trail climbed over a ridge, and Marianna saw a grizzly and three cubs on the trail ahead, about twenty-five yards away. From rangers who brought her back from the edge, and from Marianna, I put together the story of the encounter.

"They didn't see me, at first," she told me, "and I didn't try to sneak closer. I knew what a grizzly with cubs can do. I had my camera in the pack and thought they would make a great picture." She stood and watched, fascinated by the rare sight and believing that she was far enough away. Apparently the wind carried her scent, and the grizzly became agitated, sending her cubs scurrying for cover. Standing up, she faced Marianna, moving her head back and forth and trying to locate the intruder. Marianna dodged behind a tree trunk, realizing her danger, but it was too late. The bear dropped down on all fours and charged. "She came at me like a freight train. I tried to climb a tree, but she grabbed me in her jaws and pulled me down. As she tore at me I was screaming. The rest is hazy. I think she dragged me for a distance and may have gone off and come back again. When she finally dropped me her teeth or her claws scraped the top of my head and lifted my scalp."

The bear was probably frightened off by members of the church group, who started out a few minutes behind Marianna and made plenty of noise on the trail. They found her lying face down, clothes ripped into bloody tatters, and were afraid to turn her over, not wanting to cause more damage. The fleetest young men raced back to the trailhead, drove three miles south at high speed, and met a patrol car pulling out of the Lewis Lake campground. Picking up his radio mike, veteran seasonal ranger Gary Grant called the Com Center and set the rescue operation in motion.

At the trailhead, Gary loaded up with all he could carry, including a radio, three blankets, and a bulky first aid kit, and ran all the way to the encounter site. Perhaps a half hour had gone by since the bear dropped Marianna. An experienced emergency medical technician, he reported her condition to the Com Center as he began dressing her wounds, which were grievous. She was in deep shock, suffering from a sucking chest wound, broken ribs, and severe lacerations of head and body. She had lost an excessive amount of blood, her pulse was faint, and she had trouble breathing.

At the Snake River station Duane McClure, one of Jerry Mernin's staff rangers, was using his day off to repair a bridle when he heard Gary's first call to the Com Center. In two minutes he and the duty ranger loaded their patrol car with equipment, including a Stokes litter, and were underway.

"She was barely conscious when we reached her," Duane said. "I noticed her boots were off, either torn away by the bear or taken off by Gary. He was doing a beautiful job, and we were able to be helpful. I was thinking that when you see someone covered with blood on television, you know it's a fake. It hits you when you are bandaging terrible wounds. I was grateful for the training."

Jerry was attending a meeting at Lake. Called immediately to take charge of the rescue, he was on the radio for much of the time it took him to drive the twenty-six miles to the Heart Lake trailhead:

> First I called the dispatcher at the fire cache in Mammoth to prepare the helicopter crew for an immediate flight to the Lake hospital. When Gary's call came in reporting Marianna's condition, the hospital was briefed and asked to have doctors on the pad for a pickup. Other rangers were calling in asking me, "What can we do to help?" I set up a check-point at the trailhead to control rangers with equipment going in and to keep hikers and the curious out. By the time I reached the trailhead the helicopter pilot reported he was on the way to Lake.
>
> When I saw Marianna I knew it was going to be close. The rangers had done everything they could for her. She was on oxygen, her wounds bandaged, and she was wrapped in blankets. It's a time when you fiddle with anything to keep your hands busy while you wait. I sent Duane to scout a place for the helicopter to land. He found one a half mile away. It was a punishing cross-country carry for six men over rough terrain strewn with lodgepole trunks, trying not to jolt Marianna yet pushing to get there ahead of the chopper. They did it with one rest stop, an exceptional physical performance.

Marianna remembered little of this except that she was cold, breathing was difficult, and her thirst was extreme. A ranger would moisten his bandanna with water from his canteen and hold it to her lips, unable to allow her to drink. "She was intermittently conscious," Jerry said, "opening her eyes and responding weakly to our efforts to keep her courage up. She was game, but she was teetering just above the line. When we got to the landing site I knew that if the helicopter didn't come soon she wouldn't make it."

Marianna was fortunate. The helicopter landed in time. One of the two doctors was a surgeon from the University of Utah Medical Center on a one-week posting to the Lake hospital. They worked over her for a half hour in the clearing beside the waiting helicopter. Her blood pressure, described by the surgeon as "almost undetectable," improved quickly after IV tubes in both arms began to restore fluids. "You could see her gaining strength by the minute," Jerry said.

Back in the Lake hospital, which has a fully equipped operating room, they spent two hours preparing her for the journey ahead. She was taken to West Yellowstone airport by special ambulance, a traveling emergency room according to Jerry, and flown by air ambulance to the medical center in Salt Lake City. Five major operations were required during her seven weeks in the hospital.

The episode didn't end for the rangers when the helicopter lifted out of the meadow. Rangers were sent out to warn hikers of bear danger, and the Heart Lake and connecting trails were closed and posted. A Boy Scout troop camped at Heart Lake received special treatment. Duane, armed, reached the fourteen scouts and four leaders in the early evening. They accepted his invitation to sleep in the patrol cabin. "Nineteen people in a cabin fourteen feet long is cozy," Duane said. "None of us got much sleep." He escorted them out in the morning. This was a normal precaution, although the chance of running into the bear and her cubs was slim. "She was moving along, searching for food," Duane said. "Had Marianna been a little earlier, or a little later, there wouldn't have been contact. This is my third year in the district, and I have yet to see a grizzly on the Heart Lake Trail."

No one considered destroying the bear. "We flew the area afterwards, just to keep an eye on her," Jerry said. "We got a probable sighting, then she was gone." Bear 27, killed two weeks earlier, was another matter. This bear was a mother protecting her cubs, and she had been provoked. Because of continuing grizzly activity in the vicinity of Heart Lake, the trail remained closed until July 1, when it was opened to parties of four or more. I asked Jerry a question many find puzzling. Why is a mother bear so ferociously touchy?

"There must be almost as much variation in the behavior of bears as there is in humans," he responded. "All grizzlies with cubs don't react the same way. A mother with three kids in a supermarket trying to keep them away from distractions is more harried than one with three kids in a fenced backyard. Bear cubs aren't safe anywhere. The mother has to be constantly on guard, and it's stressful watching out for predators, searching for food, keeping them together, fighting off male bears who would like to make a meal of them. It's no wonder she's bad-tempered. It's surprising we don't have more accidents."

I thought the rescue of Marianna an admirably swift and disciplined effort. I asked Jerry how he would rate it. "We had some breaks. Marianna was found almost immediately, and the right people were close at hand." Then, savoring a textbook performance, he said, "I don't think any of our rangers or the helicopter crew or the hospital medical staff could have done any better. In our review of the operation we didn't have any second thoughts about the decisions that were made and the way they were carried out. Actually, Marianna is a lucky young lady."

On August 3, 1978, at the time Marianna was released from the hospital, the *Billings Gazette* printed a front-page story of her mauling, with the headline "Chased and Chewed by Bear." A two-column photograph showed her wearing a polka-dot hospital gown. Her hair was beginning to grow back, and she had huge glasses and a wide, perky smile. Below the picture was another headline, "Bison Gores Would-be Photographer." The newspaper's angle in putting the stories together was grim coincidence. Two young women badly injured by wild animals in Yellowstone were treated at Lake hospital, airlifted to the medical center in Salt Lake City, and operated on by the same surgeons. The day one checked out of the hospital, the other checked in.

Darragh Callahan, a resident of Albuquerque, had spied a buffalo lying down near the road in Hayden Valley. Visitors wrongly assume the animal is both indifferent and forgiving. Experience has proved that the buffalo always has a selected line of departure. Should this be threatened, warns Mary Meagher, he may withdraw "through or over the unwary people who sometimes nearly surround one of these bulls." Seeking to have her picture taken with the buffalo, Callahan ventured to within ten feet. He got to his feet, hooked her out of his way, and walked off to find a less congested resting place. She suffered a punctured lung, four broken ribs, a broken arm, and a broken wrist.

A teacher at the Jemez Indian Reservation, Callahan was interviewed by a reporter from the Salt Lake *Post Register* on August 3. "Ironically," she said, "the buffalo dance is a favorite of my kindergarten students. They certainly aren't the meek animals my students portray in their dances. He was a big son of a gun. I saw his horn, it was curled under, and his huge head. It was just huge. The next thing I remember I was lying twisted and face down on the ground, and I was bleeding heavily."

The first thing Marianna did after she was discharged from the hospital was to return to Yellowstone with her parents and personally thank her rescuers. She was in remarkably good shape considering the severity of her injuries, Nancy Rudolph told me. Her back and arms were criss-crossed with scars from the bear's claws, and she was still recovering from skin grafts to her thigh and buttock to replace missing tissue. She and Nancy had the same plastic surgeon. "We swapped bear stories, and of course mine paled next to hers. She had no trouble relating the gory details, and like me hasn't lost her appreciation for bears. She recoiled at the thought of killing a bear for just about any reason. Her plans are to enroll at the University of Utah to be near the medical center for the operations that lie ahead."

Marianna sought out Gary Grant, the first to reach her, whose medical knowledge probably saved her life. She also thanked John Townsley, who visited her in the hospital. She said to him, "I'm glad it happened to me and not to someone who would sue you." When Darragh Callahan spoke to the *Post Register* reporter she seemed to feel the accident was her own responsibility, although she couldn't recall seeing any signs warning that a buffalo is a dangerous creature. After giving the affair a little more thought, she sued the Park Service for twenty-five thousand dollars.

∪ ∪

Undaunted by her experience, Marianna applied for a seasonal ranger position at Yellowstone after a long recuperation. Detailed to Jerry's district, no doubt at his request, she entered on duty at the south entrance station in June 1980. That was the station through which she had passed the fateful day she hiked the Heart Lake Trail. From there she could see the ranger station where Duane McClure heard the radio report of her mauling and joined the rescue effort. He was not there to welcome her.

Two weeks earlier someone had spotted a grizzly emerging from winter hibernation near Yellowstone Lake five miles from Grant Village. On a bright, clear morning Duane started out in a canoe from Grant Village to check the den. Unexpectedly, the weather changed, and a sudden storm struck the lake. An expert canoeist and a careful person, Duane should not have been in difficulty had he stayed close to the shore instead of taking a more direct route through open water.

When efforts to reach him by radio were unsuccessful, a search was ordered and continued until dark. Next morning at daybreak his canoe was found washed up on the beach a mile from his destination. Rangers on foot and in patrol boats continued the search without result. Snow, rain, and a low overcast prevented use of aircraft. His footprints found at the den site indicated that the accident had taken place on the return journey. Searchers concluded that Duane was not wearing his life jacket, or else he wore it unfastened and lost it when the canoe foundered. He couldn't have lasted many minutes in the freezing water. Ice on the lake had gone out only a short time before. The water temperature was thirty-six degrees.

I had met Duane only once, noting his unassuming competence and cheerful outlook. His smallish frame and rimless glasses gave him a deceptively scholarly appearance. To overcome this impression, he exercised constantly, building up his muscles and gaining from his associates the affectionate nickname "Bionic Man." A ranger said, "It was one of Yellowstone's saddest days. Here was a guy with no bad habits who did everything well and had more zest for the work than anyone in the park."

It's exceedingly rare for a ranger to be killed in the line of duty, and yet three rangers crossing the Snake River on a ski patrol in Grand Teton in 1960 broke through the ice and two were lost. When I asked Jerry what might have caused Duane's death, he said, "Likely an accumulation of a number of little things, none of which by themselves would have been fatal. It was a terrible loss. Duane was everything a ranger should be. A strange thing happened a few months before. We were talking one night about this kind of possibility and agreed if it happened to either of us we didn't want a long, costly search and a ceremonial burial. Better to allow what was left to rest in peace." Duane's body was not recovered. He had been at Yellowstone six years. He was thirty-five.

8

Recruits from the Ranger Factory

You are likely to hear the name Scotty Chapman if the talk turns to the best of the early rangers. Scotty spent forty years in Yellowstone, rising to assistant chief ranger and retiring to a spread at the edge of Gardiner overlooking the Yellowstone River. "Scotty will talk about the past," Townsley told me, "but he isn't like so many of them. He'll give it to you straight." Driving into his ranch, as modest acreage is called locally, near the end of June, I passed outbuildings full of implements and vehicles that showed signs of hard wear. I figured Scotty knew how to fix things.

The low, one-story home had grown organically to a rambling log structure reinforced by stones from the river. A row of windows in the front provided an unobstructed view across the Yellowstone River into the park. I was greeted at the door by three or four hunting dogs, who swarmed around me demanding an ear scratch until Scotty worked them one by one into a back room. His wife, Louise, a serene woman whose hair and eyes had faded in the soft and kindly way that gives character to advancing years, gave me a cordial welcome from her easy chair in front of the television set.

On the other side of seventy, his wiry brown hair only beginning to show gray, Scotty had the direct look of an outdoorsman. Trimly built, dressed in khaki pants and shirt, a sheaf knife at his belt, and eyes bright behind bifocals, he suggested a Norman Rockwell painting of what America was all about in times gone by—hard work, resolute honesty, and an optimistic outlook. For hours we sat by the living-room windows and watched the play of clouds over Mount Everts as Scotty retraced his career and Louise sat absorbed in her programs.

His father had been in the lumber business, first in the Adirondack country of New York and later in the Black Hills of South Dakota, where Scotty graduated from high school. Soon afterward his father sold the business and tried farming in Colorado. "He bought some machinery, and we planted wheat. Made a fair crop for a couple of years, then the winds came along and piled drifts over the top of a three-strand fence. My father had cut a lot of big trees in his day, something I didn't take any pleasure in. For whatever reason, I decided to study forestry."

He put himself through Colorado State, working for the Forest Service in the summer, first as a fire guard and then handling grazing allotments. "Coming back to college one September from the Lolo National Forest out of Missoula I made a detour to see Yellowstone. It was something I'd wanted to do for a long time. I liked the look of it. I told one of my professors I was going to get a job there if I had to drive a truck."

Scotty reported for duty in June 1930 to George Miller, the assistant chief ranger. "He called in Harry Trischman right away and said, 'Here is your new man.'" Trischman, a Yellowstone legend, was the subject of as many rollicking stories as any individual who ever worked in the park. The son of the Fort Yellowstone post carpenter, an army scout and charter member of the original ranger force, he doubtless was as tough as old boots. He was never sick but had a habit of getting unsteady, after which he failed to report for duty the next day or days.

> Harry didn't waste any time talking, just said, "Let's go to the barn." He showed me the two horses I was to use that summer. One was well set up and gentle, one was on the wild side. I knew Harry was jobbing me, but that was all right. I'd been around horses all my life. All I got from Harry was an order to clear the Howard Eaton Trail to Norris. I checked out an axe and shovel and the supplies I needed and started out that morning. After I got twenty miles of trail tidied up, which took me a while, I patrolled, did a little fish stocking in the backcountry lakes, talked to visitors using the trails, and tried to learn as much as I could exploring the park on my off days. They didn't give a new man much training then.

I asked about Harry Trischman:

> Maybe I was lucky to start under him, and then maybe not. He was a well-fleshed fellow, built like a bear and nearly as strong. The stories they tell, most of them are doctored. But I'll say this of Harry. If he ever got tired on the trail, no one heard about it. The first time he took me along was a ski patrol to Slough Creek, out to the northeast, up one hill and down another. Just miserable going, almost more than I could take, and I was in pretty fair shape and twenty years younger. We'd take turns

breaking trail, but he wasn't one to stop on the exchange for a breather. You know what that's like, hour after hour, all day long. When we got back all he said to me was, "Now you have one you can talk about."

To discourage poaching, rangers wintered in remote cabins near the boundary lines. In the fall of Scotty's first year he was sent to the cabin on Hellroaring Creek, a couple of miles from the north boundary. On a clear and windless summer day almost fifty years later, chief naturalist Al Meban and I hiked in to Hellroaring. The cabin and a horse barn sit in a grove of Douglas fir trees a few steps up a gradual slope from the creek that comes tumbling down a narrow canyon under the steep walls of Hellroaring Mountain. Rangers of Scotty's time were expected to repair backcountry cabins, the purpose of his trip:

Another ranger and I packed twenty horses, hay and oats for them, grub for us, and enough lumber and nails and tools to put a new roof on the cabin. That was a long pack string stretched out behind us. Hellroaring is elk country. In between our chores we patrolled regularly against poachers, of which there were quite a few. We shot coyotes to protect the elk, as we thought we should in those days.

Come February they sent me to the cabin at Sportsman Lake in the Gallatins, in the northwest corner. I stayed the rest of the winter there with Art Jacobsen, a Norwegian fellow. It was really good training for me, probably the reason they paired us off. He could do a lot of things and knew how to handle himself in the backcountry. That takes time, and maybe some other things too. I learned a lot about being a ranger from Art. My second summer in the park, that was a terribly bad fire season. Several seemed sizable to me until we had the big one on the south side of the park, the Snake River fire.

Fire fighters now are given relief at reasonable intervals. Whole units are replaced after a couple of tough weeks. Not in Scotty's time. "I was on the fire line without relief for fifty-six straight days. That was harder work than I can explain. I came off feeling like a ranger. We were still horse rangers when I started out. You took pride in your equipment and in keeping your stock in good condition. Looking at a string of horses in the corral, packed for the trail, you knew a lot about the ranger. Now they're lucky if they can ride a horse, much less pack one. They have to handle people, most of the time. That's a whole different business."

The year following, 1932, Scotty married Louise, a break with tradition. Previously, rangers were bachelors. "Had to be," Scotty said, "considering the life." He and Louise wintered at the Bechler ranger station in the southwest corner, a plateau noted for waterfalls that occur where the head-waters of the Bechler River plunge over the escarpment. Their cabin had no electricity, plumbing, or much else except swarms of mosquitoes that attacked in the summer and waist-deep snow in the winter.

"We didn't see another soul, week after week," Scotty said, smiling at the memory. "Our only contact with civilization was the single-line phone to headquarters, which would usually work for a day or two after I fixed it. Patrolling the boundary was hard going, the snow up to the horse's belly, and a wind that cut to the bone. You had to dismount and hobble along to get the numbness out of your legs. Caught a couple of poachers, and it took me three days to take them to Mammoth. It would have been a lot easier had I let them go."

The next winter Louis was pregnant and went out for the birth of their son Bill, later to become a contract artist for the park and a salmon fisherman in Alaska. His carved panels of bear scenes flank the bar in Old Faithful Inn. "Louise came back as soon as the snow melted. I carried I don't know how many buckets of water from the well to wash the diapers, with the mosquitoes so bad I had to wear a net. You can't imagine the isolation, how much we had to depend on ourselves for almost everything. But I loved it, and Louise took it as well as any ranger wife." Raising his voice he called to Louise, "You loved it at Bechler, didn't you?" Patiently, she turned from the set and nodded yes, gave me a wink, and went back to her favorite soap.

Having warmed to his subject, Scotty was reluctant to see me go. It took a little while for us to walk from our chairs to the front door. En route I noticed an easel in the corner, with a table holding tubes of paint and brushes drying in an assortment of cans and bottles. Landscapes by Scotty are prominently displayed in the homes of several of my friends who have worked in Yellowstone. I told Scotty how much I liked his work and asked if he would do a patrol cabin scene for me. He said he'd be glad to oblige. The painting now hangs above my writing table. A man in a red plaid shirt carries an armful of firewood and walks up a path to a small cabin in a forest clearing. The rocky peak visible above the pines is Electric Peak west of Mammoth, highest in the Gallatin Range. It's sundown of a summer evening at the Sportsman Lake cabin where Scotty spent part of his first Yellowstone winter, learning his trade from Art Jacobsen. The colors are dappled browns and greens, the brush strokes are in soft focus, and the mood is tranquil. Mary, who knows about such things, calls it painterly.

When I drove by his place to collect the painting, he'd moved the easel over by the windows for the light. I couldn't have been more pleased. "It's that peaceful time at the close of a day on the trail," he said. "You've finished feeding the horses and staking them out, and now it's time to wash up and cook dinner." As I was writing out the check, Scotty held up the painting for one last look and gave it to me straight. He said, "I caught those evening colors just right."

∪ ∪

The crusty reception Scotty received from Trischman may have reflected the scorn of a hardened veteran for a recruit fresh out of college. George Baggley, also from Colorado State, entered on duty about the same time and received a similar welcome. In only thirteen months George was jumped to chief ranger. The old guard must have reacted to a youthful and untested boss with something more than pained surprise. It was a shrewd move by a superintendent who believed rangers should advance beyond custodial chores. Each candidate was required to submit a list of objectives for the ranger division and a plan for achieving them. George won easily in an early example of preselection.

Trischman's response was a quick-witted jest that earned a place in the lexicon of the organization. Returning one day from the Trident Plateau, an eleven-thousand-foot viewing platform in the southeast corner of the park, he met Baggley, who asked him, "When you were up there, what did you see?" Trischman must have been thinking of the future when he replied, "I looked away down south and I saw the smoke of that ranger factory at Fort Collins."

The view from the Trident, uninterrupted in all direction, runs over the curve of the earth, although not so far as Fort Collins, Colorado, three hundred miles away. Harry's nickname took hold, and Colorado State was seldom called anything but the "ranger factory," producing more park rangers than any ten colleges. "I had the feeling," George wrote me from his retirement home in Boise, "many of the rangers considered my elevation to chief to be temporary. They thought I would lack staying power. Eventually they got the resentment out of their system and came around."

In his letter to me, George conceded that his efforts to edge the rangers toward a more scientific attitude were rudimentary. "Using what little I knew I gave them some ideas about natural science subjects and we would look for examples on backcountry patrols. I had become interested in the use of enclosures and in 1930 I established a dozen plots fenced against deer and elk. They served as a control to measure grazing impact. We set up a system of recording and photographing vegetative changes. The last time I checked, the enclosures were still in use."

A few people were beginning to question the killing of predators in national parks. The Yellowstone programs had been initiated by the army in the 1890s, a reaction to the common belief that fang-and-claw predators—mountain lions, wolves, and coyotes—were the bad animals preying on the good—deer, elk, and moose. Professional hunters with packs of hounds were brought in by the army to clear the park of mountain lions, thought to be a pest to stockmen of the surrounding country.

In Baggley's time, coyotes were a source of extra income for rangers. Fur buyers made the rounds every spring, paying ten dollars a pelt. "We were still killing coyotes during the winter of 1928 and 1929," one ranger recalled. "I was stationed at Tower Falls, and it was good hunting. I made enough through my half of the hides, which we were permitted to retain, to pay more than a down payment on a new automobile." George said he must have shot twenty coyotes himself that winter before he began to have second thoughts.

He took over a staff of thirty permanent and forty seasonal rangers. The visitor count his first year was a sizable 228,000. He took time off from his administrative work in the summer to lend a hand, issuing warnings and citations to speeders—the limit was twenty-five miles an hour—and to pranksters who soaped geysers to promote record-breaking eruptions. He checked fishing creels, fought forest fires, patrolled the backcountry on horseback and the Grand Loop Road on a motorcycle, and helped construct a new ranger station at Fishing Bridge. On Thanksgiving Day 1931, he married junior park naturalist Herma Albertson.

One of my favorite photographs of the period is of Naturalist Albertson wearing the full ranger uniform and holding her stiff-brimmed Stetson to her side. She seems to be suppressing a smile as she leans against the high wooden wheel of the Yellowstone tallyho stagecoach. A few enterprising women managed to wangle appointments when the Park Service introduced educational programs in the 1920s. Marguerite Lindsley served as a Yellowstone seasonal in 1921 while a student at Montana State University. Completing her master's degree in bacteriology at Bryn Mawr in 1926, she rode her motorcycle from Philadelphia to Yellowstone. Even Harry Trischman must have been impressed.

A student and staff assistant at the University of Idaho, Herma caught the eye of Horace Albright, first civilian superintendent of Yellowstone after the army era and a towering figure in Park Service history. An amateur historian responsible for adding historic preservation to the Park Service mission while serving as second director, he believed education was one of the primary functions of a national park. He began to recruit naturalists as soon as he took over the superintendency of Yellowstone in 1919. Not many would have been tempted by the offer he made to Herma. Reading her recollection of the arrangement, I had the impression she didn't lack spunk:

The superintendent said if I was willing to come down from the university for the summer and work as a naturalist, but not have the rating of a naturalist nor the title of a naturalist, live in one of the Old Faithful cabins and be hired by the camp company as a pillow puncher in the morning for my board and room, and work for the park in the afternoon—he would like to try me out. That's what I did. I was paid as a laborer, worked as a pillow puncher, and learned to be a naturalist.

The second year I graduated to the puphouse at Old Faithful, an old cabin with one door and one window that had been moved over near the mess hall because they had a woman there one year as a cook. I didn't have to work for the company in order to have a place to sleep and I could eat with the rangers. The first thing I did was to lay out a nature trail. The chief ranger sent me a trail crew. I knew little about such things and nothing about trail crews, but together we worked out the trail.

Herma gives no particulars, yet one can imagine this enterprising young woman and a willing trail crew talking over the problems and pooling their knowledge, trying one thing and then another: "I gave talks to the visitors in the evening. I kept a flower exhibit at the lodge and at Old Faithful Inn. I hiked about fifteen miles a day to get the flowers, for they had to be gathered far away."

Construction was completed that year at Norris of the first of the park's trailside museums, prototypes of the modern visitor center. Herma undoubtedly helped plan the exhibits and present the lectures and nature walks. One of the first women in the Park Service to receive a permanent naturalist appointment, she coauthored a standard work, *Plants of Yellowstone National Park*.

About thirty years later I was stationed at the Gateway Arch project in St. Louis, and George was our assistant regional director in Omaha. Still spare and rangy, he had a twinkle in his eye and compelling logic in his discourse. Mary found him as comfortable as an old shoe. At a party we gave when he was in town he gravitated to the kitchen and ended up stirring the gravy, all the while instructing her on the fine points of glaciation, or maybe it was volcanism. A likable guy whose optimism never drained away, George was eternally curious, an attribute that may have satisfied the Yellowstone superintendent that this was the man for the chief ranger job.

9

Those Who Charm and Inform

Yellowstone's chief naturalist, a soft-spoken geologist in his mid-forties, Al Meban, grew up in North Carolina hoping he would never have to leave. Al had earnest blue eyes, ash-blond hair, a slender, bony frame that didn't fill out his uniform, and a ready smile. His voice was soft and his manner mild. He could be stubborn, though, on matters affecting the division of interpretation.

The summer he graduated from Duke with a major in geology, he decided he ought to see the West, where the rocks aren't hidden by vegetation and the geologic upheavals are more recent than in the East. At Estes Park, Colorado, thrilled by the snow-covered Rockies, he applied for a job on the trail crew of Rocky Mountain National Park. He was in luck. A seasonal ranger scheduled to report the next week had just sent his regrets, leaving the Fall River entrance station short-handed. Nearly broke, Al worked for a week in a quarry to pay for his uniform.

On his first day as a park ranger he walked into an Estes Park restaurant and met his future wife. Jean, too, had a yearning to see the West. The day after she graduated from college, she and her widowed mother packed the family car and headed for Colorado. Looking for work that would finance a summer in the mountains, they thought the gateway to a national park a likely choice. Jean quickly located a waitress job in a restaurant down the street from the hotel. Al ordered apple pie and ice cream and started a conversation with the attractive waitress. Noticing his uniform, she mentioned casually that she had climbed Little Prospect Mountain before breakfast to catch the sunrise.

The pie and her story were so good that Al asked her for a date that night. Ten days later he proposed. He returned to Duke in the fall with his bride and two years later was back in Colorado with a master's degree in geology and a longing for the Rockies and the Park Service. He drew contour lines for the Geological Survey in Denver until a naturalist position opened at Dinosaur National Monument on the Colorado-Utah border, where dinosaur bones abound and the Green and Yampa rivers have carved spectacular canyons that attract whitewater boaters. He worked under two unconstrained superintendents there, Jess Lombard and Tiny Semingsen, both saltier than fat pork. "I couldn't have started out with a better crew or less bureaucratic superintendents," he said.

The next post for the Mebans was even more remote: Lehman Caves in eastern Nevada, now a part of Great Basin National Park. They lived at seven thousand feet in a juniper and pinyon forest beside a mountain stream filled with trout; the nearest store was seventy-five miles away in Ely, population two thousand. They were now four in a small trailer, and there were seventeen other families on the party line. They hoped the next assignment would be closer to civilization and were ecstatic when a job offer arrived from the Blue Ridge Parkway, whose headquarters, Asheville, was only an hour's drive from Al's home.

They were prepared to settle down, maybe become homesteaders, yet didn't think twice when offered Grand Teton. "Heaven couldn't have been any better," is how Al remembers the three years in Jackson Hole as chief naturalist, but they all say that. The residential area is directly in front of the Tetons, the sort of view that makes employees wonder why they should bother to accept promotions. For a broadening of horizons careerists are urged to take a central office assignment. Al reluctantly accepted a regional office posting that did, in fact, broaden his perspective.

He was selected to exchange positions, for a travel season, with the naturalist of Peak District National Park in Great Britain. The cottage in which he and his family lived was built at the time the *Mayflower* sailed. The children were afraid to be alone in the drafty rooms stuffed with "spooky antiques," and moisture seeping through the stone walls had formed stalactites. Al thoroughly enjoyed his work at the Peak. He never did get the hang of starting a fire with coke, the fireplace being the village of Eyam's answer to central heating. Jean describes it as the coldest summer of her life, made memorable by the hospitality of the residents and the chance to explore England.

I jotted down these notes over dinner at the Mebans one evening celebrating July 4. First, Al and I tested a recently completed tennis court. Employees supplied the labor, materials came from the Park Service, and the result was of a higher quality than my game. My punishing serve didn't make up for a broken-wing backhand and an unreliable knee. After Al edged me out in straight sets, we retired to his house in "Lower Mammoth," the residential area down the hill from Mammoth village. It gives one the impression that a bit of outer suburbia has been transported from Denver.

Congress was the culprit. In the expansion days after World War II there had been a desperate need to upgrade housing throughout the park system. Declaring "this will cut out the frills," Congress stipulated that the cost of each unit could not exceed twenty thousand dollars. Construction costs are abnormally high in most parks because they are so far removed from building supplies and workers. Park Service architects had no alternative but to design an inexpensive and inelegant "standard plan." Duplicated everywhere, using no local materials and responding not at all to their surroundings or to local design themes, they have not graced the parks.

Lower Mammoth contains forty-odd houses, all exactly alike in four rows on two parallel streets, one-story, three-bedroom ramblers with wooden siding mostly in shades of brown. Beside each entrance is a routed sign with the employee's name in bright yellow. Each house has a garage and no basement, a modest lawn, and no sidewalk. Shrubs and trees are scarce, requiring constant watering and screening from the hungry elk. Where the narrow rear lawn ends, sagebrush and coyotes begin. If you walked out the back door and headed east, you could travel more than thirty miles before hitting blacktop.

Jean was an accomplished decorator and inventive cook. The homemade sausage she served rated three stars. One frill she missed was a dining area. Dinner guests sat at the kitchen table up against the fridge. Another mark against the standard plan is that the place to which you move is often the same as the one you left, allowing little opportunity to do something new. The most prominent object in the living room was a woodstove installed to reduce heating costs, a major item in Yellowstone. A Baldwin piano, comfortable chairs and a sofa on a colorful yellow rug, a chess game on a side table, and lots of books and bird prints made for an inviting space. Three large windows provided an unobstructed view of Mount Evans, a view, both Al and Jean agreed, that made up for a lot that was lacking in the standard plan.

Al had busy summers. The administrative details of recruiting and selecting fifty-three seasonal ranger naturalists, following strict federal regulations, are not minimal. Al had just finished putting on a one-week orientation training course for all hands, and he was responsible for interpretive programs that touched one million visitors that season. Almost that many would pass through the five visitor centers—open twelve hours a day and seven days a week—to consult museum exhibits, view films, purchase guide books, ask questions at the information desk, and pick up a copy of *Yellowstone Explorer*, a newspaper that contains four pages of things to do in the park.

Included among the interpretive programs were fifty conducted hikes, many offered daily at a dozen locations. Some programs were designed for children, and an evening campfire program was given nightly in each of the ten campground amphitheaters. Visitors could observe demonstrations of photography, backpacking, fly-fishing, and sketching and also sharpen their skills in bird and rock identification. Along with traditional activities there were also some intriguing titles on the long list: "Mud Pot Special," "Starry, Starry Night," "Chambermaid Tour of Old Faithful Inn," "Fire and Ice," "Night Walk Through Norris Geyser Basin," and "Pour les visiteurs Français."

ʊ ʊ

During the course of the evening, Al presented me with a leaflet, "The Birds of Yellowstone National Park." It was a sly reference to an exchange during my stay in Yellowstone the January before. On a walk through the snow to check the Mammoth bird feeders, Al sang out, "There's a Townsend's solitaire!" I shot back, "Who's Townsend?" Our responses may have illustrated the difference between historians and naturalists. Al was stirred by the rare appearance of this bird in winter. I was intrigued by the tribute to the man who had discovered it.

I checked up on John Kirk Townsend, who was something of a physician and more of an ornithologist. He and Thomas Nuttall, a Harvard professor and respected naturalist, set out from St. Louis in 1834 to walk the length of the Missouri River, collecting specimens along the way. Traveling mostly in the company of fur traders (they encountered Capt. William Stewart), they came near duplicating the feat of Lewis and Clark. Returning after three years, they brought collections and observations that, in the view of DeVoto, "notably enriched the American heritage." Among more than two hundred skins Townsend brought back were twenty-five species, including, of course, his solitaire.

Park Service historians and naturalists may have diverging interests, yet both have memories of occurrences so thrilling that they wished those they loved most could have been present to share the joy. One I won't forget resulted from a small newspaper notice advising that the clothes worn by

Abraham Lincoln the night he was assassinated in Ford's Theatre were for sale. It was 1968, and the restoration of the theater and construction of a Lincoln museum in the basement were well along. I was then responsible for museum development, and without knowing the asking price or where the money would come from all of us involved in the Ford's Theatre project were determined to obtain the clothes.

Responding to the notice, we learned that the owner was the granddaughter of Alfonso Dunn, a doorkeeper and trusted servant in the Lincoln White House. Not wanting to keep any reminder of the tragedy, Mary Lincoln gave the clothes to Dunn, a Lincoln favorite. They had been faithfully preserved by succeeding generations of the Dunn family, who no doubt rejected offers from many collectors. The surviving member, aged and unable to meet medical expenditures, hoped to find "a good home" for the Lincoln relics.

Much depended upon the condition of the fabrics after so many years of exposure to heat and cold and moisture, and we arranged to have them brought to Washington by the lawyer in charge of the negotiations. He walked into my office in the interior building one morning, a reserved, alert young man wearing a business suit and carrying a worn suitcase. The curators standing around the conference table were unusually silent in the presence of the garments worn by Lincoln in the last hours of his life.

Placing the suitcase in the middle of the table, the lawyer fished a key from his vest pocket, turned the lock, and opened the hinged lid. On top, carefully folded, was the familiar black cravat, or bow tie, present in almost every Lincoln photograph and not always neatly tied. When the lawyer handed it to me I had to overcome the strong feeling that it was too sacred to be touched. One by one, the lawyer held each garment up for our inspection before laying it on the table: a short vest; a frock coat with four silk-covered buttons; the long trousers—Lincoln was six feet four—with buttons in front and behind for suspenders; and an overcoat containing the only spot of color, a Brooks Brothers label sewed inside with red silk. He had worn it in the carriage on the way to the theater and slipped it over his shoulders during the performance.

We feared the clothes might be in tatters. To my untrained eye they seemed in rather good condition except for the overcoat. Most of its right sleeve had been snipped away, apparently in squares, possibly as gifts or souvenirs. The curators pointed out considerable discoloration and attrition, yet the fabrics had proved remarkably durable. The whole badly needed cleaning and preservation treatment, during which faint reddish spots on the collar of the overcoat proved to be oxidized remains of blood and the tiny red and green fragments in the vest pockets turned out to be hard candy.

Afterward I took the lawyer to Ford's Theatre, the lovely old red brick building with arched doorways on Tenth Street only a block and a half from busy Pennsylvania Avenue. Although the restoration was far along, interior scaffolding was still in place. In the basement some exhibits had been installed, including a case displaying plaster casts of Lincoln's face and hands done by sculptor Leonard Wells Volk.

Carpenters were at work as we walked up the stairs to the dress circle, down a side aisle, and through a corridor to the presidential box. Two pieces of furniture were in place: the original red damask sofa occupied by Mary Lincoln and a replica of the president's walnut rocker. The lawyer, who had become increasingly interested in the details of the tragedy, asked why Lincoln had not been taken to the White House, only six blocks away.

After the fatal shot was fired, the cry of "Doctor! Doctor!" thrust a short, handsome man wearing sideburns and mustache into a position of frightful responsibility. A recent graduate from Bellevue Hospital Medical Center in New York, Charles Leale was the first person admitted to the box. Only twenty-three but not lacking in self-confidence, he located the wound in the back of Lincoln's head, removed a clot of blood, and then announced, "His wound is mortal."

Leale rejected a suggestion to move Lincoln to the White House, favoring a closer location. Four soldiers gently lifted the body, and Leale, supporting the head, led the way down the stairs into the dimly lit Tenth Street. As the frightened and angry crowd gave way in front and closed in behind, Leale saw a man with a lighted candle motioning to him from across the street.

In a narrow room at the rear of a house owned by a tailor who rented furnished rooms, the president was laid diagonally on a bed too short, his head and shoulders supported by pillows. Although covered by woolen blankets, his skin was cold to the touch, and hot water bottles were ordered. When Lincoln's personal physician and the surgeon general arrived, they could suggest no other treatment.

The lawyer and I walked across Tenth Street to the House Where Lincoln Died, now administered by the Park Service. As we stood in the little bedroom under a stairway facing a framed print of "The Village Blacksmith" on the wall, I was again reminded that history takes surprising turns. The clothes removed from the dying Lincoln in this room more than a hundred years before had somehow made their way back to the place where, on a rainy April morning, the secretary of war said, "Now he belongs to the ages" and the bells of Washington began to toll.

The suit of clothes is now on display in the Lincoln museum, a gift to the nation from the American Trucking Association. That the garments look almost new is a tribute to the exceptional skill of the curators. I would like to say that while standing in the bedroom I thought of Old Man Storrick, but the connection did not occur to me until later. Each time I visit Ford's Theatre I go by the exhibit, grateful to the Dunn family for safeguarding the clothes. I would hope that all who see the exhibit will feel closer kinship to Abraham Lincoln.

Not long after the lawyer's visit I sat next to an outgoing young man on a flight out of National Airport. A college student who had been visiting a friend, he couldn't stop talking about the monuments and imposing buildings and green spaces of the capital city. When he discovered I worked for the Park Service he was impressed, less so to hear I was stationed not in one of the famous national parks but in a Washington office building. "Sitting at a desk every day must be a drag," he said, trying to appear sympathetic. I considered several possible responses before saying, "Perhaps."

10

Tourists of the Parks

The Federation of Fly Fishermen held its annual conclave in West Yellowstone the summer before my visit, but it wouldn't be back soon, according to a comment I heard from chief ranger Roger Siglin. "No matter how good the fishing was, everyone had enjoyed about as much of the tourist-trap, curio-shop atmosphere of West Yellowstone as they could stand for at least a couple of years."

The town hasn't turned out quite the way Horace Albright hoped it would. It began as a six-block townsite in the Madison National Forest on the west boundary of Yellowstone in 1907, the year the Union Pacific completed its branch line to the park. On lots leased from the Forest Service enterprising citizens put up makeshift stores and hotels. Soon the railroad was delivering ten thousand tourists a year to the aspiring village known as "the boundary." Chafing under government restriction—the sale of liquor was forbidden—and unwilling to build permanent structures on land they didn't own, community go-getters took their case to Washington. In 1919, the year Albright came to Yellowstone, the townsite was transferred to the interior department for the purpose of selling off the townsite lots.

A brand new superintendent at the age of twenty-nine, Albright was a confirmed optimist. No one else would have envisaged a planned community in the wilds of Montana. The land sale would not proceed, he announced, until the residents agreed to build "a very attractive gateway town, the most attractive in the country," using native stone and wood and following guidelines established by Park Service landscape architects.

The merchants were up to something else, and the result helps to explain why the West, culturally, has always been self-conscious. Albright had underestimated the absolute determination of the citizenry to rid themselves of government interference. Opposition to his dream was unbending. After five years he gave up. "We have tried long enough and hard enough to do something with this town," he wrote to the interior secretary. The lots were sold in 1924 at a public auction in the Murray Dance Hall.

Yellowstone Avenue, the town's main street, begins at the park boundary. In a stretch of one block, almost close enough to the wilderness to throw a stone into it, you can buy Woolrich shirts and jewelry from Eagle's Curios ("we've been in business since 1908"), jade and film from the Village West, pennants from Twin Bear Gifts, tomahawks from the New Pioneer Trading Company, cowboy boots from Wild West Mercantile, firearms from the Woodland Wilderness Shop, "Funny Goofy" T-shirts from the World Famous Emporium, Yellowstone pillows and plates from the Rustic Gift Shop, nymphs, streamers, and woolly worms from the Artful Angler, and a steak dinner for $5.95 ("come as you are") from Huck's Family Dining Restaurant. Driving through a relative of West Yellowstone in New England, E. B. White conceded that it had one virtue. You learned to spell "moccasin."

With an amiable swagger and an oddball charm, this prototype tourist town expresses the belligerent independence of people who have built their bars and shops the way they pleased. West Yellowstone is tacky merchandise and uncoordinated commercial impulses, a hamlet of one-story buildings, their height boosted by false fronts and slant roofs supported by log pillars. In spite of all this—and its grossly unserious appearance—I was ready for it. I wasn't running away from Yellowstone, I reminded myself, I just needed a change. I appreciate the wildness, I'm just not suited to live there exclusively.

West Yellowstone is, however, a small pleasure that soon wears off. After stocking up on necessities at the Quick Market, sampling the fare at the Chuck Wagon Cafe—nothing for Calvin Trillin here—and spending a rewarding hour browsing and listening to the fishing stories of Bud Lilly's Trout Shop—worth a detour—I had enough of West Yellowstone.

I drove the short distance to the west entrance station on an errand for John Townsley. Mulling over some ideas for a speech he was giving to a conservation group in Salt Lake City, he thought he might spark a discussion of what people expect when they set out for Yellowstone. It's a subject that has preoccupied deep thinkers for nearly a century. John asked me to sit by the duty ranger for a spell and record provocative questions, if any.

The west is the busiest of the five entrance stations, handling a quarter of a million cars each season. That must be why it's so much larger than the others. A steeply pitched roof spans four traffic lanes and shelters an office and three concrete and tinted-glass kiosks.

The seasonal ranger who answered my knock invited me to share a space just large enough to accommodate wall shelves stacked with handouts, a cash register, and room for the ranger to stand in front of a sliding panel window and for me to sit on a stool in the corner. He smiled and wished me luck when I explained my mission. "This is pretty much a money transaction. As soon as the driver cranks down the window I say, 'Good morning. That'll be two bucks, please.' He digs it out, and I hand him the literature. About all they ask for is directions. They realize I'm busy, and they don't want to hold up the line. There isn't much conversation."

A recent graduate of Sacramento State, the seasonal was saving money for a long vacation. After many weeks in the station, with no breaks to rescue lost children or escort movie stars, he was getting bored. By the time he went off-duty three hours later, he'd welcomed well over three hundred drivers to Yellowstone. All had the opportunity to ask the kind of question John wanted to hear. None did. I'd accumulated only a couple of pages of patchy notes, including doodles. "Which way to Old Faithful?" was asked seventeen times, and eleven drivers asked about the possibility of seeing bears.

Each driver received the official park information folder that includes a map; a safety pamphlet, "Hazards in Yellowstone National Park," printed on red paper; and a leaflet, "Enjoy Them at a Distance," warning that visitors have been seriously injured and killed by grizzly bears. One driver politely declined the packet, saying he'd been on the road so long his glove compartment was full of that junk. Another asked what was in the folder. Told it contained a map, he handed it back. He was just planning to drive through and come out the other side. Given directions to the nearest campground, an elderly driver with a trailer hitched behind his pickup conversed with his wife. Smiling with effort, he said, "She wants to know if it's pretty."

Two years earlier, *Audubon* magazine had decided to do a story on "the nature, purposes, and appropriate uses of the national parks" and sent one of its field editors, Gary Soucie, to Grand Teton to interview typical tourists. He talked to mountain climbers, fishermen, and retired mail carriers. He sampled attitudes in parking lots, campgrounds, and in the lobby of the Jackson Lake Lodge. He was no more successful than I, finding it "darned difficult to get the average person to come up with an opinion worth noting," and the article was never published.

He could see why the Park Service had little faith in attitude surveys.

"The commonest opinion expressed by the casual park visitor turns out to be no opinion at all. After the first several dozen such expressions, I stopped making notes or counting. Let the last response suffice to say it for the rest. 'Sure is beautiful, isn't it? We've got some right pretty mountains back in Tennessee, but nothing like this.' . . . All those things we conservationists agonize and lose sleep over, protesting or advocating in the name of the public interest, the public has no interest in, it turns out."

According to Soucie, the confusion stems "from the impossible forked-tongue mandate under which the National Park Service operated: 'To conserve the scenery and the natural and historic objects and the wild life therein and to provide for the enjoyment of the same in such manner and by such means as will leave them unimpaired for the enjoyment of future generations.'" In the draft of the unpublished article shared with a Park Service associate, he concluded, "A task fit to try the mettle of philosopher-kings dropped in the laps of a bunch of bureaucrats."

Soucie, a well-informed and friendly critic, spoke for fellow conservationists when he called the directive to balance preservation and use an impossible task. He made a plausible case that preservation must be the first and foremost goal of park management, everything else subservient. My response to that argument, however, is like Mark Twain's reaction to a persuasive preacher. The sermon began so promisingly that Twain thought it worthy of a fifty-dollar contribution. What followed compelled him to reduce that figure to twenty-five dollars, then fifteen, then five. When the collection plate was passed, he lifted ten dollars.

Against insurmountable odds, Soucie insisted, the Park Service soldiered on, compelled "to serve two masters simultaneously and equally well." It seems to me that citizens of our democracy strive constantly to balance opposing interests—the rights of the individual against the authority of the state, the need to use oil deposits against the preservation of our natural heritage. The Constitution may have worn so well because its framers declined to itemize. I trust Congress will continue to view the mandate as a statement of aspirations that cannot be bettered. The Park Service regards it as a code of honor.

Many conservationists hold "the average park visitor" in minimal high regard. Soucie was disheartened by "hordes of bewildered casual visitors" arriving at Grand Teton, "inadequately prepared to understand the parks and to reap the benefits of a park experience." I, too, regret that some people appear to drift through a park seemingly careless of the pleasures it has to offer. I prefer to think that everyone profits to some degree. There is even evidence that the most enlightened of visitors, the organized conservationists, are often hard to tell from the average kind. There was the case, for example, of a monster safari sighted in the backcountry of Grand Teton. The two hundred hikers had brought forty pack horses to transport their provender and equipment. It wasn't a family excursion sponsored by the Billings Junior Chamber of Commerce. It was an official "outing" of the Sierra Club, the spiritual descendants of founder John Muir apparently obeying his manifesto for salvation: "The clearest way into the Universe is through a forest wilderness."

They were also disregarding the damaging impact that large horse parties have on the backcountry. The iron shoes of a thousand-pound horse cut deeply into trails and damp meadows. Forty horses can eat eight hundred pounds of grass and wildflowers a day. But the Sierra Club deserves some credit. Its failure to exercise restraint resulted in stiff new restrictions on backcountry use in Grand Teton.

A more amusing incident, again involving the Sierra Club, took place in Alaska. I was traveling with Ted Swem, a principal architect of the campaign that added so many new parks in Alaska that the acreage of the national park system was doubled. In the lobby of the old Mount McKinley Hotel, in the park now called Denali, we ran into Ed Wayburn, president of the Sierra Club, and his wife, Peggy. Ed was the point man for his organization in the bruising battle for Alaskan parks. At an early hour one morning the Wayburns, Ted and I, that gifted writer and wilderness traveler Sig Olson, and a young Canadian biologist studying wolf behavior set out to observe an occupied wolf den a disheartening distance up the Toklat River from the park highway.

Mile after mile through a driving rainstorm we trudged, zigzagging from one gravel bar to another against the icy, glacier-fed current. The wolves, it turned out, had better sense than to be about in such outrageous weather. We waded the river for twelve long hours, yet as so often happens when conditions become grim—and the leader has forgotten to pack the lunches—good humor prevailed. After we reached the Wonder Lake ranger station that evening and changed into dry clothes, Sig poured us a slug of bourbon that would have tangled the feet of an Alaskan brown bear. In Alaska, he noted, routine outings become adventures.

We delivered the Wayburns to Camp Denali, an exemplary rustic camp just outside the park in full view of Mount McKinley. A few days later we drove them the length of the gravel highway across the park to the train station. They were good company, exceptionally well informed on park matters. Ted and I were kept only modestly busy fending off criticisms of alleged Park Service shortcomings. Frequent stops were made for Ed to photograph the wildlife show along the highway. Dall sheep posed on rocky outcroppings, a grizzly shambled by in search of a meal, and caribou clustered on a snowfield to escape pestering flies. Impossibly large, Mount McKinley seemed to float above the clouds, so vast, so high, so intimidating.

A little past Eielson Visitor Center we surprised a red fox, erect ears edged in black, standing squarely in the middle of the road. Ed eased quietly out of the car, camera at the ready. The fox eyed him from twenty yards away, decided he posed no great danger, and retreated slowly down the road. When Ed picked up the pace, the fox maintained the interval. It was like a scene from a Roadrunner cartoon, watched by an increasingly embarrassed wife and two Park Service hands almost weeping with pleasure at the sight of the president of the Sierra Club committing an actionable offense. The pair disappeared around a bend in the road, both Ed and the fox loping along in grand style. To her credit, Peggy was laughing, albeit ruefully. She said, "If I didn't know better I'd swear I just saw Ed chasing a wild animal in a national park."

John Townsley surprised me one time when we were brought to a halt by a traffic jam while driving through Hayden Valley. In the shallows of the Yellowstone River, a bull moose equipped with broad and heavy antlers dipped his head in the water and brought up a mouthful of dripping green plants. Instead of unsnarling the traffic, John turned off the ignition and relaxed. Noticing my upraised eyebrows, he said, "That's what they came to Yellowstone to see."

To my comment that he didn't usually look the other way when regulations were being ignored he said, "It would seem that a lot of our visitors are going about the business of seeing the park in the wrong way. But from all I can tell—and with a little help from us—the majority manage to see the important features and make enough discoveries on their own to take home special memories."

There is almost no graffiti in the park, and I've never seen anyone throw anything into the hot pools. I said that to Rick Hutchinson, the disarmingly earnest park geologist and curator of thermal features. He bet me that objects, mostly coins, thrown into Blue Star Pool since he had last cleaned it would fill a five-gallon bucket half-way. With a modified ladle he accomplished the feat in fifteen minutes. There were more than seven hundred pennies.

Among tourists of the parks the geyser-gazers of Yellowstone may be the most extraordinary—a handful of people who are seriously smitten by the play of geysers. Most visitors go out of their way to see a geyser erupt, although a generation accustomed to watching rockets blast off from Cape Kennedy doesn't react with the kind of wide-eyed, flabbergasted delight exhibited by Ferdinand Hayden, who led the scientific expedition to Yellowstone in 1871. He was unable to maintain his composure in the presence of a geyser eruption and shouted and danced gleefully.

John Wegel, a lanky, determined man with a master's degree in mechanical engineering from the University of New Hampshire, became tired of living in a dormitory and moved into the parking lot, rigging his car with a stove and refrigerator. The car has been his home ever since. On a trip through Yellowstone he was "powerfully attracted" to the geysers and was directed to Rick Hutchinson. Except for Old Faithful, he learned, long-term eruption cycles of the park's many geysers didn't exist. No one had the time to record them. He was drawn to Riverside Geyser on the bank of the Firehole River and discovered an interesting pattern. The intervals between eruptions clustered around two time periods, a discovery that helped Rick predict eruption times.

On June 21, Wegel, an unpaid volunteer, began a vigil at Riverside. He watched from a rock ledge near the crater at night, sitting huddled in a faded parka, his legs wrapped in a poncho. A headlamp strapped to his forehead enabled him to record eruption times in his notebook. Between June 21 and November 8, he witnessed 550 consecutive eruptions of Riverside, determining the average interval to be six hours, seven minutes, and fifty seconds and winning an accolade from Rick for "continuous dedication to a geyser."

It was the third summer in a row that Herbert Warren had watched Great Fountain Geyser, located along the one-way Firehole Lake Drive in the Lower Geyser Basin. It puts on one of the best shows in the park. A large crater more than fifteen feet wide and filled with clear, boiling water, it sits on a broad sinter platform. About every ten hours, surges indicate an impending eruption. The boiling becomes increasingly violent until, like a great fountain, the entire pool explodes nearly two hundred feet into the sky.

A portly, cordial, white-haired gentleman, the retired owner of a bowling emporium in Denver, Warren had been hooked on geysers since he drove a Model T Ford to Yellowstone in the 1920s. He observed Great Fountain on a fairly regular schedule, strictly for his own pleasure, paying the daily rate at the Old Faithful Inn. He flagged me down as I detoured through the Firehole Lake Drive one day on the off chance of catching an eruption. Great Fountain was about to let go, and he was encouraging drivers to stop and have a look. While we waited, I asked what it was about geysers that attracted him. He smiled and shook his head. "I can't explain it. I liked geysers the first time I ever saw one fifty years ago, and I expect I always will."

I hadn't talked with Rick about geyser-watchers for five minutes before he mentioned Hazel Decker and her fondness for Steamboat. A beloved woman from Two Harbors, Michigan, she summered for many years in Yellowstone in her later years because, as she was fond of saying, when it came to Steamboat Geyser she was not well balanced. The fortunate few who have experienced the sound and fury of Steamboat in action say it is a wondrous and fearful sight. "It literally blows its guts out," reported a Geological Survey scientist. The height of the steam phase that follows the eruption has been estimated at fourteen hundred feet.

An erratic performer, the world's tallest and most powerful geyser was quiet for fifty years before it began an active period in 1961. The curious came from all over the country, Hazel Decker among them. If the signs were promising, she would spend the days at her favorite location near the geyser, catching forty winks at night in her car in the parking lot. Until the arrival of John Wegel, she had set the standard for perseverance.

Hazel Decker was immensely likable and spent more time than the rangers telling visitors about geysers. Members of the Yellowstone staff showed their affection by building her a bench, where in comfort she could chat with passersby and keep an eye on Steamboat. An expert with a fly rod, she would slip away for a few hours of casting for rainbows on the Gibbon River, which borders the Norris Geyser Basin.

On an afternoon in July 1969, a new geyser appeared close to the Decker watching post, spouting for a short time to a height of forty feet before reverting to a pool. The official report of the phenomenon contained a rare tribute to an individual. "In honor of Mrs. Hazel Decker, who once spent over one hundred days waiting to see Steamboat Geyser in major eruption, the island of trees immediately east of the pool, where she and countless others sat patiently in anticipation, had been unofficially named Mrs. Decker's Island. Ranger Dalton (who witnessed the event) believed the new feature should be named for the person who had been Norris Basin's most faithful observer. He, therefore, gave it the name it has today—Decker Geyser."

11

Saving All the Pieces

"Yellowstone is an optimum place for a plant ecologist," Don Despain told me. "It's large enough to let the great natural systems work without interference, especially if you include the lands in the surrounding national forests. The roads and developed areas are insignificant. Some biologists consider the loss of the wolf and mountain lion to be critical. I don't. Their absence may be less important than the increase of carbon monoxide in the atmosphere, although that effect is yet to be calculated. I think it likely the food supply is the determining factor. When wolves were present in Yellowstone, the number of elk determined the number of wolves, not the other way around."

Don was unexcitable, with a shock of crow-black hair, a wide, cheerful grin, and the sturdy physique of a lumberjack, or maybe it was the checked wool shirt and laced boots he was wearing. Raised on a farm in Wyoming, he had studied botany at the University of Wyoming and received a master's degree at the University of Illinois. He held a doctorate in plant ecology from the University of British Columbia, doing his fieldwork in the Canadian arctic on Devon Island, almost a thousand miles north of Hudson Bay. It was a place, he said, where if anything happened to you no one would know about it for a long time. He was recruited by the chief scientist of the Park Service, favorably impressed by a vegetative cover map he'd prepared of the Big Horn Mountains.

Don had known the Yellowstone country since he was fifteen. That year he accompanied his father on the annual elk hunt. "It took several days of riding with a pack string to reach the meadow where we always set up our camp in Teton National Forest just south of the park boundary. Sleeping in the open, eating around the fire, listening to the talk of the adults, hiking the woods in sight of the Teton range—these are good memories. I've always liked to hunt. What I like best is after the kill, skinning the animal, dressing out the meat, knowing everything will be put to use, that's the satisfying part." Don felt no need to defend his enjoyment of hunting. Neither did another ecologist, Aldo Leopold.

We were standing on the side of a ridge two hundred yards west of the Grand Loop Road, fifteen miles south of Mammoth. It was late July. In early July 1976 the Arrow Fire had been ignited when lightning struck a spruce tree on a forested slope. Declared a natural fire that posed no immediate threat, it crept slowly along, consuming a couple of acres of grass under the trees the first day and six more acres in the next three days.

The smoke and flames of an unconstrained fire astonished the public. Drivers stopped to photograph a herd of elk grazing in the roadside meadow, the fire as a backdrop. Rangers posted along the highway explained the new Yellowstone fire policy to puzzled vacationers. On the afternoon of the fifth day, strong, southwesterly winds developed, creating crown fires in the trees and driving the flames into the meadow. Spot fires developing across the highway caused significant traffic problems.

Nothing on the slope had escaped the flames. The trunks of standing trees were black, their few remaining needles orange. Fallen trees had been partially consumed by the Arrow Fire. We kicked up dust from the ashes, and yet regeneration was well advanced. The tall stems of flaming-red fireweed and clumps of blue lupine whose slender green leaves formed pinwheels were all around us. Don pointed out lodgepole seedlings two years old and well over a foot high growing in the ashes.

He couldn't control his elation as he surveyed the signs of growth. "When we finally decided to let fires burn in Yellowstone we were going against a hundred years of history and everything we learned in school. It's only natural people think of fire as evil, forests going up in smoke, and terrified animals fleeing a wall of flames. On this fire, elk continued to graze in the meadow for several days, with smoke blowing over them. Smokey Bear has taught generations of children not to start forest fires because they burn up two-by-fours. In terms of the Yellowstone ecosystem, Smokey is the enemy. And I like two-by-fours as much as anyone."

I was kneeling, inspecting a root Don had dug that was undamaged by the fire, when something caught his eye, and he glanced up. A doe and two spotted fawns were walking toward us, their rich brown and white coats distinct against the green of the new growth. The fawns were almost toylike, with large, inquisitive eyes and miniature hoofs.

Don cautiously raised his camera, an inch at a time, for a photograph that would tell more about the role of fire than a thousand-word treatise. The shutter button failed to respond. Working the cocking lever produced a metallic clicking that revealed our presence, and the deer were off in an instant, bounding like springboks. At the high point of a stiff-legged jump the doe turned her head for one last look before the frightened animals disappeared over the top of the ridge.

The conclusion of the Arrow Fire was a bitter disappointment to Don. After the run on the fifth day that periodically closed the highway, members of the park's fire management team had considered their options. The policy specified that fires started by lightning would be allowed to run their course only if they did not threaten human life or property.

The line supplying electricity to Old Faithful village was barely a mile from the advancing fire. A break in the power line would shut down all facilities in the village. Thus far, public sentiment was supportive of the new policy. The three thousand guests from far-away places holding confirmed reservations to Old Faithful might feel differently. The decision was made to suppress the Arrow Fire. Don understood practical considerations. He also regretted the need to compromise science.

It's not that we value the concessioner's investment more than we do the resource, or that we put the welfare of the visitor above all else. But when our ecological decisions reflect political considerations, Yellowstone suffers. John Townsley did what he had to do when he gave the order to fight the Arrow Fire. But I'm obliged to say—without making a moral judgment—that a Yellowstone superintendent must develop many skills, one of them being the ability to think like an innkeeper.

As a people, our quest has been to override the ecosystem. We have allowed the original prairie grasslands to be obliterated, an enormously productive region larger than the countries of Europe. We don't know what we've destroyed, and we may not be able to find out. Scientists are searching for the clues. We are overawed by our ability to manage forces we don't understand, when you consider that calories locked up in the organic matter of the soil contain energy that moves the wind. When it comes to the land, we are arrogant when we should be humble.

The relationship that farmers had with the land is being replaced by agricultural technology, which isn't farming. Small farms are being consolidated. The large companies look at their holdings as a runway for their tractors to plant the seeds that with the aid of the chemical industry produce bigger yields so they can spend their winters in Florida or Arizona—and buy bigger tractors.

Serving as a Mormon missionary in Germany for two years, Don had encountered farmers with a different attitude:

> They have so little acreage compared to ours, and their approach to farming is land-oriented rather than machine-oriented. Their lives revolve around the seasons. They don't look at farming as a commercial operation. It's fulfilling. It continues a family tradition. It's a way of life they prefer to any other.
>
> Land is hard to come by in Germany. A man I knew was allotted a short section of an abandoned road. I can't tell you how excited he was. You should have seen his face when he brought out his first wheelbarrow load of vegetables. Somehow, I have an emotional attachment to the land like that of the German farmers. I don't know how or where I got it, but it's the reason I studied plant ecology and why I'm gratified to be working in Yellowstone.

Don was endlessly generous with his time, optimistic, fair-minded, and principled. He didn't engage in backbiting if a decision didn't go his way, but he stood his ground. His high school science teacher said he could always tell if Don didn't agree with what he was being told. He would grab his desk with both hands, push his chair back, and fix the teacher with an unblinking stare.

A scientist who talked like a naturalist, Don was also a folklorist in the field of natural history. I wish I could work the subject, say, of the lousewort, or lice plant, into a conversation. Widely distributed in Yellowstone, it was familiar to ancient shepherds because it always seemed to be present in fields where their sheep became infested with lice. Scientists, Don observed, have offered three explanations: The plant grew in all fields suitable for grazing, sheep picked up lice no matter what they ate, or shepherds are always looking for something to blame their troubles on.

Doing research on forest growth requires patience. In one experiment, Don was measuring tree growth, using a device that looked like an electric mixer but had cleats instead of beaters. They fitted over a pattern of nails hammered into pine, spruce, and fir trees in carefully selected locales. The gadget had a pointer that somehow measured outward growth. I tagged along several times, writing the numbers in his notebook as he read them off. I enjoyed being out in the woods with an agreeable companion who knew the name of everything, although I'm not sure what, if anything, resulted from the experiment. While measuring trees one day, he said, "If you consider how little we know about how a leaf grows, what we don't know about the Yellowstone ecosystem is phenomenal. So we make a few assumptions, avoid tinkering, and follow Aldo Leopold's advice to save all the pieces."

The practice of automatically suppressing all fires in Yellowstone was questioned as far back as the 1940s by a naturalist who supposedly said, "Nature doesn't get enough respect." Over the next thirty years the idea of allowing fires to burn was discussed, argued, and adopted. The theory is unassailable. Wildfire has been an essential element of the Yellowstone ecosystem since the last ice age, and plant communities have adapted to it. Some forested areas are classified as "fire dependent." In Yellowstone's cool, dry climate, trees may take centuries to decay. Fire, rather than the fungi and bacteria of wetter climates, is the agent of decomposition that instantly, rather than gradually, breaks down the organic matter.

In mature forests the sun is unable to penetrate the canopy. Birds and animals are absent, for little grows in the shade beneath. Such areas are referred to as "botanic deserts." Fire opens the forest floor to sunlight. The ash releases mineral nutrients that act on the soil like a powerful injection of fertilizer. Charred trunks retaining heat from the sun melt the snow and lengthen the growing season. A luxuriant new growth of vegetation sets the table for wildlife.

If the objective is to keep Yellowstone natural, you cannot do without fires. Their suppression may be linked to the steady decline of nutrients in Yellowstone Lake over many years. Since the Divide Fire of 1976, however, samples taken from the South Arm of the lake have shown a sharp increase in nutrients. Obviously, minerals leached from the ashes by rain and melting snow were carried by stream flow into the nearby South Arm. "We thought we found the cause," Don said, "but the nutrient increase was so large we could hardly believe the figures. There could be other causes."

Don and William H. Romme, who has done research on Yellowstone's fire history, had begun a study to determine the nature of the fire cycle. One day in his office Don covered a blackboard with drawings of pine trees while explaining his "working hypothesis." The cycle takes several hundred years. It is not an accumulation of lesser fires until all of the park has been burned over. The cycle ends, and begins again, with a conflagration. Essentially, the forest will not burn until it's ready to burn.

Self-pruning lodgepoles, the park's major species, dominate the regeneration. They grow tall and close, resembling a forest of wooden columns with minimal foliage on top. There is little fuel in a young forest, and the probability of fire is close to zero. The Divide Fire of 1976 hurled burning brands into an adjoining century-old stand of lodgepoles. The plentiful lower branches of spruce and fir provide kindling and a ladder that conducts ground fires to the canopy. A conflagration occurs when the necessary weather conditions oblige: severe drought, extremely low humidity, and continuously high winds.

It's difficult to explain why the Park Service has never given scientific research the priority it deserves, except that superintendents find it hard to divert funds to long-term research when the sewage system is leaking into the river or potholes need to be fixed. A half-dozen studies going back to the 1960s have identified the need, yet the improvement is gradual. Don suggested that although the natural fire policy was a giant step forward, it would be strongly advisable to know a great deal more about fire ecology. Lack of scientific knowledge has worked against the Park Service commitment to maintain park ecosystems and natural processes — and not only in Yellowstone. The information base had improved at the time of the 1988 fires, but I think it fair to say that Yellowstone did not have the science it needed at a critical time.

12

As Long as the Knees Hold Out

The story of smoke jumpers—they parachuted into Yellowstone for the first time in 1945—is covered in a richly detailed account of the daredevil pilots who pioneered air travel in the northern Rockies. Their brash slogan is the book's title, *Fly the Biggest Piece Back*, written by Steve Smith. After a ride, a real winner, in the open cockpit of a World War I airplane, Bob Johnson, the hero of the narrative, knew nothing else would do but to fly.

He helped the Forest Service develop the technique of smoke jumping. That venerable agency has no peers when it comes to fighting forest fires. The Forest Service was using airplanes to locate fires in California in 1919, making free-fall drops of food and equipment in the 1920s, and clearing strips to land fire fighters in the 1930s. In the summer of 1925, a Forest Service fire boss recruited thirty men from the bars and pool halls of Missoula to fight a blaze in Idaho's Clearwater National Forest. They were trucked to a ranger station at the end of the road. With a pack string carrying food and equipment, fording streams and climbing over steep ridges, they were three days on the trail before reaching the fire.

After years of careful preparation, the Forest Service dropped smoke jumpers on a fire for the first time in July 1940. Bob Johnson was a month behind. In August he lifted his Ford Tri-Motor from the Missoula airport, with four smoke jumpers aboard. They were wearing two-piece, felt-padded jumpsuits, football helmets equipped with wire masks to protect the men's faces from tree limbs, ankle and back braces, and logger boots. They were attacking the fire in less than an hour from takeoff. A veteran Forest Service ranger said, "I'd fought fire the hard way. I worked in that

backcountry of Idaho for seven summers chasing smoke on foot. I used to
look at those old hawks sailing over and think, 'My God, if I could get over
the mountains like that what a thing it would be.' "

Before I met Jim Sweaney all that I knew about fire fighting I'd picked up
in a one-day training course put on by the Natchez Trace Parkway ranger
staff while I was stationed at Vicksburg. The fire we fought wasn't much,
the old ranger in charge was scared to death that it would get away from us
and burn into private land, and I scorched a pair of uniform pants so badly
that it cost twenty dollars to replace them. I'd introduced myself to Jim
early in the summer and hadn't caught up with him again until I saw him
standing outside the fire cache early in August. He shook hands, gave me
his private smile, and said yes, it had been a little while. In all my trips to
Yellowstone I'd never been inside the fire cache, and Jim was agreeable to
showing me around. The building looks like a massive barn. Two hundred
feet long, with high stone walls, it was built by the army as a cavalry stable
for a hundred horses.

He led the way around a spick-and-span fire engine, a Superior Ford
900 at least as old as Jim and ready for action. The polished red hood was
higher than my head, and as we walked by Jim casually tested the handle
of a fire axe mounted on the side under a rack of metal ladders. The park
maintains nine fire engines to protect its several hundred buildings.

A forestry graduate of the University of Montana, Jim signed on with
the Forest Service as a fire control aide. At the first opportunity, he volunteered for the parachute school and became a smoke jumper. "There's
nothing like it," he said, and I thought I detected a wistful note in his voice.
Eventually, he realized that his knees couldn't take the jumping anymore.
Hearing that the park forester job was open in Yellowstone, he applied.

Jim, a low-slung man in his late thirties, met authority half-way by wearing a uniform shirt. A little below average height and heavier than when
he was jumping, he had thinning hair and glasses with sturdy frames. He
had the reserve and dry sense of humor befitting a countryman who grew
up in Deadwood, South Dakota, a reliable, low-key professional with an
exhaustive knowledge of the particulars of fire fighting.

The fire cache is divided into offices and a variety of storage rooms.
Wooden walls, painted white, are a reminder of the stable era. We passed
a door marked CORRAL OPERATIONS that had a horseshoe hanging above.
A yellow telephone slip on a nail said, "West needs Hay," "west" being
the local term for the west entrance station. The seventy-five horses and
pack mules brought in from winter range every summer are used for ranger
patrol, trail maintenance, and fire fighting.

I examined a fire shelter made from aluminum foil. It's a last resort if the wind changes direction and you're trapped, Jim said. Shaped like a blanket, the foil reflects the heat, and there are tabs to fasten it tightly to the ground. The fire is supposed to burn right over you, causing no damage that can't be treated with Unguentine. "The general feeling is it should come with a ration of butter so you can baste yourself," Jim noted.

One room was full of equipment packaged for air drops: backpacks, chain saws, and two-person crosscut saws. Boxes of fire-resistant suits were piled high on tables, bright yellow shirts and dark green pants. Disposable sleeping bags made of paper were marginal, Jim said. "They're better than nothing, but what you really need on a cold night in the mountains is a parachute." A large crate cushioned by innertubes for an air drop was stenciled "10 MAN TOOL UNIT." It held shovels, canteens, headlamps for night work, and the most famous fire-fighting tool ever invented. The Pulaski is shaped like a double-bitted axe, except that at the working end it has an axe blade and a grub hoe back to back. No one knows the origin of the name, but, as Jim said, it sounds right for the work it does:

> You fight a fire with a Pulaski by digging a trench eighteen inches wide between what's burning and what isn't. That's about as wide as you can make it, efficiently, and if you scrape away all the duff and get down to bare earth it will stop a ground fire. Rather than beating a fire to death, although that can be done with a small one, you contain it and let it burn itself out. Fires mostly slack off at night when the temperature goes down, humidity goes up, and the wind tapers off. But if the fire is in a place with a good fuel supply and wind begins to supply it with oxygen, you'd think someone was feeding it kerosene. It just takes off, the flames leaping up into the tree tops, the wind throwing branches ahead, starting new fire. Then it's out of control. There isn't a thing you can do to stop it. Fire fighters don't put big fires out. They put themselves out when they've burned everything up or the weather changes.

The Bryams Intensity Scale calibrates the energy of a forest fire. Containment by fire fighters is no longer possible once the reading passes one hundred on the scale. The 1967 Sun Dance Fire in Idaho, one of the big ones, had a reading of twenty-two thousand.

Wall shelves holding freeze-dried and canned food were nearly empty. I picked up a can labeled "Ration C Meal, Individual," containing spaghetti and beef chunks in tomato sauce. Jim pulled a face. "All the good stuff is gone this late in the summer. We have to eat the discards before we can order a new supply." There seemed to be a lot of little flat cans. "We call them 'the inedibles,' like this ersatz peanut butter. About all you can do with it is stir in insect repellent and use it for canned heat."

On the bigger fires, crews are fed by catering companies serving steak and pie à la mode from mobile kitchens. It's expensive, but if you feed people well they work better. Fire fighters hike back to camps that cover acres and look like military posts. A radio and telephone communication center is set up, trucks and trailers and electric generators are parked everywhere, and plastic tarps are tied to trees to provide office space and shade.

For a big fire you need an army, Jim said as we inspected two cartons, each the size of an upright piano and marked FINANCE CHIEF KIT and FINANCIAL PLANS KIT. All over the West, fire-fighting teams are standing by in base depots. It takes only a telephone call to start them on their way. Smoke jumpers stationed at Boise have as much chance of being dropped on a fire in California as they do in Idaho. If the smoke jumpers can't do it, more and more crews are called in. They come from many agencies, including the Park Service. A number of Yellowstone rangers are on call, drawn I guess by the excitement and the extra money. All fire fighters must carry a red card, proof of training and experience.

The basic fire-fighting unit is a crew of twenty people. A fire boss orders as many as needed. On a major fire, an incident commander is in charge, aided by a staff responsible for planning, operations, fire behavior, and air support — everything from guarding valuables left in camp by fire fighters to obtaining infrared photographs taken by high-altitude airplanes at night to show the extent of fire perimeters and delivering the photos to the incident commander early the next morning.

Jim explained the tactics:

There is always a designated fire boss, even if only two people are involved. Whatever the size of the fire, he's in complete command. If the initial attack by the smoke jumpers fails, the fire goes to class three. An experienced fire boss and several crews are dispatched. There's a lot of inefficiency at the start as you try to find your way in strange country and the air drops are trying to find you. If this isn't enough, the fire goes to class two, the fire line is divided into sectors and hundreds of people are involved. Then, if everything goes to hell, it goes to class one, with an incident commander. People are coming in from everywhere, guys who haven't seen each other for years. That's one of the few nice things about fighting fire.

On that scale, it isn't an efficient operation. One day the fire takes off and leaves everybody behind. The next day it may look containable. The fire boss must be on the safe side, sending for reinforcements when the fire is running, discharging crews when it seems to be under control. It

happens that as the fire gets contained and the fire boss starts to demobi-
lize, half the equipment he ordered and a lot of people are still coming
in. You have to keep detailed financial records and accurate payrolls for
hundreds or thousands of people who are constantly arriving and leaving.
You have to send out checks for the number of meals served by caterers,
for each piece of equipment purchased, or lost, or burned up, and for
the 727s and 747s chartered to transport the crews. It really doesn't take
much of a fire to cost a million dollars.

∪ ∪

The initial calls for smoke jumpers go to centers jointly funded by the Forest Service, Bureau of Land Management, and the Park Service. The one
serving Yellowstone is an unembellished cinderblock affair sitting on the
edge of the runway of the West Yellowstone airport and painted green and
blue, with a loft to hang parachutes. When the crew of smoke jumpers stationed there hasn't been called out on a fire for thirty days, a training jump
is obligatory. Jim wangled an invitation for me to ride along.

The briefing was held in a room lined with tall lockers. The twelve jumpers sat on boxes of gear and upended trash cans, cocky, mid-sized, and
young. Ed, the jump boss, a little older and more intense, pointed out the
target on the wall map, a small clearing near Cougar Creek west of the airport and surrounded by tall trees. He began by reviewing the drill for a
tree landing. They had heard it as often as seasoned travelers have heard
flight attendants give their safety spiel, and took it no more seriously.

"As you approach," Ed cautioned, "aim well down from the top of the
tree. Ideally, your canopy will drape over the top, giving you a good hang
up and an easy descent. Remember, don't drive in on the wind line. Drop
off to one side of your target and slip in. Otherwise, if you miss the tree
you'll hit the ground like a brick. Streamline your body for contact with
the tree, legs together, hands on the risers or down along your legs. There
are some dead trees in the area, but no bad snags—I don't think."

His disclaimer drew a derisive comment. "Bet you ten bucks Walter hits
a dead tree." The experience, I gathered, is best avoided. You either get
jabbed by a jagged limb or part of the tree is broken off by the impact and
falls on you. Ed warned against landing in a larch, another brittle speci-
men. "How do you tell a larch?" someone asked, vaudeville style, receiving
the inevitable answer, "It's the one you hit first."

Next to me, a jumper thin as a wire told me of the time he realized he
was approaching his target tree too fast and at the last moment elected to
lift over. He couldn't quite raise his legs high enough. They caught in the

tree top, and the jolt turned him upside down and collapsed his chute. Falling down through the tree, he said to himself, "Aw shit, this is it," just as the shroud lines caught over a limb and stopped him, his head a few feet from the ground. "I swung there a bit, quivering, before I could detach."

The briefing over, Ed helped me into a yellow jumpsuit, then buckled me into a reserve parachute. The pros took big orange bags out of their lockers, casually spilling the contents on the floor. The top of the jumpsuit has a high collar in back to keep the shroud lines from catching under the helmet and breaking your neck. A knife in a red sheath is taped on top of the front reserve chute to cut the lines in an emergency. A large pouch on the right leg, tied with a drawstring, holds the let-down rope used to make your way down from a tree landing.

At the "grease rack," whose design was borrowed from the standard service station model, we tested our leg muscles with a half-dozen jumps into a layer of wood chips. My first effort to turn and roll sideways after I hit was met by fake applause and a falsetto barb. "Oh, that was *good*, for a writer." Finally Ed said, "Everybody loose? Ready to do it?" Another humorist, of which there seemed to be an oversupply, called out, "I can't seem to get it right. Maybe I should stay down today." I could only assume that the cornball humor was for my benefit, although it may have been a way of easing tension.

Twelve jumpers in blue helmets and wire masks, the spotter, and a literary observer in an Irish walking hat marched in single file across the runway to a white DeHaviland Twin Otter. I sat just forward of the open door on the starboard side. My back was against the shoulder-high bulkhead partially separating the passengers from the pilot. The jumpers sat in two rows facing me, bulky with reserve chutes strapped to their chests and the big ones on their backs.

The jump went smoothly at twelve hundred feet. One jumper waited quietly, completely relaxed, right leg on the outside step, gazing intently at the target area before he jumped. Another, who could scarcely wait, never stopped doing knee bends. After the last man jumped, we dropped down closer to tree level, and the spotter kicked out two boxes of equipment, the chutes opening instantly. In the fly-by I stood with the spotter in the open door and held tightly to the white enamel rod along the opening. Most of the chutes were in the small clearing, two or three in the trees. A good grouping, the spotter commented.

Remote sensors are now used to detect fires and plot their courses, but smoke jumpers don't depend on space age technology to hit their target areas. They use a homemade device, a "streamer," a ten-inch length of Number 9 wire to which is attached a strip of orange crepe paper. The wire descends at the same rate as the jumper, the fluttering paper making the flight path visible. We made a couple of preliminary runs over the target, the spotter dropping a sequence of streamers while making note of terrain reference points.

Jim said there is a superstition about the effectiveness of Number 9 wire. It's the same grade once used as a telephone transmission line to the fire lookout towers. As the lines were replaced by radio communications, sentimental smoke jumpers salvaged the wire for streamers. I noticed that most of the jumpers closely followed their descent. Jim's comment was, "I always watched them. They could tell you a lot about what was going to happen."

The jumpers carry a supply of streamers to send messages back to the plane by arranging them on the ground to form code letters. I have Jim's old copy of the Visual Signal Code, a wallet-size card issued by the Forest Service. He said that in the course of my travels I might need to signal a passing airplane that "I need power saw" (SS), "helicopter landing spot nearby" (H), or the sign of a successful jump, "personnel OK" (LL).

Brought back to the center by truck, the jumpers tossed their parachutes on the long tables and began repacking them. Banter ended, replaced by silent concentration. "Packing helps to create total trust," Jim said. "You sign your name to the chute, and no one knows who will pull it off the rack for the next jump." When the guy who told me of hitting the tree finished his chute I asked him how long he intended to keep jumping.

"Three of us have been together now since we went through jump training in Boise six years ago. We've had some rare experiences. There's an attraction about this life that makes it hard to leave. The money can be good if you get on the big fires, sometimes enough to live on the rest of the year. Once I was able to bum around Europe for six months. Winters I work the ski resorts. Now I'm ready for something else, if I could find a job that appealed to me. I tried marriage two years ago, but that didn't work out. I have a need to find a real job."

"That's happened to a lot of us," Jim said later when he talked of his own experience. I had the feeling that those days were some of his best:

> Jumping is a confidence-builder. You take pride in being a smoke jumper. There's a closeness among jumpers you don't often see. I enjoyed the life. I enjoyed it a lot, in spite of the monotony. Sitting around the base you can't wait to get on a fire. Once there you can't wait to get back. Fighting forest fires is nothing but hard dirty labor.
>
> Smoke jumping is a delivery system. It's worth the cost because almost all fires start small. The trick is to get people on them fast. Getting out afterward carrying a hundred pounds of equipment is as wearing on the

knees as jumping. The accident rate for jumpers isn't bad, maybe two per hundred jumps, usually curable injuries.

The rate for aircraft is a lot worse. When the fire is burning hot, the air is unstable. Tankers heavily loaded with retardant come in just above the tree tops, and the planes tend to be antiques. In one fire season several years back the Forest Service lost eight planes, 10 percent of its fleet. The most dangerous part for smoke jumpers is coming back to base late at night in the back of a truck. That and riding helicopters through the canyons.

13

Between Earth and Sky

The rusting railroad plow stands in a cluster of alpine fir high on the shoulder of Mount Washburn not far from the Chittenden Road. According to Aubrey Haines, it must have been unhitched and discarded by a teamster when construction of the road up the mountain was completed in 1905. It is as obscure a place as you could find for a memorial to the man who supervised construction of Yellowstone's Grand Loop road system. The purpose of the road, said Hiram M. Chittenden, was to provide just such vantage points where a person might come "through all future time, and study the handiwork of Nature as it lies outspread before him from the summit of Mount Washburn."

One of the few spur roads that lead off the Grand Loop, the Chittenden Road was built for stagecoaches and later used by automobiles and buses. An enlightened management restricted it to hikers many years ago, presumably to restore tranquillity to the scene although the strain on brakes and transmissions could have been a factor. The surface has since weathered into a dirt pathway like an abandoned country lane. In the park's vast network of trails there may not be three and a half more rewarding miles.

An old volcano with a bare peak topped by a fire lookout tower, Mount Washburn is the highest point, at 10,243 feet, in a mountain range shaped like an amphitheater. Deep snows block the upper part of the trail into July. Then a snowblower labors up the former roadbed and slices a passageway. A maintenance vehicle takes a seasonal ranger and his load of supplies and food to the tower, and the Chittenden Road is open for the short season. Aubrey's story of the plow encouraged me to make the climb on an August day that started well and then went from bad to worse.

The angle of the mountain looks moderately steep from the parking lot, mostly open meadows with a few bands of pines lower down, wild and craggy above timberline. That the road was designed by an engineer is obvious. It slants back and forth in long tangents, never deviating from the prescribed gradient. Chittenden thought the road "an exceptionally difficult piece of work." Much blasting was required, sending rocks rolling down the mountainside on crews below.

I would recommend the hike up Mount Washburn for the beauty of its wildflowers alone. The summer before, the state of Wyoming had polled travelers to ask what they had enjoyed most, and the result was surprising. A large number were impressed most of all by the extraordinary flower show in the Rocky Mountains. Mount Washburn's slopes are almost like gardens, flower upon flower, color upon color, like dabs and smears of bright paint. I should have brought along a botanist.

Two winded but talkative elderly women who had stopped to catch their breath and debate the wisdom of continuing put names to a few of the flowers: yellow balsamroot and cinquefoil, blue harebell and larkspur, the flat white tops of cow parsnip. "It's like the palette of an artist who works in all colors and all shades," said one, as we admired the display. "Have you ever seen anything to compare?"

Enchanted by flowers all about me, I almost stepped on a large gray bird that had feathered feet. I noticed the orange splash above the eyes and white throat markings. Making clucking sounds, it showed no alarm. I continued for a minute or two, then dutifully slipped off my pack and sat on a ledge. In *Birds of North America* I found a picture of the chickenlike critter; it was a blue grouse, often called a fool hen because an edible bird that doesn't stay well out of reach lacks good sense.

By the time I was halfway to the top, all the lofty ridges of the Mount Washburn range were below me, green and thickly wooded. I didn't like the looks of a cloudbank in the western sky that neither advanced nor retreated. A mountain bluebird hovered like a kestrel, poised to swoop down on an insect. The caustic croak of a raven riding an updraft startled me as I inspected the still-distant tower through binoculars. In the silence, the unexpected sound seemed to be coming through an amplifier.

Above timberline, the stunted white-bark pines, whose limbs cannot grow on the windward side of their trunks, gave way to outcroppings of rock and dwarf bushes at an elevation that is exposed to arctic gales. Rounding a switchback, I saw ahead a band of bighorn sheep, ewes and lambs, some lying down, some cropping the sparse, dry grass. They studied me as I advanced, coal-black eyes peering out of white faces, the short, slender and slightly curved horns of the ewes so unlike the massive full-curl horns of the monarch rams. In no great hurry, the resting animals got to their feet and in single file strolled out of sight over a saddle.

After hiking up Mount Washburn some years earlier, I had to admit to a geologist friend that I hadn't noticed the glacier scars on the rocks near the summit. Reminding me that Yellowstone is often called a geological park, he mentioned with pride that the Geological Survey had assigned sixteen scientists to conduct extensive studies in the park for *The Geologic Story of Yellowstone.* Why, I asked, would it take so many people?

He took me seriously, a failing of his kind, and yet his response suggested that geologists are deserving of sympathy. An infinite number of natural forces have successively altered every particle of Yellowstone, he informed me (and I'm compressing his explanation considerably). The evidence of every change was buried or removed by the next spasm. Then the glaciers rearranged what was left. I thought a naturalist presenting an evening campfire program put it even better. He said that explaining the geology of Yellowstone is like walking into the last scene of a movie and trying to figure out what has gone before.

Finally, the trail began to spiral around the rocky summit. The sky had turned gray, and the wind was a definite factor. Suddenly the square shape of the tower appeared, grown in size, a glass box on a platform. The site had originally been scraped flat to provide parking for horse-drawn vehicles and later for turn-around space for automobiles.

From the comments I'd heard around Mammoth, the seasonal ranger who had been on duty in the lookout tower for the past few summers operated in the style of Grover Whalen, New York City's famous greeter. "Lookouts generally run to solitary souls," a ranger told me. "This one's different." A casually dressed young man with a beard, large rimless glasses, and the kind of guileless face that fills old ladies with sentiment and supervisors with suspicion stood waiting at the top of the flight of stairs. I almost expected him to say, "Of all the lookout towers in all the mountains all over this land, you had to pick mine." Instead, he said, "Doug Haake. I've been watching you for the last half hour. Couldn't decide whether you were enjoying the scenery or just played out. Come in out of the wind."

Views from high places are better experienced than described. From Doug's aerie at the apex of Mount Washburn I had the feeling of being slung between earth and sky, with the panorama of a good part of Wyoming and Montana spread out below. No wonder the eagle soars, someone has said. Yellowstone was green forests and blue lakes and distant snow-laden mountains in all directions. The peaks of the Beartooths lay to the north. The Absarokas swept the eastern horizon, climbing to elevations above thirteen thousand feet in many places. On the west were the rocky summits of the Gallatins. In the near foreground the upper wall of the Grand Canyon of the Yellowstone showed some of the color that gave the river its name. Farther south the entire shoreline of Yellowstone Lake was in sharp focus. A hundred miles beyond were the peaks of the Tetons. Looking over my shoulder, Doug said, "It's a climax view."

For the ten- or twelve-week fire season Doug would live in a square room fifteen feet on a side, with glass walls, a linoleum floor, and no closet space. The furniture arranged around the perimeter formed a continuous work and storage space: a small table with a red-checked tablecloth held a pair of binoculars and a *Handbook of Emergency Medical Lore*, a double bed had a rolled-up sleeping bag on top of a faded blue quilt, and a bookcase was crammed with paperbacks. There was also an old four-burner electric stove and a couple of wooden chairs, originally blue. On the floor against a side wall were a tape deck and speakers and a professional first aid kit equipped with layered shelves, like a fishing tackle box. On the floor was the radio communication equipment, and the refrigerator and electric heater were in the rear. Numerous messages of good cheer and social commentary were taped to the walls: "The Golden Rule of Arts and Sciences: Whoever Has the Gold Makes the Rules."

An Osborne firefinder sat on a stand in the center of the room. The equipment is named for William B. Osborne, who as a young forester from Yale conceived the idea of building permanent lookout towers and invented the device that took the guesswork out of locating fires. Two metal sights rotate around a circular map of the park. Spotting a fire, the operator lines up the sights on the base of the smoke and relays the map bearing to the fire cache. Similar information from lookouts on Mount Sheridan to the south and Mount Holmes to the west enable the fire dispatcher to pinpoint the fire by triangulation.

By the middle of this century there were more than five thousand lookout stations, mostly in the West. The lonely, monotonous duty attracted all kinds and had a special attraction for writers, from Jack Kerouac to Edward Abbey. Now, active lookout towers are as scarce as covered bridges. The era ended when it became cheaper to send out an airplane after every thunderstorm, lightning being the cause of nearly all fires. Doug said that it takes a little practice before you can tell a forest fire from a family cookout.

Over a couple of hours a dozen or more hikers entered the tower and took by-golly looks at the world below. They were welcomed by a friendly ranger whose responses to their questions were as quick as treated charcoal. Doug was sinewy and cheeky and crackling with energy, and when he smiled you noticed a lower tooth that had taken its own direction. There's little going on in Yellowstone he hadn't heard about. He knew everybody's business, mine included. As keen as mustard, Mary would say.

A graduate of Miami of Ohio, Doug was in his third summer at the lookout tower, his sixth as a Yellowstone seasonal. "I'm going to keep coming back until they say, 'You're hired,'" he said when I asked his career plans. In every park you meet aspiring seasonals like Doug, men and women with attractive personalities, intelligence, and strong motivation who return year after year, determined to hang on until they can "go permanent." The rest of the year Doug worked on a mobile intensive care unit in Billings as an emergency medical technician, hoping to improve his credentials. Inability to bring in people with Doug's promise because of continuing budget cuts is a loss that concerns everyone.

Before leaving, I copied a sign that Doug had posted on the door of the tower. I repeat it here in its entirety:

NOTICE
Answers to Commonly Asked Questions
1. I'm fine how are you?
2. 10,243 FT. (3,112 m.)
3. No, I live here all summer.
4. Fire lookout.
5. Really, all summer.
6. 3.5 miles.
7. Good looks and fantastic personality.
8. Billings, Mont.
9. Single.
10. 6 yrs.
11. They bring up water. I brought up all my food for the summer.
12. In the pan.
13. In the pan.
14. In the pan.
15. A dinner date.
16. Never.
17. Sometimes.
18. I will, thanks.
19. Great, I'll be here.
20. Have fun, bye.

This piece of Haake whimsy played well on Mount Washburn, prompting smiles and comments from all. The questions are mostly obvious. Numbers 12, 13, and 14 were responses to those interested in where he washed his dishes, his laundry, and his person. Numbers 16 and 17 were catchalls for those who asked whether he ever became tired of the view or of the constant stream of visitors. Under hard interrogation Doug admitted that the questionnaire was a cover whose single purpose was to attract female companionship. "There's a lot riding on Number 15," he said. Not only did it produce desirable results, but many who responded also volunteered to bring the meal.

"Doug," I said, "you're putting me on." His eyes strayed briefly to a demure, dark-haired young woman sitting on a chair in the corner, boots propped on the electric heater and reading a Ngaio Marsh mystery. She had rewarded me with a winsome smile when I told her Marsh was one of my favorites. Trying to slip Doug the needle, I said it was beyond me why engaging young women would hike all the way up Mount Washburn to have dinner. "For the star show," he said solemnly. "Everyone says it's the best north of Kitt Peak."

I didn't like the look of the sky as I began my descent. "Storm brewing," Doug had advised. Earlier, the bank of clouds off to the west seemed as distant as a range of hills. Now they filled much of the sky, purplish and powerful. Wind gusts were strong enough to blow me off course. I was making for the shelter of a grove of alpine fir when the squall struck and the rain came sheeting down.

My windbreaker was better than nothing, but not by much. Soaked to the skin and chilled to the bone by the knifing wind, I took refuge under a conical fir. Fingers stiff from the cold had trouble with the zippers, but I managed to open the pack and exchange the useless windbreaker for a pullover.

Rather quickly, the rain gave way to whirling snow that turned the ground white. Preferring snow to drenching rain, I started on down the trail. In another mile the storm had blown through, and I finished the hike in warm sunlight. A light breeze helped to dry clothes and carried the fresh, clean smell of wet pine needles.

I silently blessed Hiram Chittenden, an engineer with imagination, who deserves a place among the truly remarkable figures of Yellowstone's history. After graduating near the top of his West Point class, he began his career with navigation and flood control duties on the Missouri River. A photograph taken at the time shows a man of evident refinement, with a carefully trimmed Van Dyck beard and a contemplative expression. You would guess him to be an intellectual. He was recalled from a vacation trip in Europe in 1891 to take charge of road and bridge construction in Yellowstone.

During a two-year tour he built a section of road across "that chaotic wilderness" between Old Faithful and Yellowstone Lake. He surveyed the route with a hand level, a five-foot staff, and the assistance of two laborers. As a base mark, he fastened a white cloth to a tall tree on the Continental Divide. After the park's construction funds ran out, he returned to river improvement duties. In his leisure hours he wrote *The Yellowstone National Park*, which introduced me to Yellowstone.

He came back to Yellowstone for his second tour resolved on a new approach. Instead of asking Congress for funds each year to do one more road section, he proposed that the Grand Loop and entrance roads be accomplished in one continuous operation. Persuasive as well as gifted, he guided "Uncle Joe" Cannon, speaker of the House of Representatives, through the park in 1901 and sold his vision to the crusty, tightfisted custodian of the U.S. Treasury. Yellowstone received five hundred thousand dollars a year for the next three years, a stupendous amount of money in those days, enabling Chittenden to complete the entire Yellowstone road system.

We are so accustomed to giant earth-moving equipment capable of slicing through a mountain range that it's hard to comprehend Chittenden's task. He smoothed a roadbed through rugged mountain terrain using only horse-drawn scrapers and plows, black powder, and hand labor. The work required 250 teams of horses and almost a thousand men wielding shovels and picks, husky recruits from local ranches and transients arriving each spring carrying their bedrolls. In later years the road was widened and upgraded for automobiles, alignments and grades were improved, and the developed areas bypassed. But the Grand Loop is still largely the road built by Hiram Chittenden and his crews in three summer seasons nearly a century ago.

The night before, in my snug apartment in Mammoth, I had promised myself that I would search out Aubrey's plow on the way down Mount Washburn. The storm distracted me, and the pledge was forgotten until I reached my car in the parking lot and saw Aubrey's book on the back seat. I didn't feel a bit like starting back up the trail. A little thought convinced me that it would clearly make more sense to give Aubrey a call in a day or two and get precise directions rather than go looking behind every clump of alpine fir on the south shoulder of Mount Washburn.

14

A Place That Takes You Back

The Park Point patrol cabin seemed small and unremarkable viewed from the lake, the red stain on the logs badly faded, the single window on the side wall off-center, and a weatherbeaten stovepipe sticking above the pitched roof. Facing southward, it stood in a small clearing halfway down the eastern shore of Yellowstone Lake, a solitary outpost at the edge of an unbroken forest that rolls away over higher and higher ridges. "On a peaceful summer day," John Townsley said, "it's hard to imagine what a welcome sight that cabin can be in January when you have skied down the lake, fighting wind and blowing snow all the way."

Declaring that I would never really understand the ranger heritage until I'd spent time in a patrol cabin, John had tried several times to schedule a visit to Park Point, but it hadn't worked out. Near the end of my summer in Yellowstone, on an August day that felt more like mid-October, we were on our way, traveling from Bridge Bay marina across Yellowstone Lake in a white Bertram cruiser with a searchlight and blue dome light mounted above the cabin and the name "Ranger" painted on the stern. Included in the party "for indoctrination," as John put it, were his new assistant superintendent, Ron Wrye, and a newcomer to the Denver regional office, personnel officer Doug Murphy.

Before we docked, John pointed out the landmarks: Frank Island four miles west, with tiny Dot Island in the background; Promontory Point to the south, dividing the lake's two south arms; and, west of it Flat Mountain, a tall peak overlooking the much smaller Flat Mountain Arm.

"If you include the surrounding mountains and tributary streams," John said, "Yellowstone Lake is a national park in its own right, probably less altered than any other big lake in the continental U.S." The lake, as clear as tap water, is busier and more dangerous than it looks. Canoeists are warned not to venture from the protected shoreline and to be mindful of squalls. Those who paddle the hundred-mile circuit and are not excessively disheartened by mosquitoes and biting flies have a good chance of seeing moose, elk, coyote, buffalo, beaver, otter, and muskrats, as well as California gulls, white pelicans, cormorants, mergansers, ospreys, and peregrine falcons.

At the cabin, a couple of hundred feet from the dock, John unfastened a padlock at the side window, swinging the heavy shutter open to let in some light. He had more trouble with the front door, covered with metal to discourage hungry bears. Above it was a white metal sign with green letters — "Park Point Patrol Cabin" — and a rusting horseshoe. A porch overhang protected the entrance from snow accumulation. Pushing the door open with his shoulder, John stepped back and said, "Welcome to the past."

I expected a rough-hewn interior offering shelter and little else. Instead, it was as neat and tidy as if it came fresh from the hands of an energetic housekeeper — or museum curator. A lot of necessary things — tools and equipment, beds and bedding, and cooking gear — were compactly arranged in a small space, about ten by fourteen feet. Almost all of the articles hung on the walls, there being no other place to put them. John's right, I thought. It's a place that takes you back.

Fascinated by the array, I took time during our stay to sketch the layout. Several large items did occupy floor space in front of the east wall. There was a square Majestic cookstove ("almost impossible to replace any more"). Beside it for quick heat was a small woodstove not much larger than its pipe sitting on a metal pad in front of aluminum foil insulation tacked to the wall. Alongside was a table holding a wash pan, bucket, and, in a cup, a bar of soap. Under the table was a woodbox filled with finely split kindling, and a garbage can marked "Stock Feed" held oats and had three heavy black rubber pans on top labeled "Good Year Rubber Trough No. 50."

On the east wall were two tea towels on a string behind the green Majestic stove; three cooking pots, from medium- to large-size; a baking pan and a dipper; four iron skillets, from medium-size to huge; a first aid kit, claw hammer, and hand axe; an assortment of pliers, wrenches, and screwdrivers; a double-bit axe in a leather holster; and a handsaw. On the west wall were a long-handled shovel and a bell on a loop of picket rope; next to the window were more picket ropes with straps and hobbles, two chairs, a mirror, and, leaning against the wall, three metal cots. On the north wall were firewood stacked high around a double window, a pair of snowshoes, and an orange crate nailed to the wall and containing the Park Point patrol cabin library: paperbacks by Alistair MacLean, James Michener, and Louis L'Amour and old issues (going back to 1962) of *Playboy*, *Mad*, *Outdoor Life*, *Sports Afield*, and *Life*. On the south wall beside the front door were two shovels, one for snow and one for digging; a red fire extinguisher; a box holding rolls of toilet paper and insect spray; and a large food cupboard lined against mice. On top of the cupboard was a box labeled "Emergency Medical Supplies," along with a Coleman Stove and a bag of cement mix. The door of the large cupboard opened outward to form a table. On the bottom shelf were plates, cups, and bowls old enough and heavy enough to have been army issue; a tray of knives, forks, and spoons; cooking spoons and spatulas; and more.

I will offer only a few examples of the surprising amount of food stored in the cupboard. On the top shelf were Bisquick and Cheerios, a box of instant dry milk that made fourteen quarts, Log Cabin syrup and Pream, Yuban instant coffee and Kool-Aid, boxes of Tide and plastic bottles of Satin Sheen detergent, steel wool soap pads and brown paper hand towels, and more. On the next shelf were Carnation, IGA, and Pet evaporated milk; quick-cooking oats and farina and rice; Janet Lee macaroni and cheese dinners; Robbins tea bags; strawberry, lemon, and butterscotch Jell-O and instant vanilla pudding; Tang packets ("it's popularity is fading"); and more. On the next shelf were Swiss Miss hot chocolate and regular grind Country Club coffee, Smuckers preserves and IGA jellies, Mountain House freeze-dried specialties ("everybody prefers cans"), and more. I have greatly condensed the inventory. By actual count, there were ninety-six items on three shelves. On a trip to Mary Mountain patrol cabin, chief ranger Roger Siglin surveyed the stores in that cabin and found 140 items.

Canned goods are kept in the grub box, or root cellar, located under the cabin floor to prevent freezing. The box held only cans of pork and beans, chili and beans, beef stew and luncheon meats ("the ham goes first"), and assorted fruits and vegetables. John explained that the sparse larder was due to the season. All cabins would be restocked by boat or pack train in the fall. These rations, he said, are for work parties, patrols, and emergencies. It occurred to me that the cabins are stocked with an ungodly amount of provisions considering how few emergencies there are and how rangers are always complaining that they have so little time to spend in the backcountry. At least they don't waste taxpayer money on gourmet fare.

The immutable cabin routine, John noted, is in part a legacy of the army rule of doing things by the numbers. "There's a way to split kindling and a way to make the beds." He pointed to the three mattresses hanging over a long wooden pole suspended from the ceiling, woolen army blankets, and thinner blankets, called "sheets," carefully folded over the mattresses. He gave us the drill for storing the bedding, which I forgot to write down. You fold the blankets and sheets twice lengthwise (I think), but I can't remember the most important part, the way the creases—or was it the folds?—go.

The army's bloody-minded ways did have something to do with survival, John said. Five soldiers are known to have died of exposure on winter patrols. He lifted the stove lid and showed us how the previous occupant had laid the fire with paper, fuzz sticks, and kindling. On the side of the stove, a short pine stick with holes drilled into it held a half-dozen kitchen matches upright. "In the old days a person might arrive from ski patrol exhausted, or maybe there had been an accident. Laying the fire this way was critical. Now, it's a courtesy. And a tradition. It can also be amusing. When you lay the fire in the morning before you leave the stove may still be hot. More than once I've heard the fire go whoosh! just as I was going out the door."

Six "snowshoe" cabins were built by the army in 1890 to put soldiers on equal footing with the wily poachers. (The Norwegian ski, eight to ten feet long, was then called a snowshoe.) Patrols were so successful that the number of cabins was increased to nineteen before the turn of the century. One of them was at Park Point. It recalls a time of grim winters and hard country, of isolation and boredom. As one who knew the life said, "too little mail and too much of the same faces."

There are now thirty or so active patrol cabins, with the additional construction done by rangers from plans carried in their heads. They still handle repairs and build replacements. Some cabins, not including Park Point, are occupied in the summer by seasonals to monitor backcountry use. All are used intermittently by maintenance crews doing trail repairs and by rangers on various missions. Cabins are for official use only, with the permission of the district ranger. It is understood, although not in writing, that they belong to the rangers.

Cabin happenings and comments on conditions in the backcountry are recorded in the lined pages of cabin logbooks, a practice initiated by the military. Each individual or party using a cabin is expected to make pertinent observations. Leafing through the pages and looking for familiar names is a lot like browsing through an old picture album. It's a pleasurable part of cabin routine.

As might be expected, Jerry Mernin watched over the patrol cabins like the conscience of Yellowstone. To leave a cabin in less than apple-pie order is to risk ostracism. At the moment he and John Townsley were feuding over custody of the logs. Believing them to be historical documents, John wanted them deposited in the archives and replaced with photocopies.

He'd encountered obstinate resistance. The rangers preferred the look and feel of the originals. "We're not backing down on this one," Jerry told me. "The originals give you direct contact with people you have known or known about. That's continuity to me. Put the copies in the archives. Leave the originals in the cabins."

On our return to Mammoth, John took the Park Point log along, to be replaced by a copy. It was an example of the heavy-handed, arbitrary style of management to which he frequently resorted, one that did not endear him to his subordinates. His father, with all of his good qualities, had expected his orders to be obeyed—and without a lot of conversation. So did John.

With time remaining before dinner, John was impatient to get started on a large tree that had blown down on the Thorofare Trail a few hundred yards from the cabin. I enthusiastically declined his offer to join the work party. I said I wanted to sit down with the Park Point log. It would be easier to hike the twenty-eight miles to the Thorofare patrol cabin than to work opposite John on a crosscut saw.

I found a comfortable seat in the sun on a stack of firewood and leaned back against the front wall of the cabin. Intermittently I would gaze out over Yellowstone Lake, the most majestic feature of the park. It would take a lifetime, John said, to witness all of the lake's moods, from serene calm to violent hostility, when its surface is covered with whitecaps. I could hear in the distance the ring of an axe and the two-stroke rasp of the misery whip. Butterflies flickered over the stretch of grass in front of the cabin, searching for flowers, vanishing momentarily as they landed and folded their wings before fluttering away. Two ground squirrels raced by, the leader holding his narrow margin all the way to the nearest lodgepole.

The green-bound ledger contained many hundreds of entries going back twelve years. Mostly they were matter-of-fact in tone, with frequent comments on the weather and a mention of workaday events. Others were chatty, descriptive, or wry. "In the six days we have been on this trail sighted only three elk," the south district trail crew reported on July 10, 1967. Moose were plentiful, the creeks full of spawning trout, but "dead elk along the trail probably died of loneliness."

An appreciative ranger saluted the view across Yellowstone Lake in October of that year after a snowfall the previous day. "A beautiful morning. Warm and comfortable in the sun. Mount Sheridan is wearing a frosting and a bald eagle is working his way back and forth along the shore. At 11:30 ice is still falling from the trees as it thaws out from yesterday." Nearing the end of a thirty-four-mile ride, Jerry Mernin checked out the cabin the same month and gave it a passing grade. "Stopped by for a snack on way from Thorofare to Ten Mile Post—to be a long day—was impressed by and grateful for the substantial supply of wood left by the maintenance crew. Thanks, Red."

Orville "Butch" Bach reported a close call on September 6, 1972: "Ran into a sow with cub at fifteen feet despite much noise—sow charged—thank God for trees nearby." Bach had received permission to use the patrol cabins while doing research for his *Hiking the Yellowstone Backcountry*, published the following year in the Sierra Club Totebook Series.

In his book, a valuable and concise guide, Bach mentions that cutthroat trout can be observed on spawning runs at the mouth of Meadow Creek, where it empties into the lake about a hundred yards from the cabin. At first light on the morning of July 10, 1973, a ranger was lying on the rocky beach, watching a procession of cutthroats only a few feet away straining to cross the sand bar blocking the mouth of the creek. She cheered one on for a half hour before it struggled over the barrier. "I was lying so close they would splash water on my face. It was one of the rarest sights, evoking the most unique emotions, I have ever experienced."

Vandalism of patrol cabins is virtually unknown, but grizzlies, with their incredible sense of smell, are attracted by the faintest odor of food. According to the old saying, if a pine needle falls in the forest the eagle sees it, the deer hears it, and the grizzly smells it. A ranger stocking lakeside cabins with food arrived at Park Point on October 15, 1973: "Clear Yellowstone fall day. Relieved to find cabin intact and not rampaged by bear as at Cabin Creek and Trail Creek." Those two patrol cabins are located about ten miles south of Park Point on the opposite sides of the Yellowstone River valley, where the stream empties into Yellowstone Lake.

By the time of the next entry, a week later, the grizzly had paid a visit to Park Point. "Door frame broken, teeth and claw marks around door, woodpile a mess, edge of roof shingles torn off—but bear unsuccessful. Saw fresh tracks of large grizzly sow and cub when hiking in." The following year a member of a trail crew working out of Park Point noted that after a pack horse died, "Bear dragged carcass into trees, dug hole, covered it entirely with dirt. We will be going to campsite 5L14 each evening to warn campers of increased bear danger."

Not all people who enter Yellowstone's backcountry regard it with reverence. "Turned around a horse party (eighteen stock) that was going to camp without a permit," indicated that a few are heedless or harebrained. So did "cited boat party for no life jackets, no camping permit, & dog." Even those with the best of intentions can wear the backcountry down if there are too many of them. In the summer of 1967 Jerry Mernin noted, "Area in pretty good shape considering fairly heavy use." In 1972 a ranger observed, "Many backpackers (too many!). Signs of many illegal campsites. The Point area could use a great deal of regular patrolling. To remain in present condition and usage will mean the loss of a beautiful area."

The last entry but one was a jaw-dropper. Not expecting anything so skittish, I assumed it to be a plant, maybe to give Mernin a conniption. I meant to show it to John but didn't. He would have probably threatened bodily harm to the ranger who entrusted the Park Point key to Carl and the temptress Sonika. "It's beautiful here," she wrote, "quiet and dream-like. I love nothing more than to awake after a great night's dream & hop into the cold crisp water. My body always feels real tingly and alive as do my thoughts. I feel comfortable and welcome here & beautiful. I love how I feel outside in the sun, barefooted & half naked." There was more, but let us not intrude.

At dinner the whopper steaks were pan-fried to perfection, rare and juicy, with a side of John's trademark thick-sliced potatoes and onions. Afterward we were content, sitting on logs around a campfire that leaped and sputtered as the resin bubbled out of the pinewood. Stars appeared in the darkening sky, and we listened to the who-who of a circling gray owl. For openers, and because John is a thoughtful host, he asked me if I'd en-countered a mention of Park Point in any of the historical narratives I'd been reading.

By chance I had, in Osborne Russell's *Journal of a Trapper.* A Maine farm boy who ran away to sea at the age of sixteen, Russell entered the Rocky Mountain fur trade in 1834 and joined a brigade led by Jim Bridger. He stayed in the mountains for nine years until the great westward migration began, keeping a journal that may be the most unembellished and reliable narrative of the trade.

Bridger set out on the fall hunt from the 1836 rendezvous on the Green River, taking sixty men and dispatching Russell and a small party to set a course for Yellowstone Lake and await his arrival. With fifteen men Russell trapped through Jackson Hole to the upper Yellowstone River and went into camp near the present Cabin Creek patrol cabin. There Bridger joined up, and the full brigade moved along the eastern shore of Yellow-stone Lake. Anyone lucky enough to have been present at Park Point on August 18, 1836, would have witnessed one of the grand sights of the fur trade era: a procession of seventy-five trappers mounted on spotted Indian ponies. The men would have been wearing wide-brimmed slouch hats, long coats called "capotes," heavy shirts, and buckskin breeches and moccasins; the rifles across their saddles would have been at the ready. They were a tough, case-hardened bunch led by Bridger, the mountain man personified and the greatest romancer of the West.

The tree removal operation that afternoon reminded John of a similar incident when he was a Yosemite ranger. A big red cedar had fallen on a trail near a backcountry cabin in his district. "That's your job," the chief ranger told him. "Cut it up and get it off the trail." John decided that there was an easier way. He drew a supply of blasting powder, cut down saplings and spaced them around the cabin to shield it from flying debris, and set the charges. The explosion exceeded his expectations by a factor of ten, blowing out every window in the cabin. He told the chief ranger that the tree had been taken care of, not mentioning the windows. "I heard you had a little trouble," the chief ranger replied. "You can draw the glass from the storehouse but don't do the work on government time." John laughed. "I lost a couple of weekends, but I learned a little about glazing."

John continued by paying tribute to several rangers he learned to admire while he was growing up in Yosemite:

> Sam King was one. He put in a number of years as a campground ranger—promotions were few then—but he stood out, becoming the first superintendent of Saguaro National Monument. The custodian before him must have been a low-profile kind of guy, and nobody in Tucson knew the Park Service was around until Sam reported for duty. I was traveling in the Southwest sometime later and stopped by monument headquarters to see him. He asked me had I ever been to a Rotary luncheon, and I said, "No, I'm sure I haven't." And he said, "Well, I'll take you to one."
>
> If you've ever gone to a Rotary luncheon, you've never gone to one with a man in tennis shoes and a business suit, who, on the way to the luncheon, hitched the water trailer to a dump truck and went by way of the golf course for a load of water so he wouldn't have to make two trips. The tennis shoes were for climbing up on top of the water trailer. And then he proceeded to park the rig in front of the largest hotel in downtown Tucson, with a goodly number of Rotarians helping him squeeze it in. And as he walked through the lobby you could see groups breaking up so they could say hello to Sam King. He had an exuberance about him that you could feel.

John rearranged his considerable bulk on the log seat and positioned his legs comfortably. It was story time. We weren't impatient as the hours passed, captured by his memories and by the companionable noises of the fire. The outline of the cabin would fade in the darkness until someone threw more wood on the glowing ashes and the fire would flare again. I was able to make a few notes. I also referred to John's oral history interview in the archives and may have added a few touches he forgot to include.

I'd never heard John talk much about his father, Forest Townsley, and I asked him how "the Chief," as he was known throughout the Park Service, had become Yosemite's first chief ranger. He said that his father had suffered from an infection as a child on a homestead in Nebraska, a condition so severe his parents loaded their possessions on a wagon and moved to the healing springs at Sulphur, Oklahoma.

Bought from the Choctaw and Chickasaw tribes by the federal government, the thirty-odd sulphur springs and 640 acres were designated Platt National Park (a dubious move not corrected until the area was expanded and renamed Chickasaw National Recreation Area) when Oklahoma was admitted to the Union in 1906. John's father was employed by the park as a patrolman. A few years later the position of superintendent became vacant. John gave us his version of a letter of endorsement for his father submitted to the secretary of the interior by a local politician:

> The reasoning went something like this. Number one, my father was not only a good patrolman, but he was also an excellent cement mason and had been building the bridges in the park. If he succeeded to the superintendency he could continue the patrol work and the bridge construction and the superintendent's job, all in the body of one man. And further to qualify him, he had his own house, which would allow them to sell the superintendent's house and use that money to pay his salary. Lastly, to the best of the supplicant's knowledge, he was a pretty good Republican around town.

He heard of a ranger vacancy in Yosemite in 1913, was accepted, and promoted to chief ranger in 1915. John recalled:

> I suspect the real love of my father's life was horses. He had a little ranch near Mariposa, thirty miles from the park entrance, where he bred horses. We were always horse poor. Sometimes it would be six or eight or up to twenty, but there were always horses around.
>
> I'm sure he expected me to be the kind of horseman he was, and he would take me along on trips with him when I was eight or nine. He was riding and I was running along behind. We used to go to Merced Lake, about fifteen miles from the valley, and he didn't like pack mules to carry too much weight going up the steep stretch out of the valley. But when we reached Nevada Falls, if I wanted a ride all I had to do was get on one of those big packs resting on a set of sawbucks. He called that tag along, going back to his youth, I guess, when that was common for kids.
>
> One night we were bringing a stallion he called Ranger One from the

ranch at Mariposa to Big Meadows up the Colterville grade, the first
stagecoach road into the park. It was steep and narrow, and there were
drop-offs and many places cars couldn't pass. It was about two in the
morning—it was always that time when we were coming home from
the ranch—and he said, "Well, the old Studebaker will never pull the
horse and trailer up that hill. You get out and lead the stallion. I'll drive
ahead, and we'll load him back on the trailer at the top." I can remember
pretty vividly the moon and the stallion and the narrow road and nobody
around. Nothing occurred, but I was about nine years old, and my heart
was in my mouth.

There is a photograph of John's father standing beside Eleanor Roosevelt at a picnic lunch in Yosemite's Mariposa Grove of giant sequoias. In
full uniform he was a tall, powerfully built man who held himself proudly.
The resemblance to John was striking. John remembered the occasion.
His father had escorted Mrs. Roosevelt and her party on a camping trip
into the backcountry. To show her gratitude, she invited the families of the
rangers who had accompanied her—young John included—to a "social" at
the Ahwahnee Hotel. She was so taken with Chief Townsley that she wrote
two of her syndicated "My Day" columns about him and the camping experience.

In his father's day, John said, Yosemite was a favorite destination of the
Hollywood movie colony, easily accessible while New York was three days
by train. The film people enjoyed his father's company, he thought, because he was able "in a personal way to share his love for Yosemite. I think
they were very much struck by his honesty." One of John's prized possessions was the old family guest book containing the names of many of the
stars of the silver screen. One suspects that John's father decided early on
that self-reliance and diligence—and being himself—were his strong suits.

My dad liked to fish and had been involved in the planting of golden
trout in the high barren lakes in the early years. These fish achieved phenomenal growth. Upper Fletcher Lake near Vogelsang Peak had a nice
population of goldens, not real large but they still retained their color,
and it was one of my dad's favorite places in Yosemite.

One day in August of 1943 he got a county health nurse who was a
close family friend and a couple of rangers and simply stopped what he
was doing and said, "We're going to Upper Fletcher and go fishing."
You almost have to assume that he was going to get there one more time.
They got to the lake, and he caught two fish, and then he went over and
sat down on a rock and passed away. I choose to think he had a prior

heart attack or sensed one was coming. It was characteristic of him that instead of going to bed or to a doctor he went to a place that was eleven thousand feet high and did what he wanted to do and that was that.

Many more stories followed. After a while, to ease cramped legs and a numb bottom, I strolled off from the fire to observe the sky. The half-moon was of lesser wattage than the Milky Way, a glittering river of cold white stars flowing across the sky. What, I wondered, is the attraction of tales about people you have never met? It must be that we love beyond the telling things that have vanished and the brief contact with people we wished we had known.

As we prepared to turn in, John insisted that his guests take the three cots. I accepted gladly. After seven or eight miserable nights on sandbars floating the Charley River in Alaska a few years earlier, I'd decided I'd had enough. I carried a cot and bedding out under the overhang, and John unrolled his sleeping bag beside me. "What if a hungry grizzly should come calling?" I asked. "Ah, if a hungry grizzly should come calling," he answered, making it sound like an event worth waiting up for.

I had trouble falling asleep. The sounds of the forest were unfamiliar. The moon entangled in pine branches cast dark shadows, and just before I dropped off I thought I heard the wailing call of a loon far out in the lake. The rustling that awakened me was not in the trees but from a large and indistinct shape advancing toward me. I was on the point of yelling to John that his desired guest had arrived when a shaft of moonlight revealed the presence of a mule deer.

When I threw back the covers at daybreak, my bare feet landed on grass stiff with frost. John didn't stir. From my pack underneath the cot I pulled out a turtleneck, corduroy pants with the extra pockets where important objects can be stored if you have any, thick wool socks, and a down jacket. Lacing my boots, I went out into the morning light.

A thick morning mist blanketed the lake. In the east, the mountains were purple against a brightening sky. Keeping to the shoreline, I moved at a brisk pace. The western sky turned from gray to pale yellow to light blue. Returning to the cabin area, I could hear someone ask John, "Do I have the creases pointing in the right direction?" Beside the cabin a blazing fire was sending up smoke signals. A charitable soul had lined up a can of Carnation and a jar of sugar on a handy log, and a blackened old coffee pot was catching the heat from the coals.

It always happens when you find yourself way off in the middle of nowhere on a bracing morning and catch the tantalizing smell of coffee brewing over a fire. It makes you realize how simple your wants really are. I warmed my hands around the thick mug and sipped steaming cowboy coffee laced with cream and sugar. The mist was lifting all around the lake, the exposed surface sparkling in the rising sun. Never had coffee tasted so good. Never had the world seemed so exceptional.

15

Take Down Flag & Feed Horses

Four years after my summer in Yellowstone, on September 19, 1982, Mary and I flew from Dulles Airport to Denver, drove over Trail Ridge Road in Rocky Mountain National Park, staying the night in Granby. It was the first day of a pleasurable week enjoying the fall colors in the Colorado Rockies. It was also the day John Townsley died in St. Vincent's Hospital at Billings.

I didn't see John during his year-long illness. I had received several reports, including one from director Russ Dickenson. "John made a trip to Washington to see me last winter after he learned he had terminal cancer. He told me all he knew, down to the estimate of how much time he had left. He wanted to stay on the job as long as possible, or, as he put it, so long as he gave good measure. He didn't want sympathy and didn't give me an opening to offer any. He finished the conversation by saying he didn't want to hear another goddamned word on the subject."

By summer John was losing weight steadily and driving to Billings for chemotherapy. "They're turning me into a DuPont product," he commented. Later in the summer, after he was hospitalized, Russ traveled to Billings to see him. "Weak as he was he insisted I crank up the bed so we could talk. He started out whispering but somewhere he found a little reserve of energy when I told him of the latest Park Service news. His mind was clear but he seemed to have turned inward."

The memorial service was held in the broad, green median of the boulevard at Mammoth. John would have called it a super day, with a few high clouds in a blue sky. Regulations permitting the American flag to be flown at half-mast on federal reservations only to honor national figures and when specifically authorized were ignored. The park's huge ceremonial flag was flying at half-mast. Twenty rangers in full uniform were drawn up in a semicircle behind the flagpole. John's family and a few old friends sat on folding chairs facing several hundred people standing under the cottonwoods. In keeping with John's known preferences, the service was informal and nondenominational.

John and Elaine's two sons, Forest and David, and their daughter, Gail, sat with their mother. Gail had not returned to college in order to be with her father, working as a waitress for the concessioner as her mother had done in Yosemite before marrying John. Gail told a friend that she had not really known her father until the final months and that he had taught her about courage.

David was in the uniform of a Marine Corps officer. The summer I lived in Yellowstone he had just graduated from Cornell and was training hard for a berth on the U.S. eight-oared shell in the coming 1980 Olympics. He survived all but the final elimination trials. Those who had known John in his youth said David was the spitting image of him when he entered the Marines in World War II. In his remarks David said that his father had always told him it was important to be able to speak well in public. He apologized for his performance—judged by all to be blameless—saying that although he had been practicing hard he wasn't there yet.

Forest, named for John's father, was a teacher in the Denver school system. He said that his father seemed to be interested in almost everything, seldom returning from a trip without bringing a remembrance. The family was suffering the consequences of John's curiosity. They were in the midst of sorting through the bits and pieces he had squirreled away, unable to figure out why so many unrelated items were important to him. They had found a hoard of ski wax, for example, that Jerry Mernin thought would supply the entire ranger staff for years.

Ken Ashley, a prototype ranger and one of John's oldest and closest friends, recalled that he and John and a couple of other young rangers had formed a kind of fraternity while serving together at Yosemite early in their careers. They had the misfortune to work for a crusty supervisory ranger who felt obliged to spell out all instructions in excruciating detail. If he went to town for one day he would post a list of the same old duties. The last item was always "Take Down Flag & Feed Horses," and it rankled the most. Insulted and then merely exasperated by constant repetition of the obvious, they eventually appreciated the absurdity of their position and adopted TDF & FH as their rallying cry.

All went on to successful careers. In correspondence or talking on the telephone, they would sign off with "TDF & FH." I encountered the slogan for the first time in the Park Point log, in an entry dated February 2, 1977: "A great occasion! John Townsley, Glenn Gallison and Ash Ashley ski together once again after a quarter of a century. Lake surface made for superb skiing. TDF & FH!" The entry caught my attention partly because Glenn Gallison and I had attended a training course together during his tenure in Yosemite and become friends. John explained the origin of the slogan and then picked up the log and read the entry, savoring the memory.

In Ashley's narrative in the archives he speaks of the time he and John finished checking the snow gauges at Tuolumne Meadows during a Yosemite ski patrol. "We were feeling good, and we just skied right down into the Valley, forty-two miles in one day. John and I always got a kick talking about that trip." He ended his remarks at the memorial service, and lost his composure, when he said, "Goodbye old friend. TDF and FH."

U U

The week following the memorial service I drove from Bozeman to Yellowstone under clouds that hid the mountains and threatened more snow. I was attending a meeting of the naturalists, historians, and archeologists of the Rocky Mountain region. Back in July when I accepted an invitation to speak, I'd hoped the occasion would provide an opportunity to see John.

The young man behind the Hertz counter in the Bozeman airport said that several inches of snow had fallen during the night, but the temperature was above freezing and I shouldn't hit anything worse than slush on the way to Yellowstone. The snow hadn't melted at all on the long upward slope to Bozeman Pass. Some drivers were putting on chains in the parking bays marked for that purpose. My little Nissan performed an extended and graceful fishtail going over the pass, and I feared for the steep grades in Yellowstone.

Conference sessions were held in the auditorium of the Mammoth Hotel, a spacious room with polished, hardwood floors. An enormous map of the United States all but covers one wall, and inlaid wood of varying colors designate the states. Spanish galleons under full sail lurk offshore. Rows of gray metal folding chairs faced the carpeted stage. Entering the room, I heard the pleasant din created by colleagues glad to be together again. They came from parks as distant and diverse as Glacier on the Canadian border, with its famous Going-to-the-Sun Road, and Hovenweep National Monument, New Mexico, whose standing towers built by pre-Columbian tribes in the Four Corners area are twenty-five miles by graded dirt road from the nearest highway.

One of the objectives of the conference organizers was to brighten the outlook of the participants. On a sad and profoundly unjust day for the Park Service two years before, president-elect Ronald Reagan had met with Jim Watt, who hoped to be appointed secretary of the interior. In his allotted fifteen minutes Watt described what he would do to the bureaucrats and environmentalists. By Watt's own account, Reagan's reply was, "Sic 'em." Addictively combative and a master of the genial insult, Watt declared upon taking office, "I will bend the employees of this department to my will." A Park Service old-timer said, "He must be kidding. Even the director wouldn't dare say that."

The organizer of the conference hoped that my keynote address might give participants a lift. By reminding them that the Park Service had accomplished good things in the past and would surely do so again, I may have diverted them momentarily. Of much greater concern were the severe budget and manpower cuts imposed by an administration committed to getting government off of the backs of the citizens.

The deputy regional director, Jim Thompson, welcomed the participants to the conference. Temporarily serving as Yellowstone's superintendent, Jim had a disconcerting habit of speaking candidly. For the foreseeable future all parks would be on short rations, he said. Orders from the department were to do more with less. The next summer, for example, Yellowstone would be hiring a hundred fewer seasonal rangers, naturalists, and maintenance workers than it had two years earlier. He said that every Friday afternoon he and regional director Lorraine Mintzmyer set aside five minutes to discuss good news. Mostly they had to stretch the material to fill the time slot.

That night at a barbecue supper, with help from Jim and Lorraine, spirits picked up. Pinto beans, beef, tomatoes, and chili peppers achieved fusion, the keg beer was so satisfying that you didn't mind the paper cups, and Jim slipped the strap of a guitar over his head and had every toe in the room tapping. Lorraine broke into an exuberant clog dance, the high point of the evening. Principled, capable, and warm-hearted, Lorraine had started at the bottom and overcome obstacles not encountered by male colleages.

I had distributed a questionnaire to the participants in advance of the conference, not knowing what to expect, and I shared the results as a part of my remarks. The final question invited respondents to make a general comment on their predicament. Said one, "We are bloodied but undefeated." Said another, "All you can do is pull up your socks and get on with it." There was also plenty of frustration. As someone wrote, "Transfers and promotions are things we read about in history books." But the old mystique was clearly evident. Another said, "The greatest part of working for the National Park Service is my pride in what the Service is and stands for." "This organization is still full of people with high ideals, social consciousness and creativity. They respond to the slightest encouragement," volunteered another. Implicit in their comments, or so it seemed to me, was an appeal: Spare us the political ideologues who use their power over government agencies to settle old scores.

The second day of the conference was the kind of day you don't venture out unless you have good reason. It was wet and cold, the blustery wind bringing swirling snow flurries. I checked the weather bulletin in the chief ranger's office and quickly abandoned my plan to tour the park. Snow was falling in all locations above seven thousand feet, which takes in most of Yellowstone south of Mammoth. Both Dunraven Pass to the east and Craig Pass south of Old Faithful were closed. A good time to get acquainted with the chief ranger, Tom Hobbs, I decided.

On the morning of September 30, the official end of the fire season, his office was a busy place. Fifteen fire control specialists were being terminated. The three fire towers were being mothballed and the lookouts taken out, some by pack train. The seven-person helicopter crew responsible for helicopter operations was also being disbanded. Between June 15 and that day, the big chopper had been used on fires, search and rescue missions, and medical evacuations. The money kept in reserve to handle an emergency was given to Geological Survey researchers, who would use the helicopter for five hours that day to calibrate instruments measuring thermal flow in a distant geyser field.

Tom welcomed me, explained that he had a few things to do, "mostly a matter of going around with a pointed stick, tidying things up," and invited me to sit in on the proceedings. His office was supplied with government-issue furniture: a desk equipped with three telephones and several armchairs around a coffee table. On the walls were the usual ranger artifacts: possibly the largest rack of elk antlers ever found in Yellowstone, a six-foot-high map of the park marked with red, black, and yellow grease pencil, and a battered wooden sign on which the words "Pitchstone Plateau Trail" were barely legible. The elements had fretted away most of the paint, and something, no doubt a bear, had knocked off both ends of the sign.

For more than an hour Tom worked steadily through his agenda, consulting with staff members standing by. One of them invited me to go up to the lunchroom for coffee. He talked about the demonstration when Watt had visited the park that summer:

> Conservationists, including many concession employees, were waiting
> for him at Old Faithful. His aides were beside themselves. You can't be-

lieve their attitude toward people who are against Watt. They demanded the rangers keep them and their signs out of camera range. What a hope!

There were crews from the major television networks, from Denver and Salt Lake, even one from West Germany. It was a media event and there were some great signs, like "Save a Tree! Axe Watt!" The best cartoons were in the dormitories and the hotel kitchens. Almost every concession employee signed a Sierra Club petition calling for Watt to be fired. I didn't sign because I didn't think it would be ethical. There's no use getting bent out of shape by Jim Watt, but appointing him secretary of the interior was an act of contempt.

The staff ranger would, I said, have enjoyed the demonstration against President Richard Nixon at the dedication of the Museum of Immigration in the base of the Statue of Liberty. It was July 4, 1972, and Nixon was gearing up for his reelection campaign. The celebration drew a large crowd, mostly pro-Nixon but with a lively group of young people carrying anti-Nixon and anti-Vietnam War placards. The master of ceremonies was regional director Chet Brooks, a historian by training known to be loyal but not compliant. Having parachuted into France on D-Day, he wasn't easily intimidated. Nixon's supporters greeted their hero with chants of "Four More Years!" They were drowned out by the shouts of "No More! No More!" That was music to my ears, Chet said, only partly because the young man leading the opposition was his son.

By the time I returned to his office Tom had reached the last item on his list. Bear 81, a grizzly, had smashed the windows or pulled off the doors or wrecked the interiors of eight vehicles in the Bridge Bay campground. He had also banged up two motorcycles and totaled a canoe for no known reason. In the discussion of alternatives one ranger proposed a simple solution. Close the Bridge Bay campground, reopen the Grant Village campground twenty miles down Yellowstone Lake, and move the residents of Bridge Bay to Grant Village. Tom thought a long moment of the dislocations involved and then said, "Let's give Bridge Bay back to the bears." It took a while to work out the necessary arrangements.

When John had selected Tom to replace Roger Siglin two years earlier, he must have liked his size—extra-large. He was well above six feet, big-framed and avuncular. One of the reasons I took to Tom was that he resembled a favorite teacher, an English professor at Gettysburg College, and had the same relish for good language and fondness for the word *gentleman*. He had grown up in "the hills of West Virginia," the son of a biology teacher, and was a graduate student in botany at the University of Kentucky in 1961 when hired as a seasonal at Mammoth Cave. He became a spelunker, helped map new caverns, and decided that he liked ranger work. The next summer Appomattox Court House needed a botanist to help restore the historic scene. A few months later, in time to celebrate Thanksgiving at Mesa Verde, he joined the ranger ranks.

"When John talked to me about this job I had reservations. I knew the stories of what he was like to work for." He smiled and said it wasn't until he came to Yellowstone that he heard the one about the ranger at Mount Rainier John had tried to recruit for Yellowstone. "The ranger turned down John's offer, saying his children were doing so well in school he and his wife didn't want to move them for a few more years. The real reason came out when a friend asked him why he turned down a promotion and a chance to work in Yellowstone. He said, 'I'm too old to work for John Townsley. After all, I'll be thirty-five next year.'"

That Tom had his own differences with John was confirmed, I thought, by what he left unsaid. He was about the only ranger to whom I'd talked who didn't lash out about something John had said or done. Tom's role, standing between an impatient and demanding taskmaster and a ranger staff aggrieved by John's ways, must have put some extra bricks in his knapsack.

He never sugarcoated his orders and like all perfectionists he was hard to please. But I could not have imagined the man's intensity, and I admire what he did for this park. He was never casual about Yellowstone.

Watt was pushing the Forest Service to approve more than a hundred and fifty leases filed by oil companies that would have opened the Washakie Wilderness, just outside Yellowstone, to roads and oil rigs. All superintendents had been warned by the director that if they opposed secretarial policy they did so at their own peril.

Despite the ban, when John was asked for a public statement about the Washakie he didn't equivocate, Tom said, and read from a document on his desk: "The long-term effects created by the impact of energy development would be devastating to the critical wildlife habitat and would destroy the wilderness value in this wild, remote and incredibly scenic area adjoining Yellowstone National Park."

I asked Tom how John got along with Watt, and he told me of the VIP snowmobile tour that John had arranged for the local congressional delegation. It was Christmas week, a time when members of Congress are home and receptive to free vacations. The distinguished group included Sen. Malcolm Wallop and Rep. Dick Cheney of Wyoming, two representatives from Idaho, a governor, and Jim Watt, along with spouses and aides. The tour began with breakfast for twenty-five in John's kitchen.

As you would expect, John dressed for the occasion—in long johns and overalls. It made quite a picture, John at the stove in his bare feet, frying bacon, everyone standing around drinking coffee and watching. He used slab bacon, cutting the slices three times as thick as the store variety. He had a big old camp fry pan, well-blackened by smoke, that covered two burners. Those who knew the drill ate the bacon out of the skillet as fast as he finished a batch. Those who didn't had a story to tell.

He did the eggs the way we often do around a campfire for easy handling. You tear a hole in the middle of a thick slice of bread, frying the egg and bread together. One of the congressmen tried his hand, at John's urging, and burned the bread. John said that was just the way he liked his toast, gave himself a generous helping, and filled the plates of the people next to him.

There were some high jinks when Jerry Mernin and I introduced them to their snowmobiles, but they soon caught on, and away we went. The weather was made to order, the wildlife was plentiful, and the exhilaration level was beyond our expectations. After dinner that night at the Snow Lodge in Old Faithful we sat on the floor around the piano in the lobby, singing Christmas carols. John made a welcoming speech, the kind of thing he did so well. He went around the circle, greeting every person by name, thanking each member of Congress and each aide individually, recalling some specific instance when they had been of help to Yellowstone. You would have been proud of him that night.

The next morning Watt was showing off and somehow managed to run off the road and bury his machine in a snowdrift. This after boasting he was good enough to earn a living as a ranger. I got the feeling he's much given to falling into traps of his own making. He took a razzing from his companions that went on for a long while. On most matters John was loyal to the secretary, his commanding general. I thought he might do something to even things up.

He stopped the procession at West Thumb to look at the colorful hot pools and maneuvered Watt's principal tormentors to the head of the line. Approaching Bridge Bay, he signaled the leaders to take Gull Point Drive, a spur road seldom plowed that runs along the shore of the lake. They turned off, sailed along for a little, and almost disappeared when they hit the deep snow. You should have heard the ribbing they got when they crawled out. Jerry and I could have killed John. It was hard labor to get those machines back on the road again. After the tour I said to John, "That was an unusual thing you did at Gull Point."

He said he felt bound to support Watt because he was the secretary of the interior, and that Watt was a nice enough guy to be around, mostly, except when he was pushing his political agenda. John seemed to be searching for something else to say that would give Watt a little but not too much. Watt's companions were undoubtedly aware of what John had done and why he did it. I can't say the same for Watt, who doesn't deal in subtleties.

∪ ∪

Walking out of the administration building to my car, I didn't like the look of the dark clouds as they tore this way and that, spitting snow. Sometimes, but not this visit, fall in Yellowstone can be glorious. The roads are almost empty, the villages deserted, and the air invigorating. You hear strange sounds, the wild clamor of Canada geese who have decided to stay the winter and the bugling of a bull elk watching proudly, or fearfully, over his harem. The red and brown shades of willow and alder are nothing like the brilliant colors of eastern hardwoods, but the shimmering gold of the aspen lights up the hillsides.

Leery of how the car would perform but wanting to see something of the park, I set out on a test run to the Golden Gate, five miles to the south and a thousand feet higher. Halfway to the top, in an abundance of snow, I was having difficulty maintaining headway. I was sitting in front of a control panel borrowed from the space shuttle, and I had no traction. I made it to the top, a triumph of prayer over physics, and headed back to Mammoth.

Driving down officers' row past the superintendent's residence, I noticed that John Townsley's nameplate had not yet been removed from beside the front door. I'd seen him for the last time at a dinner party here two years earlier. According to my notes, it was August 26, 1980, and the other guest was Joan Anselmo, the newly appointed information officer. It's a demanding job. Anything that happens in Yellowstone attracts media attention. A dark-haired young woman who looked as though it would take a lot to upset her, Joan had earned John's trust.

Elaine, who served an elk roast that put steamship round to shame, had taken courses at the Yosemite Institute that summer, and she proudly corrected John on a point of geology. John was wearing his special string tie, the one with the gold moose head on the clasp. He stood at the head of the table and smiled down on us, drawing his carving blade expertly over the sharpening steel and telling us of the time he had dressed out an elk with a pocket knife, or maybe it was a nail clipper.

After dinner, cupping a wine glass in those massive hands, he said he'd just received a letter from the Park Service patriarch, Horace Albright, enclosing a *Los Angeles Times* story he'd discovered in his files that reported the death of John's father. We trooped across the entrance hall to the library, a warm-looking room lined with bookshelves, comfortable chairs, and a painting of John's father above the fireplace. The headline of the clipping, "Yosemite Park Ranger Chief Dies on Fishing Trip," was followed by a subhead, "Forest Townsley, Known to Great, Collapses on Shore of High Lake."

I'd never seen the family guest book, and at my request John took it down from the shelf, a large, old-fashioned volume with a brown cover. As he was putting on his Ben Franklin reading glasses, one of Eleanor Roosevelt's "My Day" columns, written in April 1940, dropped out. I copied one paragraph: "Chief Ranger Townsley gave me five perfect days of camping in the High Country and an unforgettable day in the Valley. He has the kindest face I know and the most humor, yet the eyes look you so straight in the face that I should hate to meet up with him if I had wished to hide anything. He gives you a sense of strength — one of those men you would like to have with you in a tight place."

The entries, on pages ornamented with scrollwork, were not chronological. People could sign wherever, many electing to sign next to an old friend. "My father was not an autograph seeker," John said. "It didn't matter whether I was having a birthday party and a kid signed it or whether it was the president of the United States. No one was invited to sign unless there was a nice meal, shared by all, and a personal relationship."

I didn't need to inquire whether President Jerry Ford had been given the opportunity to sign when he came to Yellowstone during his 1976 campaign against Jimmy Carter. It was billed as a "return home" because Ford had worked as a Yellowstone seasonal in 1936, and his son Jack had done the same. John introduced Ford, who promised, if elected, an appropriation of $2.5 billion for the parks and wildlife refuges. Although grateful for his election-time conversion, Park Service people figured he did well to get through his speech with a straight face. He had never lifted a finger to help the parks during thirty years in Washington. "I didn't gather from talking to him that Yellowstone was a milestone," John said.

Leafing through the guest book and tracing the signatures with a finger, John called out a few names. "Here's Tom Mix, the most popular cowboy of silent pictures. Here's Jean Harlow, who had It, and Shirley Temple who didn't. Here's J. Edgar Hoover and the Crown Prince of Japan, and, God Almighty, here's Rin Tin Tin." He paused over the name of Luther Tibbs. "Luther helped me out of a scrape once. Some day I'll tell you a great story about Luther Tibbs. Here's a cartoon by John Barrymore." Cleverly done, it showed the famous Jeffrey pine on Sentinel Dome in Yosemite and Barrymore, his arm around John's father, and was captioned, "Chief, on a clear day you can see Catalina."

The Ford mention prompted John to reach for a box of photographs taken during a visit by another president, Jimmy Carter, in 1978. Vacationing with his family in Grand Teton, a park not renowned for its fishing, Carter was persuaded to combine a day of sight-seeing with some serious fishing in Yellowstone. The Carters arrived by helicopter at the Southeast Arm of Yellowstone Lake "ready to fish and dressed like tourists," according to John, who was waiting with Elaine to greet them. In the pictures the president, who looked relaxed, is wearing denim pants and a white polo shirt and carrying the rods in metal cases. Rosalyn Carter wore a red T-shirt, white slacks, and white tennis shoes without socks. The tranquillity of this remote corner of the lake was preserved when the helicopter carrying the pool of reporters and photographers was stranded by mechanical difficulties.

There was a complete lack of tension once introductions had been made, John said. The Carters were friendly and curious, interested in everything they saw. Eleven-year-old Amy seemed remarkably unaffected by the punishing scrutiny of the White House press. John speculated that her nanny, Mary Fitzgerald, may have deserved some of the credit. "You're falling asleep," Mary told her sharply as the cutthroats took their time biting. "I am not, I'm trying not to scare them away," Amy retorted. Excited to have caught the first fish, she was aggrieved a little later, after reeling in a sizable cutthroat, to learn of Yellowstone's thirteen-inch maximum limit. "Why do I have to throw the big ones back," she demanded. "I've never fished anywhere that you had to throw the keepers back."

The lunch served on a picnic table beside the lake was pronounced "a winner" by the president. Elaine had prepared her special potato salad, fried chicken, and chocolate chip cookies. Amy politely asked to help and was given the chore of sprinkling sunflower seeds on the potato salad. She shook the dispenser so violently the salad was immersed in seeds when the top came loose. Mary Fitzgerald came to the rescue, the excess seeds were removed, and Elaine's spirits soared when Rosalyn asked for the potato salad recipe. John took a liking to Amy. "Quick, spirited, and outspoken," he said, recognizing a kindred spirit.

John also had a special treat for the occasion. He mentioned to Carter that no president had ridden a horse in Yellowstone since Teddy Roosevelt in 1903. Two horses were handy, should the president be interested. "A wonderful experience," Carter told him after they cantered along the shore of the lake, "one I will long remember."

Yes, John said, it was a super day. The Carters had gone on to Old Faithful, enjoying every minute of their walk through the geysers and their conversations with fellow tourists. But something seemed to be eating him about the presidential visit. Slamming the box of photographs back on the shelf, he came out with it. "Jesus Christ! Can you believe it? Two of my rangers put in for overtime pay on the day the president visited the park!" As he went on stowing away the guest book carefully, I said to myself, "John, you're old Park Service, and there can't be many left like you."

∪ ∪

I find I've written more about John than I'd planned. He was certainly an intriguing personality, yet there were many Park Service people as worthy of being profiled. He had impressive qualifications, but if a poll had been taken of his peers to pick the best superintendent he would not have won.

Many reasonable people in Yellowstone heartily disliked him and his management style. "He can be an unfeeling bastard," said one ranger. "If he wants a thing done he says 'Do it.' He couldn't care less how many twelve-hour days it takes. Maybe he remembers to thank you and maybe he doesn't." Tom Hobbs saw both sides of John. When Tom's young son was severely injured and required prolonged rehabilitation, John could not have devoted more time or shown more compassion. But one day he caught a ranger in full uniform wearing his hat indoors. In the busy lobby of Old Faithful Inn John dressed him down like a drill sergeant. The ranger was so stunned he never did take off his hat. "A lot of us felt John's wrath," Tom said. "He seemed incapable of saying 'I'm sorry.'"

To keep the record straight, the Park Service would not have demanded a reckoning from the Yellowstone Park Company had John not been the tenacious advocate. For too many years, General Host, the corporate owner of this derelict concession afflicted with a terminal case of fustiness, had delayed maintenance indefinitely while racking up profits. "Not because of good service or quality facilities," a Park Service study team commented, "but because the thousands of visitors who enter Yellowstone National Park have no other place to eat or sleep. Without a captive audience, and in a competitive situation outside of the park environment, the company could not survive." With the approval of Congress, the Park Service bought out the Yellowstone Park Company in 1979, leasing the facilities to a reputable firm and requiring restoration of the great old hotels to their original condition. Food and lodging are now first class, for which John deserves much of the credit.

Whatever his faults, John knew what parks are for as well as any of us, and he tried always to give his colleagues a sense of the true worth of their calling. If asked to write his epitaph, I'd say: This gifted second-generation ranger and keeper of the institutional memory blew the dust off so many of the old stories that when he died it was almost as though a library had burned to the ground.

Part 2

The Fires That Wouldn't Die, 1988

16

A Summer of Fire

There was nothing unusual about the 1988 fire season—at first. The Rose Fire, ignited May 24 by a lightning strike during a thunderstorm, didn't survive the rain shower that came along a few hours later. Three more fires of little consequence flared briefly during the next month. Observation, the handiwork of a thoughtless camper near Old Faithful, was quickly extinguished by a ranger. The next two, Crystal and Cougar, also the result of lightning strikes, soon fizzled out.

On the afternoon of June 23 the lookout in the fire tower on top of Mount Sheridan radioed the fire cache: "I have a smoke to report." He had sighted a puff of smoke rising above the trees near the southeast edge of Shoshone Lake in the south central section of the park. By long custom the person discovering a fire names it, usually for the closest map reference point. The lookout called his fire "Shoshone," a name the fire cache duty ranger wrote on a wall chart beneath those of the four other fires of the season. A ranger immediately hiked in to take a look.

That evening the park's fire committee, which included ecologist and fire behavior specialist Don Despain and chief ranger Dan Sholly (who followed Tom Hobbs), reviewed the ranger's report. Located about a mile from the lake and near the channel connecting it to Lewis Lake, the Shoshone was the size of a small suburban backyard, smoldering in a ragged patch of lodgepole killed by pinebark beetle. After looking at weather predictions, the fuel supply, and the terrain downwind, the committee designated the Shoshone a natural fire.

Yellowstone's fire management plan requires monitoring of all natural fires. The next morning, a biologist and a fire specialist arrived at the fire site, carrying a food supply and sleeping bags. The fire was less than an acre, winds were light, and the Shoshone seemed unlikely to amount to much. The day following, lightning started a fire in the Gallatin Mountains in the northwest corner of the park. The Fan Fire quickly consumed several hundred acres of forest, but its location was remote, no buildings were in danger, and it too was allowed to burn.

In 1972, the year of the Yellowstone Centennial, the Park Service had set sail like Columbus into uncharted waters by allowing natural fires to burn under prescribed conditions. In 1988 reporters used the unfortunate term *let-burn* to describe the policy, suggesting a foot-on-the-desk indifference to the consequences. The policy contained restrictions. Fires would be allowed to burn only if they were ignited by lightning and if they did not threaten life or property. Fires started by humans would be suppressed. The superintendent could order suppression of a natural fire at any time. All natural fires would be monitored closely and suppression ordered if conditions changed.

In the sixteen years between 1972 and 1988 the new policy caused little concern. Of 235 natural fires, all but fifteen burned fewer than a hundred acres, eight burning more than a thousand acres. The largest fire burned 7,400 acres. A total of 34,157 acres was burned, about 1½ percent of Yellowstone.

The northern Rockies and many parts of the West had been in a drought for a number of years before 1988. For Yellowstone the signals were mixed. In the six years preceding 1988, July and August rainfall was 200 percent above normal, yet the winter snowfall was well below. Over this period natural fires burned only a thousand acres. Spring rainfall in 1988 seemed ample, 150 percent above normal in April and almost 200 percent above normal in May.

Twenty fires were ignited by lightning in the month of June. Half went out after burning only a few acres, but June rainfall was barely 20 percent of normal. The park was rapidly drying out. Fires were being reported everywhere in the northern Rockies. For this region of the Forest Service, 1988 would be the biggest fire season since 1910, even without Yellowstone.

As a part of the fire management plan, relevant conditions were being measured at twenty-six stations in the park, including the moisture content of fuels, the speed at which fires were likely to travel, and how hot they would burn. By early July, fire behavior specialists who analyzed the data were becoming uneasy. At some point a threshold is crossed, after which fires will take off. Unfortunately, a threshold equation doesn't exist.

Storms over the July 4 weekend bringing lightning but no rainfall set off the Miller, Amethyst, and Lava fires. They were followed by Mist on July 9, Pelican and Cone on July 10, Raven and Clover on July 11, and Falls on July 12. Some of these fires grew rapidly. Clover in the northeast burned three thousand acres in two days. Red, ignited July 1 on the shore of Lewis Lake, burned toward the Shoshone four miles away. The media was finding little merit in the natural burn policy. Neighboring communities demanded it be scrapped.

On July 14 chief ranger Dan Sholly and two fire aides were making a helicopter survey of the Clover and Mist fires in the rugged mountain terrain of northeast Yellowstone. A strongly built, battle-scarred veteran of Vietnam and a second-generation Park Service employee, Sholly was the right man in the right place. He'd fought his first forest fire in the same section of Yellowstone twenty-five years earlier. "Action-oriented, high energy, strong opinions" a colleague said of him. "Fire gives him as big a rush as anything. Talk about intense!"

Sholly had more than the fires on his mind. George Bush, vice president and soon to be the Republican presidential candidate, and his pal James Baker III, who would be his campaign manager, were going to hide out in Yellowstone during the upcoming Democratic Convention and get in a little trout fishing. The Coal Creek patrol cabin in a secluded valley under Little Saddle Mountain was to be their snug retreat. A new food storage unit had been installed, and the floor touched up with fresh paint to hide the worst stains. In deference to Bush's high station, the blankets were changed. Sholly had flown to Cody that morning to discuss security with the Secret Service.

Flying over the Calfree Cabin, seven miles north of Coal Creek, Sholly saw the Clover Fire was barely a half-mile away and coming fast. He landed, sent the helicopter off, and with his two aides moved the woodpile to a safe distance, dug a passable fire line around the cabin, and burned the underbrush with flares. Surrounded by fire, they made their way to a meadow close by and reached for their fire shelters. There were only two. Sholly shared. Forty-five minutes later the three crawled out, leaving two green rectangles in the black meadow. The cabin survived. The Bush-Baker trip was canceled.

The Yellowstone information office issued its first map on July 15. Perimeters of the nine fires listed enclosed eight thousand acres. That same day the National Weather Service predicted that precipitation for the next thirty days would be somewhat less than normal. Smoke from fires in remote areas of the park drifted across the Grand Loop. National forests bordering the park had adopted a natural burn policy in designated wilderness areas. The Forest Service began to suppress some of its fires, notifying Yellowstone that it would no longer "accept" fires burning across the border.

To those watching on their television screens, Yellowstone was on fire and no one seemed to care. The impression that national parks are the country's crown jewels was fixed and familiar. The idea that they would be allowed to burn was met with disbelief. The Park Service explanation—fire is as important to the ecosystem as the sun and the rain—sounded educational and therefore impractical. "We were going around happy-faced with stories about how great fire is," superintendent Bob Barbee, who had replaced John Townsley, acknowledged. The explanation was the spoonful of sugar to make the medicine go down. "Then the fires got bigger and bigger and bigger."

The burn perimeter on July 21 reached seventeen thousand acres. The largest previous fire was only a thousand acres larger. The Red Fire swerved around Lewis Lake, threatening the campground. Clover and Mist were about to combine. Assistant chief ranger Gary Brown, who observed the strange behavior of the Red Fire, burning against the wind and over an area that had burned not many years before, said, "In my mind, things were different."

In Barbee's beginning days with the Park Service as a Yosemite junior naturalist he was favorably regarded, by most, for his youthful impudence and glancing wit. Now he faced the most difficult choice of his career. Had the time come to abandon the policy he had so resolutely defended and begin fighting the fires? Or should he wait, letting the fires grow and putting his trust in the summer rains that had not failed in six straight years?

Judging that the risk of fires burning out of control at a time of critical fire danger outweighed other considerations, "on July 21 Barbee decided to suppress all existing and new fires" and called in the fire fighters. "I had the feeling," Barbee said to me later, "we were moving out into the unknown." The same day the Clover and Mist fires merged into what would become the second-largest fire of the summer.

Five hundred fire fighters were on duty in the park within forty-eight hours. In the previous month the Shoshone Fire burned a couple of hundred acres. It erupted the day after Barbee made his decision, burning thirty-five hundred acres in one day. Grant Village on the western shore of Yellowstone Lake was directly in its path. Most of the buildings are of wood construction with cedar shake roofs. By the time the incident commander arrived to take charge, ashes were falling in the village. The evacuation of the three thousand guests and employees was a Park Service first and a measure of how rapidly a fire could move.

Two hundred and fifty fire fighters cleared a wide swath through the pines at the edge of the village, removing lower limbs and the fuel on the ground. Fire engine crews called in from town and city fire departments hooked up to fire hydrants. They saved the village. Flames high in the tree tops surged over the fire line but were knocked down just short of the buildings by powerful jets of water from hoses. Expecting the worst as the fire reached the village, the caterer moved his trailers to the lakeshore. That evening he moved them back and served a steak dinner. Only one building was destroyed.

On July 22 a man with a permit from the Forest Service was cutting fire-wood a few hundred yards outside the park's western boundary. Before getting into his pickup and driving away, he flicked his cigarette butt into the dry grass. By that mindless act on a windy day in a period of extreme fire danger he ignited the North Fork Fire, the largest of the summer. The wind drove the fire into the park. Smoke jumpers quickly airborne were unable to jump because of high winds.

At the beginning of this fire, as it burned into the park, a district ranger denied a request from the fire fighters to use bulldozers, causing a controversy that continued all summer. The blade of a bulldozer digs a fire line wide and fast. It also digs more deeply, scraping away the mineral soil and producing scars that last longer than the effect of the fire. The twelve-foot line carved by a bulldozer can stop a ground fire. It is of no help in crown fires that spot far ahead. What a national park didn't need, Dan Sholly said, was the "all-out southern California approach," attempting to save expensive residential property by using earth-moving equipment indiscriminately without any concern for how much damage was done to the landscape. "That kind of destruction would not be tolerated in Yellowstone."

The people who fight fires are a nervy bunch, drawn by the physical challenge, and the pay, of a hazardous occupation. Their creed is simple: jump fires fast and hit them hard. They came to Yellowstone from all over the country, accustomed to using any tactic that would succeed. They regarded the Park Service stricture to go "Light on the Land" as nutty logic. A September 5 story in *Time Magazine* headlined "We Could Have Stopped This" quoted a disgruntled fire fighter who claimed that the North Fork could have been stopped cold by bulldozer lines initially, but "they wouldn't let us do it."

The North Fork nearly took out the town of West Yellowstone several times, and its citizens blamed the Park Service for their sufferings. The man who commanded the North Fork Fire said that although bulldozer lines might have been tried, it was his belief that they would not have held. He noted that the pilot of a tanker dropping retardant in the initial attack had seen spot fires being ignited far ahead of the fire. Even if dozers had been used, he said, "The end result would have been the same. An escaped fire." In other situations where bulldozers were deemed essential by incident commanders they were used, cutting many miles of fire line in the park, mostly to protect gateway communities.

Although I might disagree with fire fighters on the effectiveness of bulldozers at the start of the North Fork, I salute their courage and tenacity. Photographs taken in 1988 that show them coming off the fire line with goggles pushed up on their hard hats, faces streaked with sweat and grime, and eyes glazed with physical exhaustion remind you of pictures of miners coming up from the pits after an explosion. Crews are supposed to be relieved every couple of weeks to go to town, have their laundry done, and maybe drink a few beers. Replacements aren't always available.

Thomas Hackett, reporting for the *New Yorker* on October 2, 1989, described an experience with the Redding hotshots that provides a sense of what fire fighting is like. The Forest Service maintains about fifty elite crews, called "hotshots," seasoned men and women who are mostly employed by the land-managing agencies or come from Indian reservations. One day in August, Hackett's crew from Redding, California, was flown by helicopter "into a smoky war zone" next to the Firehole River. "The meadow lay under a somber pall reminiscent of a solar eclipse," Hackett noted.

He could hear a deep rumble from the fire hidden somewhere ahead in the smoke. Taking orders over his walkie-talkie, the crew chief marched the twenty men and women for a mile down a service road through the pine forest. Dressed in flame-retardant yellow shirts and green pants, boots, and hard hats, each carried a Pulaski, a back pack, a canteen, and a fire shelter fastened to their belts. With the crew chief's shout of "strike and move," the team began to dig a fire line using a technique as old as the Pulaski. In this case they were preceded by sawers cutting branches and swampers raking away sagebrush bushes, twigs, and needles to mark the line.

Crew members line up one behind another an arm's length apart. At an even pace and without looking up, each person takes a swipe with his or her Pulaski, turns over a chunk of soil, and steps ahead. At something rather less than a normal walking pace, depending on the terrain and the receptiveness of the soil, they dig a fire line a foot and a half wide, enough to stop a ground fire. Few professions are so exhausting and so dangerous. When smoke reduces visibility, communication becomes critical. "We always try to keep the fire in our face and never let it flank or get behind us," a crew chief explained. "You must know at all times where you are and where the fire is."

It took an hour of punishing work to cut a quarter of a mile of line, Hackett wondering to himself the value of "a mere scratch in the dirt." The plan, someone explained to him later, was to tie in with the line a crew ahead was cutting and then start a backfire. "But as the fire jumped over the river we could feel its wind whirling and whipping. Three-hundred-foot flames—rising three times as high as the tallest trees—lashed at the sky. Firebrands ignited small fires, called spots, beyond our line."

A burning ember landed on the roots of a fallen tree, and before any-one in the crew could respond the log was consumed by flames. A woman behind Hackett kept yelling, "Bump up! Bump up! Let's go! Let's work!" Hackett was bushed from swinging his Pulaski and had trouble keeping on his safety glasses. "The smoke seared and scalded my throat; my eyes teared and my nose ran uncontrollably. The roar of flame grew so loud that I could hardly hear a warning that someone called when a snag crashed less than ten feet away." There was nothing that could be done, he realized, "to contain, let alone extinguish, the kind of fire we faced while we were dig-ging the fire line. Within five minutes the blaze had coalesced into a fire storm—the kind that has been studied in the interests of knowing what would happen in the first hour or so of a nuclear war—and as the twisting winds sucked the surrounding air and drafted upward in a tight convection column the fire seemed to gather still more energy and power. It was as if we were standing on the fringes of a hot tornado." The line was abandoned in the confusion of falling trees and dense smoke. There were moments of terror as Hackett and a crew member "slipped through the fire and into the black" and made their way to safety. "I know that's what we did," Hackett says, "but even an hour later it still seemed unreal."

As reported by Alan and Sandy Carey in *Yellowstone's Red Summer*, pilots flying air support had similar experiences. "At one time I had fourteen heli-copters in the air in the same area, and felt the situation was getting mar-ginal," a flight controller with twenty years' experience said. "To establish a higher degree of safety, I pulled everyone down, modified some of the patterns and frequencies, and sent them back up again." Small helicopters lowering canvas buckets could dip a hundred and fifty gallons of water out of streams and lakes, the big Chinooks many times that. One bucket at a time, helicopters dropped ten million gallons of water on the Yellowstone fires. "At times it was almost like the Tet Offensive," said one of several helicopter pilots with service in Vietnam.

Often the choppers were used to support fire crews digging lines in front of an advancing fire. In one instance they carried fire crews into a tight landing zone then dropped thousands of gallons of water to bring up the moisture levels behind the fire line. "We began flying buckets at daylight and continued all day; Captain Stone was flying N664 and we were rotating out of the same dip point averaging five-minute round trips with two thousand pounds of water each trip. The smoke was thick, about a quarter of a mile visibility, and it became increasingly difficult to take a deep breath without choking." The line failed to hold. "The heat of the fire forced its way into the cockpit—flames were running about two hundred feet above the trees. The ground manager gave the word to pull out the ground people to prevent injuries, and over the radio I could hear the bitter tone in his voice as he admitted defeat to a raging fire with a two-mile front, driven by high winds, roaring down the drainage."

∪ ∪

By the end of July, fires covering a hundred thousand acres were being fought by fifteen hundred fire fighters. Forest fuels contained as little as 2 percent moisture, far less than kiln-dried lumber. "The probability of ignition during this period was well into the nineties," said one fire analyst. "This means that when an ember lands on the ground, there is a 90 percent probability that it will ignite. When you're trying to fight a fire, 50 percent is considered alarming and anything above 60 percent is considered extreme." A satellite image showed smoke billowing all the way across Wyoming and Montana into North and South Dakota. The incident commander of the North Fork said, "We could be in for the siege of 1988."

Area Command, a group of Forest Service and Park Service officials coordinating fire strategy and resources, assembled a half-dozen of the best fire behavior specialists in the country at the beginning of August. Accustomed to telling an incident commander where his fire might be in twenty-four hours, they were asked to predict how much the Yellowstone fires would burn in the next month. For two days they fed all of the relevant data into their computers—weather patterns going back several decades, the age and species of trees that might be affected, and known fire response to various conditions—and ran their models. On August 2 they made their forecast, using map overlays to show projections for August 15 and August 31. As they spoke, some of the fires were burning beyond the

August 15 forecast. In the next five days the fires exceeded the August 31 forecast.

The biggest media event in Park Service history swamped Joan Anselmo's information office. "The office went from normal to out of control almost overnight," she told me later. "We were serving two hundred media representatives a day when things were tense. There isn't any way to satisfy that many reporters. They were often unhappy with us and had cause. They wanted up-to-the-hour information on all of the fires, and the incident commanders were too busy to keep us informed. Yellowstone is news everywhere. We installed phone banks to respond to calls worldwide. We had to bring in fifty information officers from other parks. Our office was open from six in the morning until midnight.

Joan felt the reporters had their own problems. "So many asked the same question. 'Where can I see the biggest flames?' As a result, newspaper readers and television viewers received an exaggerated impression of the extent of the fires." Conrad Smith of the Ohio State School of Journalism, whose special interest is environmental reporting, came to the same conclusion. He used the Yellowstone fires as a case study of how television news accounts shape public opinion. Flames, he noted, photograph well. Reporters, accustomed to covering urban fires treated the fires as a "disaster" story, looking for victims and someone to blame.

Smith found that the reporters for ABC, CBS, and NBC had committed basic journalistic errors, projecting "the inaccurate impression that Yellowstone Park had been lately reduced to ashes" and fanning the political controversy about the fire policy without explaining the origin of the policy and whether it really made a difference. Of 861 Yellowstone news scenes on the three networks, only one was visually related to the reason why the fire policy was adopted. In addition, there were newscasts "incorrectly suggesting the natural burn policy was still in place long after it had been abandoned."

Among the examples of "unfair reporting" Smith discussed was one that embittered everyone in Yellowstone. Photographers constantly searching for moonscapes found few. Even the hottest fires generally left trees standing. At first glance, an area of several hundred acres on the highway between Norris and Canyon seemed a real winner. Every tree was down, and the earth bare—but not because of fire. Back in 1984 a windstorm had uprooted the trees and laid them out in windrows. The North Fork conveniently charred the trunks and burned away the groundcover. So one evening Tom Brokaw looked up from his anchor desk and told viewers that Yellowstone National Park was being destroyed "by the fires that will not die." Roger O'Neil, standing in front of the purported moonscape, pronounced a benediction: "This is what's left of Yellowstone tonight." As they say in the business, it was a story too good to check.

ʊ ʊ

The fires that kept tourists away further aggravated what at best is a nervous relationship between Yellowstone and its neighbors, environmental protection colliding with market imperatives. The Park Service and the residents of gateway communities each look at Yellowstone and see park values differently. In a change of roles, the locals were accusing the Park Service of killing the goose that lays the golden eggs. Barbee was the cause of it all, according to a typical story in the *Bozeman Chronicle* on September 4. The owner of a medical supply business in West Yellowstone was training a hose on his wooden office building. "The park has the resources to put this fire out. The attitude around town is vigilante lynch mob. If you took a popularity survey Barbee would come in last." In the same story, a motel owner said, "I don't think that Barbee realizes how he has affected our lives by not putting the fires out. A lot of businesses, including ours, will not be able to make the large payments at the end of the season we are supposed to make on our motel because the fires have ruined the tourist business." Across the street at the Western Inn, the marquee sign announced "Welcome to West Yellowstone Barbee-Que."

A meeting of a hundred Cooke City and Silver Gate residents, attended by Barbee, was the subject of another *Chronicle* story, also on September 4. A former Air Force pilot, dissatisfied with fire-fighting efforts, was leading an effort to bypass normal procedures. He claimed that an Air Force reserve unit "had two squadrons of bombers loaded and ready to drop multiple loads of retardant" if someone would give the word. Dan Sholly explained that retardant alone would not stop a big fire. A call to Washington determined that "while the Air Force reserve does have a fire-fighting capacity, the units are not on any kind of alert." Meanwhile, seven hundred signatures had been added to a petition that said, "Let's face it—the top man in Yellowstone Park blew it and willingly let the fires get out of hand."

Rep. Ron Marlenee of Montana maintained his record of opposing every environmental measure. He called natural burning a policy of locking it up and letting it burn. Both Wyoming senators, Alan K. Simpson and Malcolm Wallop, put the blame on Park Service director Bill Mott and called for his resignation. On the floor of the Senate, Simpson echoed the doomsday pronouncement of Roger O'Neil and charged that the ground in Yellowstone was sterilized and blackened to the depths of any root system in it. After a look at the fires with Barbee, however, he straddled the fence, saying that the fine line to be drawn was to allow nature to do her mysterious work while still protecting those who make their livelihood from the forests.

Cecil Andrus had been a dedicated friend of the parks while secretary of the interior under President Jimmy Carter, but the former Idaho governor ridiculed natural burning, saying any westerner knows you don't let fires burn in July and August. The record showed that during his tenure at interior sixty-seven fires had been allowed to burn in Yellowstone, fifty-three in July and August. The incumbent secretary, Donald P. Hodel, was at odds with the conservationists on most issues, yet he had approved the fire policy and didn't back off. He was supportive of Barbee, within reason, and at a trying moment he said that what the people in Yellowstone needed most was understanding of the difficulties they had faced, along with support.

Bob Barbee apparently came close to losing his cool in public only once. He told me about it later. A politician, best unidentified, flew over the North Fork Fire one day with him and then held a press conference. To a reporter who asked if he felt everything possible was being done, he replied, "Frankly I'm convinced that if enough men and equipment were utilized that fire could be stopped." He went on to say, "I know how government works and I expect more could be done to fight these fires, but a tremendous bureaucracy is in motion and possibly no one wants to upset the apple cart."

After the press conference ended, as he and Bob were walking to the patrol car for the drive to the airport, he asked, "How did I do?" Politicians are notably touchy about criticisms from federal employees, but Bob was steamed. He said, "In all candor, those guys trying to put a line around the North Fork deserve our thanks. What they are doing would test anyone's endurance. They have been busting their asses to get it done, and you just gave them a royal vote of no confidence."

When a reporter stopped the politician for one more question, Bob joined a veteran ranger in the patrol car. Rangers like to think of themselves as tough birds, old pros. This one had been worn down by too many sixteen-hour days. He was tired of being second-guessed by self-appointed experts relying on thirdhand information. "Let the fucker walk home," said Dan Sholly.

Ʊ Ʊ

Moisture was being diverted from the northern Rockies by the abnormal behavior of the jet stream. Lightning from dry storms ignited many blazes.

By early August the fire cache wall chart listed forty fires. A cold front with gusting winds hit the park on August 15. Fire fighters confident that the approaching North Fork could not sweep over the high bluffs and adjacent rivers at Madison Junction could only watch as it mounted the bluffs and hurdled the Madison, Firehole, and Gibbon rivers in a day.

On Saturday, August 20, a day they would call Black Saturday, Barbee and the North Fork incident commander met with citizens of West Yellowstone. A month had passed since the squabble over use of bulldozers at the beginning of the North Fork Fire. It was still burning off to the east, making an occasional jab toward the town. Some mornings inversions blanketed the town and closed the airport. These were days of scorching heat and acrid smoke, and the testy audience asked questions for hours. Since Park Service policy was to suppress man-caused fires, why didn't they put out the North Fork? Why didn't they bring in those big water bombers and drown the fire like they did in other parts of the country all the time? As Barbee walked out of the convention hall at one o'clock, he was met by winds of thirty miles an hour. A reporter saw him look at his wife and let out a sigh that said, "Oh, God!"

The fires that day were sprawling, chaotic, and terrifying. Helicopters and air tankers were grounded by high winds. Under these conditions, "Trees blew down and the fires began to make their own winds, with hot air from the fires rising rapidly upwards, while new oxygen rushes in from the bottom to fuel the flames, which in turn drive the fires to new heights." Fire fighters could only protect buildings and helplessly watch flames consume the forests.

Turned back when the road to Mammoth north of Madison Junction was blocked by fire, Barbee, his wife, Carol, and Joan Anselmo drove south. "It was a scary trip with many detours that lasted into the night," Joan said. "Coming into Old Faithful we could see huge convection columns in all directions that must have been thirty or forty thousand feet high. It was an unbelievable sight. At West Thumb, frightened visitors who had been turned back by the road blocks were milling around. Bob helped the rangers reassure them and get the situation under control, despite the fact that the Shoshone Fire was making a run in our direction."

On Black Saturday, eight major fires in Yellowstone burned sixty-two thousand acres, with a hundred and sixty thousand acres burned in the greater Yellowstone area. No one had ever seen anything like it. A salient of the North Fork pushed eastward across the park, forcing the evacuation of Canyon village three days later. The North Fork had grown so large that the eastern portion was renamed Wolf Lake and given its own fire fighters and command staff. Storm Creek "acted like a runaway train." The Clover-

Mist Fire now covered a perimeter twenty miles wide and half again as long. The Lake Hotel closed for the season because the view of Yellowstone Lake was permanently obstructed by smoke. Canyon Village never did reopen.

After three days of undiminished winds, beginning on Black Saturday, a quarter of a million acres had burned in the greater Yellowstone area. The fires seemed to have taken on a new dimension, burning at will. It was the same throughout the northern Rockies and Pacific Northwest. Smoke obscured the sun in Seattle and turned sunsets red in Chicago. Plumes from the Yellowstone fires could be seen from the space shuttle. Not counting Yellowstone, Montana was fighting ten major fires, Idaho almost as many, and California close to twenty. The supply of fire fighters was getting dangerously low. Yellowstone was asked to give up a thousand, with replacements to be furnished by the army and marines.

All summer, fire bosses had been employing the tried and true method of fighting fires. You contain them by digging fire lines, working the flanks to prevent spreading, and pinching off the head when the weather is favorable. But this perimeter control strategy had failed. At one stage, of two hundred miles of fire line dug, twenty miles held. The North Fork Fire was not delayed by the Grand Canyon of the Yellowstone River. At several locations the big fires were bearing down on park developed areas and gateway towns. At a meeting of all fire officials the day after Black Saturday the strategy was changed. Henceforth, in the disposition of available resources, incident commanders would concentrate on the protection of life and property.

ꙅ ꙅ

Some of the fire fighters assigned to the defense of Silver Gate, at the northeast entrance to the park, and Cooke City, two miles down the road, had to be supplied by pack train. The two hamlets that supply tourists with food, lodging, and T-shirts are crowded into a canyon between the Beartooth and Absaroka ranges, an area of steep canyons, heavily forested ridges, and mountain peaks above ten thousand feet.

Extremely vulnerable to forest fire, they were caught between two monsters. Storm Creek Fire, ignited on Forest Service land to the north, headed south on Black Saturday, making an incredible run of ten miles in three hours against the wind. To the south, Clover-Mist covered almost as much ground and followed a northward course. Both were getting dangerously close to the two mountain communities. The day after Black Saturday, twelve hundred infantrymen from Fort Lewis, Washington, were flown to

Yellowstone, taught the rudiments of fire fighting, and rushed to a camp outside Cooke City.

Residents of Silver Gate and Cooke City were not on the best of terms with fire officials. The Storm Creek Fire had been burning for nine weeks, and Clover-Mist for seven. Residents believed fire suppression efforts were tardy and unproductive and blamed their predicament and loss of income on Park Service and Forest Service inertia. They took no stock in official pronouncements, including one by an incident commander reported in the *Casper Star Tribune* on August 28: "There is no more threat to Cooke City and Silver Gate at this time."

Shortly, there was only one more ridge between the Storm Creek Fire and the towns. With bulldozers, chain saws, and hand tools, fire fighters hacked out a fire line seventy feet wide running from one side of the canyon to the other a half-mile out of Silver Gate. Jellied gasoline dropped by helicopters started a backfire intended to consume enough fuel in front of the fire to stop it. Hundreds of fire fighters stood by to keep the backfire from jumping back over the line. Winds funneling up the canyon picked up burning brands from the backfire and carried them far behind the fire line, starting a new blaze that fire fighters couldn't control. It burned along the ridge toward Silver Gate, missing the buildings by fewer than a hundred feet.

Ironically, if that is the term, the Storm Creek Fire never did burn into the backfire or further threaten Silver Gate and Cooke City. The backfire that backfired became one more grudge issue between the townspeople and the fire strategists. It was also the subject of gallows humor, including the following example.

Question: How does the government put out a fire in your kitchen?
Answer: They backburn your living room.

U U

While fire fighters fought to protect a half-dozen gateway towns and park villages, the defense of a single building, Old Faithful Inn, attracted the most publicity. Completed a decade before the first automobile entered Yellowstone, it had become an American icon. For most of the summer it appeared to be safe. The point of origin of the North Fork Fire was fifteen miles to the west, and prevailing winds sent the fire to the north and east. On Black Saturday a containment line that had held for a month on the extreme south flank of the North Fork gave way. The blip burned steadily southward toward Old Faithful, eight miles away.

By the evening of September 6, it was less than a mile away on a line that would take it over a wooded ridge a quarter of a mile southwest of Old Faithful Inn. The incident commander thought the topography was in his favor. "We expect it to break over the ridge and back down the hill. A backing fire (one that advances into the wind) is a much easier fire to control." The next morning, the forecast indicated that winds would shift and grow stronger. On a bright, clear day the inn was closed, and visitors asked to vacate their rooms by 10:00 A.M.

Fire fighters prepared to stop the fire before it reached the village, and engine crews were ready to hose down building fires. Parking lots between Old Faithful Inn and the ridge would act as a firebreak for the old landmark, and a recently installed deluge system was capable of sluicing down the roof and walls. Sometime before 4:00 P.M., smoke began to boil up behind the ridge. Bombers could be seen flying in low and dropping retardant. Big Huey and Chinook helicopters dipped water from the Firehole River and sewage lagoons that had been filled with fresh water, wetting down trees ahead of the fire. Spot fires began to appear on the crest of the ridge.

A reporter for the Mutual Broadcasting System watched from the Old Faithful parking lot as a Forest Service lead plane dipped its wings, guiding a four-engine aerial tanker that dumped half of its load of sticky pink retardant on each of two passes down the ridge line with no apparent effect. Choking in the thick smoke, the reporter and several other correspondents dashed into the Old Faithful Inn, borrowing napkins from the dining room tables and fashioning smoke masks. Suddenly, the ridge disappeared in a welter of smoke and fire. At that moment, Alan and Sandy Carey, who had hiked up to Observation Point on the other side of the geyser basin, snapped an end-of-the-world photograph later made into a classic poster that hangs on the door of my study. As the wall of flames rolled down the ridge, reporters ran for parking lots. "Coals pelted our backs," said one, "and fist-sized firebrands flew by our heads." A *National Geographic* reporter yelled his impressions into a tape recorder: "4:04 wind about fifty miles an hour. . . . Fire is to the left, right, and center. . . . The roar sounds like a continuous jet takeoff. . . . Now we're completely surrounded by red flames. Sparks everywhere. . . . There's fire now in the nearby trees. . . . It's obviously jumped the line." All who were present spoke of the eerie amber light caused by sunlight partially penetrating the thick smoke, the pellets of fire whizzing in all directions. The *National Geographic* reporter termed it "a scene that only Dante could have imagined."

The wind tossed burning brands over the parking lot, the inn, and the geyser basin, starting fires on a ridge a mile away. There, the Careys were taking photographs, unaware of their danger. An order came over the radio: "Come down now. Don't take the trail, there's fire on it. Head straight down." They skidded and scrambled down the ridge through smoke and ash. "By the time we got to the level of the inn, we could see fire fighters everywhere, their yellow shirts neon in the thick haze, checking for embers and hosing down buildings."

The fire passed in an hour, bearing off to the northeast. Twenty cabins were lost, and several other buildings damaged. Old Faithful Inn was saved, in part, by the invasive parking lots that so many had criticized. The incident commander said that in fires, as in military engagements, it helps to be lucky. A wind shift of two or three degrees, and the inn would have been destroyed. "No amount of engines or water would have made any difference. We were right on the ragged edge."

ʊ ʊ

For as long as fire fighters assemble, the North Fork Fire will be remembered and stories told of its stunning fury. Don Despain called it "a natural force, like a volcano or a hurricane. Even when there was no wind, it rumbled like a locomotive. It came in from Idaho and did what it was going to do and there was nothing we could do about it." On an evening two days after it grazed Old Faithful, Joan Anselmo watched the North Fork bear down on park headquarters at Mammoth, fifty miles to the north. "It looked like a thousand campfires in the hillsides."

Once more, fire fighters chopped down brush and trees around the buildings, and engine crews unrolled hoses. Hotel guests were replaced by journalists, and Park Service families were evacuated. A spokesman for Area Command gave an ominous weather prediction for Saturday, September 10: "Today, if we get the forecasted winds, people will see fire behavior situations that they've not seen in their careers."

At 11:45 A.M. the control tower at the West Yellowstone airport clocked winds of forty-five knots. But something about this storm was different. Moisture-carrying clouds began to fill the sky, and humid winds had a calming effect on the fires. In his informative narrative *Summer of Fire*, Jim Carrier notes that the man who spotted the Shoshone Fire in June was among the first to realize that the long nightmare was over. From his vantage point on Mount Sheridan the lookout wrote in his journal, "Rain fell for an hour beginning 2 A.M. Rain and hail. Turned cold."

It had been fifty-two days since Barbee ordered the fire fighters in, a period of no appreciable rainfall. Six dry cold fronts had blasted through Yellowstone, each accompanied by winds of twenty to forty miles an hour and gusting to sixty and even seventy. No one could have anticipated back in July when the National Weather Service advised that precipitation would be a little less than usual that the summer of 1988 would be the driest in the history of the park.

"All we ask for is just a little bit of rain," Barbee said soon after ordering the fires suppressed. "We'd settle for half an inch—one of those days you always have in the northern Rockies, where it's gray and cruddy and everybody bitches and moans about the weather. That's all we want." On Sunday the Mount Sheridan lookout wrote, "The station was fogged in all day and snow started falling about 8:00 and continued most of the day. 19 degrees."

Large, wet flakes whitened the charred path of the North Fork, covered the roof of Old Faithful Inn, now closed for the season, and lifted the spirits of thousands of beleaguered fire fighters. In West Yellowstone a jubilant disc jockey played "Jingle Bells" over and over and over again. Three inches of snow and rising humidity subdued the fires of 1988, one natural process yielding to another.

∪ ∪

Although the fires made no more runs they did not die immediately. A lot more work was needed to contain and smother them. Crews turned over smoldering stumps and logs, extinguishing every smoke, until the last line was declared cold in late October. Meanwhile, the sizable task of mopping up began. The sites of the extensive camps set up for all major fires, more than a hundred helicopter landing areas and fifty backcountry spike camps, had to be restored and all trash and equipment carried out. Hundreds of miles of hand-dug fire line and thirty-two miles of bulldozer lines dug in the park were filled in and raked back to their original contours to help reduce erosion.

Crews with chain saws cut down hazardous snag trees along the trails and highways. An unlucky fire fighter, killed by a falling snag in a neighboring national forest during the mop-up, was the only fatality. A tragic loss, but the toll could well have been much higher. The animal population also suffered relatively few casualties: nine buffalo, four deer, two black bear, two moose, 257 elk out of a population of twenty thousand, and no recorded loss of grizzlies, bighorn sheep, or antelope.

Except for one day, the park remained open—at least part of it—every day. Rangers who closed some entrance stations and sections of the Grand Loop, and who removed people from jeopardy constantly, might have welcomed an order to close all entrance stations permanently, as no doubt would the fire bosses. Visitors who did brave the smoke and came closer to fire than they planned had a rare experience. Against large odds, not one was injured. But the cost in terms of the number of acres burned was gigantic: almost a million acres, close to half of Yellowstone National Park. The North Fork alone, ignited by a careless smoker, burned nearly half a million acres. A lot of the curious visitors who toured Yellowstone in October were amazed that so much of the park was untouched, but all were saddened by mile after mile of blackened meadows and dead trees.

Fears had been expressed by persons in high places that large parts of Yellowstone had become sterile. Scientists worked to complete a soil survey of the entire park before snows covered the landscape. They found that only one-tenth of 1 percent had been sterilized. In virtually all of the burned area, roots and rhizomes were alive and healthy. "The ecology is sitting under the ground just waiting," said soil scientist Henry Shovic.

Lodgepole pines that cover most of the forested area of the park have developed an ingenious strategy to survive the frequent fires. Seratinous cones sealed by a resin coating remain on the tree until opened by the heat of a fire. Within days, seeds attached to tiny wings flutter down to the forest floor, as efficiently, someone observed, "as though they had been spread by a crop duster."

In the ashes of a lodgepole forest Don Despain placed a metal grid at random intervals and carefully counted the seed wings. Using the back of an envelope, he calculated their number at fifty thousand per acre. In other areas where he repeated the exercise the count was as high as a million seeds per acre. Deer mice and red squirrels would account for many, and some would not take root, but in a few years young lodgepole saplings would thickly cover the forest floors.

The largest fire suppression effort ever carried out in the United States cost a record $120 million. More than twenty-five thousand fire fighters, civilian and military, and more than a hundred fire trucks and a like number of helicopters and tankers were involved in the greater Yellowstone area. Still, the fifteen interagency teams that jointly prepared *The Greater Yellowstone Postfire Assessment* concluded, as had Jim Sweaney ten years earlier, that fire fighters don't put the big fires out: "There is a widespread if informal feeling that the massive fire-fighting efforts probably did not significantly reduce the acreage burned."

17

The Resource Is Wildness

On a comfortably warm July day in 1989, with a sun beaming down so obligingly that a cynic would have rejoiced, I drove through the south entrance of Yellowstone. A flyer received at the station, "Welcome to the New Yellowstone," told me I was fortunate to be witnessing the regeneration of the park. In truth, it was easier back in Reston to agree with Barbee that "there was no ecological downside to the fires" (and to keep reminding Mary not to call it destruction) than to view with pleasure the charred forests along the south entrance road. In some places the trees looked like graphite sticks and the ground like the contents of a charcoal grill. The abruptness of the change in the landscape was disorienting.

I felt better after viewing the exhibits on the fire at the Grant Village visitor center, particularly the one containing a relevant quotation from Bob Marshall. One of the great figures of the wilderness preservation movement, Marshall had expressed his reaction after hiking through a burned forest in 1927: "There were some scenes of desolation that pretty nearly drive an imaginative person crazy—A pessimist would conclude that one summer's fires destroyed more beauty than all the inhabitants of the earth could create in many years, while an optimist would go singing through the blackened, misshapen world rejoicing because the forest will look just as beautiful as before—in two or three centuries."

The anniversary of the Grant Village evacuation occurred during my visit. Many who had been chased out of their rooms by the Shoshone Fire returned for a "Reenact the Evac" celebration. A physician from Pittsburgh, Henry Wessel, was nervous about what he would see. His response would have pleased Marshall. "I was pleasantly surprised," he told a *Billings Gazette* reporter in a July 24 story. Asked about the rebirth of a national treasure, he said, "It's not a rebirth, it's a metamorphosis. The park didn't die and was resurrected. It's not a wilderness that was destroyed. It's changed in some interesting ways."

On the drive from Old Faithful to Mammoth I was seldom out of sight of the North Fork burn. Yet if I had mounted a motion picture camera on the hood of my car, clicking off a picture every ten seconds, no two frames would have looked the same. Around one bend everything in sight seemed cooked, except for a single living tree that would act as a seed bank. Around the next, there was only a smudge on a far ridge. Pushed by light winds, flames will dart and hopscotch, burning in random designs. Ridges showered by flying embers showed the familiar mosaic pattern of black splotches rimmed with orange on green. Wherever trees had been killed but not consumed by surface burning the needles had turned orange, the characteristic color of a dead forest.

The blooming of Yellowstone after the snows melted in the spring was beyond all expectations. A park naturalist called the flowers "the best ever." To my untrained eye they were abundant and piercingly beautiful against the sooty black tree trunks. Meadows that must have resembled asphalt parking lots a year earlier had grown back completely. Lupine added touches of silvery blue to a blackened forest floor, and purple larkspur almost covered the side of a hill. With the help of a flower book I identified a few more: bright yellow cinquefoil, pinkish sticky geranium, and blue harebell. The tall, purplish-pink fireweed, named for its ability to invade burned areas, was everywhere.

Alongside the Firehole River a hawk slowly quartered a meadow on the far bank in a gently rocking, effortless flight. Hawks and owls benefit from fires that burn away foliage and expose mice and voles. Bird populations in lodgepole forests increase dramatically as the new vegetation expands the food supply. From a population of fewer than twenty pairs of breeding birds per square kilometer before a fire, the number would grow to more than a hundred pairs in the developing forest. I saw a half-dozen yellow-streaked pine siskins competing with a chipmunk for seeds under a stand of dead lodgepoles.

I saw many elk grazing on the new grass. Because of the loss of forage and severity of the winter, a great many elk had died, upward of five thousand out of a population of twenty thousand. Many concerned people wanted the park to provide supplemental food. The urge to feed starving animals was understandable, and the explanation that it made no sense in a national park was unfathomable to some. They wrote angry letters, and Dan Sholly received a death threat. Thousands of elk die every hard winter in Yellowstone. Scientists from a dozen universities had noted that demands for supplemental feeding "would put pressure on limited winter range, producing either higher mortality later on, or more likely, increased and continuing pressure for feeding programs."

Responding to criticism, chief scientist John Varley, whose appointment had enabled Mary Meagher to return to research, observed that six thousand elk calves had been born that spring and that the herds would quickly recover. Scientists agreed that the elk carcasses would provide needed food for many species, including grizzlies and eagles, both of which are endangered species. There is no down side to the trade-off. Buffalo carcasses are reserved for the bears, the only animals with claws and teeth strong enough to rip through the tough hide.

About half the Grand Loop Road was outside the fire perimeters. The most popular features were relatively unmarked: Mammoth Hot Springs, Old Faithful and all the geysers, Fishing Bridge, and the Grand Canyon of the Yellowstone River. The spectacular drive along the north shore of Yellowstone Lake had escaped the flames. The lovely section of the Madison River between Madison Junction and West Yellowstone had not. At some of my favorite places I had to remind myself of Barbee's frequent pronouncement that "scenery isn't greenery."

I have seldom passed Gibbon Falls, five miles north of Madison Junction, without stopping for a look. Gliding over a sloping ledge of brown volcanic rock, the Gibbon River plunges eighty-four feet into a deep and forested canyon. The falls are almost as broad as they are wide, and as you view them from the parking area the eastern flank of the Purple Mountains presents a dramatic backdrop.

Now the prospect was more somber than stirring. All of the mountain rising behind the falls had been burned, as had the entire hillside across the canyon that slopes upward to a summit called Gibbon Hill. Somehow a narrow band of green trees along the river just above the falls was spared. From Gibbon Falls northward for some miles on both sides of the road the burn extended as far as the eye could see. I marked it on my map as "a bleak stretch."

Where the Crow and Blackfoot quarried black glass from Obsidian Cliff sixteen miles south of Mammoth, a small stream flows through a narrow valley. The ridge opposite the cliff was burned as near to a crisp as makes no difference. All that remained on the slope were charred splinters of what were tree trunks, the few still standing tilted at odd angles, the rest strewn on the blackened soil.

I joined a man and woman of about my age who were standing in front of one of the wayside exhibits installed that year. "The hillside should not have burned again so soon," the message began. Set on fire by lightning in 1976, a recovering lodgepole forest not yet old enough to produce seeds was thought to be too green to burn. Yet on a day of near-hurricane winds it had been completely consumed. "Regeneration will occur here, but it may be different from other burned areas of the park. Research scientists will be watching with interest." Looking at the barren ridge, the woman said to no one in particular, "I don't care what they say. It won't be as pretty again in my lifetime."

ᴗ ᴗ

After interviewing Bob Barbee for an article that had appeared in the *New York Times Magazine* in December 1988, Peter Mathiessen wrote, "Barbee is a big, genial, ruddy man, who after the most trying summer of his life has not quite lost an ironic sense of humor." Alternately delighted and astonished with the cards life had dealt him, Bob, a bright and funny conversationalist, spoke in jest, candidly. His troubles must have finally ended when the snows put the fires down in September, I said. "Last winter was the worst since the twelfth century," he began. "Elk died in significant numbers, and when spring came six hundred buffalo decided to migrate to Livingston. Would-be hunters deputized by the state opened fire as they crossed the boundary. The public expected me to declare war on Montana. It wasn't my year."

Bob didn't like to talk to people from behind the big square desk he used primarily to stack things on. We sat on comfortable bentwood chairs with orange plaid backs and seats at a small, white table holding a few papers and a telephone. Hanging on the wall beside us was a framed painting of two wolves captioned "A Howling in America's National Parks." A quotation from Aldo Leopold ended with the thought that "you cannot love game and hate the predator. . . . The land is one organism." As we were getting comfortable, he recalled my letter to him at the time of his appointment reminding him that the Yellowstone job could be a bully pulpit. Favoring me with one of his staccato laughs, he said that it had proved to be so the year before, except that the give-and-take of daily press conferences came close to being a contact sport.

Barbee often spoke of his undergraduate days at Colorado State as "the glory years of a hot-shot skier." Almost thirty years in the Park Service hadn't changed him all that much. Never reluctant to speak his mind in defense of the right as he saw it, he'd done so with such wit and glee that he'd made many friends and few enemies—until 1988.

After graduation and seasonal work at Rocky Mountain, he caught on at Yosemite as a temporary photographer. At the time, Ansel Adams and his wife operated a photo shop in the valley. "Here I was," Bob will say, "a beginner privileged to be in the company of Ansel Adams, and he treated me like an equal." With the help of the Yosemite superintendent he entered the Park Service by what was then a well-traveled back door, working as a tour guide at Carlsbad Caverns and praying for a break. He and his associates likened their situation—measly wages and ramshackle housing in the middle of the New Mexico desert—to servitude in the French Foreign Legion. After a year the Yosemite superintendent recalled him, and from that unpromising debut his rise through the ranks was steady, including a posting to Colorado State for a master's degree in resource management.

After John Townsley's death, competition was intense to become his successor as superintendent of Yellowstone. Then superintendent of Redwood, Bob didn't think that he and Yellowstone were a fit and didn't apply. He received a call from the director, Russ Dickenson, who said most of the applicants were nearing the end of their careers.

> He wanted someone younger with energy and fresh ideas, and he offered me the job. All at once my negative feelings disappeared. I said I'd take it, without talking to Carol first on this one.
>
> Russ hadn't discussed the selection with my regional director, Howard Chapman, knowing what his reaction would probably be. Howard preferred an old reliable because he is one. I knew when I called he would be touchy because he hadn't been consulted. When he told me he thought I needed more seasoning before I'd be ready for a big job like Yellowstone I couldn't hold back. I said, "Goddammit Howard, I'm forty-six years old! I've worked in eleven parks and been superintendent of four. By the time I get enough seasoning to suit you I'll be sixty. You still think of me as that smart-ass kid you knew in Yosemite twenty-five years ago."

Howard Chapman was a prototype straight-arrow ranger, but his considerable accomplishments did not include telling jokes about his work. Both he and Russ were products of a system that tolerated in-house critics while schooling superintendents to keep personal opinions to themselves. The choice of Barbee, incurably mirthful about the sacrosanct, was unexpected and caused some conversation among the old guard.

Bob traveled to Washington to pay courtesy calls on members of the Wyoming delegation and meet the secretary of the interior:

> Jim Watt said there was only one thing he wanted me to get straight about Yellowstone. On his first trip to the park the concessioner invited him to have a picnic lunch—and served him a three-course meal on a

tablecloth. Next time he wanted a sandwich and an apple. Nothing else. Did I have that straight? If he had any other concerns about Yellowstone he didn't mention them.

The stories they tell about Yellowstone, that everything is hidebound by tradition, aren't all exaggerations. Townsley is supposed to have said, "First you abhor it. Then you accept it. Then you like it." He was partly right. Everything here seems to start out a breech birth. But I have a good staff, some really first-rate people, and I couldn't ask for better support. Last summer we fought a war together.

You can read about it, but you had to be there to know how it felt. There was high-level hysteria in the gateway communities, and some of the merchants were lobbing grenades. It got so personal and so spiteful that for my family's sake I had to take my nameplate off the door. I told the staff, "Don't be defensive. Don't take things personally. Show dignity. Empathize."

Stopping at Old Faithful on my way to Mammoth, I struck up a conversation with a lanky young ranger named Deborah Bird. With her green sunglasses fastened by a black elastic band, quick, outgoing, and attractive, she reminded me of my daughter Kim—except for the pistol on her hip. After talking to her, I didn't doubt that she knew how to use it.

I asked about the day the North Fork Fire nearly destroyed the village. She said, "It was a scary scene. At one point I thought the whole housing area would go. Two weeks earlier I'd moved into the loveliest Park Service house I'd ever lived in. I was afraid I'd lose everything I owned. I knew my husband would rescue what he could, and he started with my dog and cat."

Debbie grew up in Modesto, California, working for the Yosemite concessioner and for the Park Service as a seasonal during junior college. She took a clerk-typist job for a year in the San Francisco regional office, then started as a ranger at Sequoia and was a supervisory ranger at Glen Canyon. She married, and when she was transferred to Yellowstone her husband was employed as a trails maintenance foreman.

"We were moving people who had lingered too long to safe places, and then a couple of us were sent to close the road and set up a barricade. All of a sudden and out of nowhere the flames crossed the road just ahead. It was incredible that no one was injured. As stressful as it was, I didn't fear for my own safety, maybe because I was focusing on what I had to do. After the fire passed I drove around until midnight, checking that everybody was accounted for, watching the fire until it torched the trees on the skyline."

A day earlier, when Debbie and her district ranger had debated whether to close Old Faithful Inn, its manager had listed the reasons why he hoped it wouldn't be necessary to evacuate six hundred guests. The North Fork incident commander, who kept his fire shelter handy at the height of the fire storm, had been optimistic and recommended the inn not be closed. The district ranger agreed. At ten o'clock that night Barbee called, ordering Old Faithful Inn evacuated the next morning. "All of us were upset," Debbie said, "but we knew the pressure Bob was under. We felt so protective of him we would have done anything to spare him more grief. As it turned out, he made the right decision. I'm only a GS-9 ranger, but I think he's a great superintendent."

At the Chuck Wagon Cafe in West Yellowstone, where I stopped for coffee after leaving Old Faithful, a couple of friendly local types sitting next to me at the counter fed me invented anecdotes about the fire. Describing the effect on the Gardiner tourist trade, one said, "Things got so bad a woman sent her husband out looking for road kills to put meat on the table." I thought Bob might be amused. He wasn't. Nor were any of the other staff members. Some of the slurs had not been forgotten, like the editorial saying that "Barbee has ridden a dead policy into hell."

And yet the swiftness of postfire attitudinal change was amazing, Bob said. The substantial rise in tourist traffic had about wiped the slate clean. Two members of Congress who had called for Barbee's scalp seemed to have forgotten him. George Bush and Sen. Alan Simpson dropped by for a look. They expressed disbelief that a green meadow through which they walked could have burned a summer earlier — until they squatted down with John Varley and saw the ashes under the grass.

I mentioned to Bob that the media critics had changed their tune. A May 29, 1989, issue of *Time* on his table contained a story titled "Springtime in the Rockies." The last vision of Yellowstone that most people had carried into winter was that of an "environmental Armageddon," a reporter noted. "Yet Yellowstone still lives and is as wondrous as ever." After predicting death and disaster the year before, Bob commented, "Reporters are into atonement and rubbing ashes on their foreheads."

A *Washington Post* story on July 23 by T. R. Reid, an environmental writer, contained an unequivocal apology, a *nostra culpa* offered on behalf of all reporters who covered the Yellowstone fires. "If the first job of the media is to convey accurate information," he wrote, "then we failed our job." Reid thought that the fires of 1988 had been the most dramatic in the nation's history. "Faced with this singularly gripping and important story, we blew it." Now that the smoke has cleared, he concluded, "a somewhat chastened herd of journalists has descended on Yellowstone to note dutifully the positive effects of last year's fire storm on flora and fauna, to film the lush green of new life in the meadows, and to state that reports of the park's death were greatly exaggerated."

A few of Bob's more pungent remarks were unsuited to the printed page. I include one gibe because it was so well deserved. Alston Chase, in his relentlessly nagging *Playing God in Yellowstone: The Destruction of America's First National Park,* accused the Park Service of being Yellowstone's worst enemy and said that over the previous seventy years nearly every conceivable mistake that could be made in wildlife management had been made by the Park Service in Yellowstone. Chase holds a doctorate in philosophy from Princeton University. A member of the same department at Colorado State University, Holmes Rolston III, had this response. "Chase's work would be philosophically and biologically more productive with the distortions and misquotations, the vituperative allegations and innuendo, the scorn and rage removed." Chase continued to chastise the Park Service during the summer of 1988. "Alston," said Bob when the name came up, "crawled out of his slimy cave to bayonet the wounded."

"I wouldn't say Bob was unaffected by the abuse he took," a member of his staff said. "He did lose a little of his bounce. But more than anybody else he tried not to let it get under his skin." I noticed in our conversation that Bob seemed more puzzled than angry that people could say such nasty things. He believed a public debate useful because it would force people to consider what they wanted Yellowstone to be. Too many of them are not well informed. Gov. Thomas Kean of New Jersey, for example, had offered to ship a million seedlings—none native to the park—to help with reforestation. Bob was heartened by the results of a poll of park visitors taken that year. One-half felt the fires were a natural phenomenon rather than a disaster, one-quarter thought the reverse, and one-quarter was undecided.

Had I asked Bob whether mistakes were made in 1988 I'm sure he would have reeled off several, maybe some of his own. He had final approval over the strategies of the incident commanders and often had to decide among options they presented. It was an immensely difficult position. Predictions of fire behavior and weather changes suffered from inadequate knowledge. As to the natural burn policy, I think it fair to say that the people who drafted it back in 1972 did not have a conflagration in mind. They were conditioned by the facts that in most years Yellowstone is too wet to burn and that there hadn't been a truly big fire in the park's history. It is likely that future fires will be allowed to burn only after a more systematic study of such factors as drought and weather conditions. The allowable buildup of fuels adjacent to developed areas will be studied, and the legitimate concerns of communities on the boundaries taken into account.

As we parted, Bob noted that people were beginning to reflect on what had happened and why. The majority, he thought, were aware that he and the fire fighters could have done little that would have changed the outcome. Nature deals the last hand. "None of us would have wished for fires of such magnitude, but the future is exciting. There has never been such an opportunity to study the regeneration of such a vast area. Two hundred scientists from universities all over the country will be conducting research. Imagine how much more we will learn about Yellowstone. Everything that has happened reinforces my conviction that the role of this park is to be a repository for natural processes."

ꙋ ꙋ

One day I toured the park with the chief naturalist, George Robinson, who had sandy hair, a short, pointed beard, and the enthusiasm of a cheerleader and was a veteran of many assignments. He had grown up in places such as Lassen Volcanic and Yosemite, where his father was a naturalist. At Harpers Ferry Center he worked as an interpretive planner. No one had more ideas. He stopped the car to show me his latest, a children's discovery trail, and led me through a broad meadow brightened by flowers. Patches of bare earth around stubby, dead stems marked where sagebrush had burned. A strip of blackened trees was wedged between the meadow and a hill. In a low spot a small grove of aspen had escaped the flames.

He envisioned a boardwalk with exhibits, elevated to protect the vegetation and low enough for wheelchairs. The project was a response to the large number of letters and contributions sent by young people anxious to help restore Yellowstone. "Our aim will be to appeal to a child's sense of wonder and curiosity about the natural world," George said. He saw it all in his mind's eye, pointing out the exhibit sites, exulting over the stories that could be told. The dead trees ahead of us weren't just standing there: Wood-boring beetles had followed the smell of smoke to them, woodpeckers would tap that food supply until they moved on to another burned forest, and their excavations would then become nests for chickadees and sapsuckers. "Children will walk back in time, experience the fire, and witness the regrowth. Look over there! Perched in that aspen! A mountain bluebird! I was hoping for a three-toed woodpecker!"

South of Tower Falls, George and I sat for a time on a rocky outcropping in warm sunlight, looking down into Antelope Valley. Visitors would be able to understand fire ecology so much better if we could tell them the story of that valley, he remarked, but you couldn't line the road with exhibits. A broad indentation of grassland and pine stands, the valley is prime grizzly habitat. Isolated dead trees in the foreground and splotches of black that speckle the woods were reminders that fire had swept the valley on September 7 the year before.

Steve French and his wife Marilynn, independent grizzly researchers who had studied and filmed the grizzlies in Antelope Valley for six years, were present that day. French shared his diary entry with a reporter from *Smithsonian Magazine:* "My legs were weak. . . . Fire absolutely everywhere—up to the ridge, all in the upper meadows and interspersed trees, all below. The meadows were circled in fire rings. Trees were exploding/crashing/echoing constantly . . . I can't imagine anything surviving in this entire drainage." A physician and the head of emergency services at the hospital in Evanston, Wyoming, French had became interested in grizzlies after doing his internship at Yellowstone's Lake Hospital and treating people mauled by bears. Ever since, he and his wife had spent their summers observing and photographing grizzlies in Antelope Valley.

In the next few days after the fire French was unable to raise a signal from two radio-collared grizzlies he'd been tracking. At first he feared both had died. The male had merely moved off a short distance, however, and soon the female returned to her favorite mineral lick. Meeting French in the valley in the spring of 1989, the *Smithsonian* reporter had listed what French had seen during the first few weeks of the season: "Three pairs of grizzlies courting and mating, two or three grizzlies digging biscuitroot or hunting for elk calves or scavenging winter-killed carcasses, a couple of males passing through looking for females; a herd of 175 elk, with a total of about five hundred elk scattered across the valley at one time; moose, bison, bighorn sheep, a lot of small mammals, all sorts of raptors, mountain bluebirds, a blue grouse in rut, sandhill cranes—at which point I ran out of paper."

The same day that Antelope Valley burned, an ornithologist in Hayden Valley fifteen miles to the south could hardly believe his eyes. He counted forty ferruginous hawks skimming through the heavy smoke. It's a species native to the prairies and rarely seen in Yellowstone. Living in a fire-prone environment, the birds had associated the drifting smoke from Yellowstone with a plentiful food supply—rodents displaced by fire. They must have followed the smoke trail to its source.

∪ ∪

Don Despain's office upstairs in the administration building would be difficult to describe and even harder to inventory. Let's call it working space for a field scientist. My only question would be, If he had another armful of books and papers, where would he find space? Don's black hair had developed streaks of white since I last saw him, and his beard was grizzled. He wore comfortable clothes, a wool shirt, worn jeans, and high boots. He had the same cheerful smile but displayed it less often. An innocent remark he had made the year earlier had been widely quoted in the press and had put the Park Service in an embarrassing position. Knowing how he had suffered, I didn't mention the subject, but he wanted me to know how the incident had happened.

He had been laying out a series of research plots as the fires advanced, using the standard Darbenmire method of marking the corners with metal posts and subdividing them according to prescribed measurements. Trees and plants were then tabulated and photographed. After the plot burned, new growth would be recorded at prescribed intervals. One day, accompanied by a reporter, he was laying out a plot near the Gibbon River in the path of the approaching North Fork Fire. The trick is to place the plot as close as possible to the fire. Otherwise the fire may swerve, and there goes your experiment. The North Fork, however, didn't change course, and Don couldn't contain himself when it reached his plot. He yelled, "Burn, baby, burn!" He didn't expect that his words would receive prominent display in newspapers that didn't mention the research plot; the stories conveyed the impression that "burn, baby, burn!" reflected the attitude of the Park Service toward the Yellowstone fires. To a public frustrated because the fires were not being contained, the phrase conveyed an image of scientists applying impractical theories with disastrous results. "It still hurts," he said.

He had been vindicated by publication of a four-year study of how a lodgepole forest evolves, an investigation that resulted from a collaboration with William D. Romme, forest ecologist at Fort Lewis College in Durango, Colorado. Yellowstone, they found, is not burned over randomly by a succession of small fires but by conflagrations that occur every two or three centuries after the forest has passed through four distinct stages. In the final stage, overmature lodgepoles dying off are replaced by spruce and fir whose branches, extending to the ground, supply fire ladders to the canopy. A conflagration then occurs whenever conditions are favorable: severe drought, sustained low humidity, and recurring storms carrying lightning, high winds, and no precipitation. The fires of 1988 were inevitable. Tree rings indicated the last previous conflagration took place in the early 1700s. Despain and Romme concluded that "the fires of 1988 represented a nearly natural event in the ecological history of the Greater Yellowstone ecosystem."

Don spoke modestly of the study, which had received good reviews, saying it was a tiny piece of an enormously complicated puzzle. Grinning broadly, he said that he anticipated a lot more surprises. His outlook echoed Einstein's comment that scientists are happiest when things aren't turning out the way they expect. A few years later John Varley would say, "For a long time as the aspen continued to decline we've wondered what was needed to make them reproduce, and now we know. Wet ashes." Don pointed out that Aldo Leopold did not publish *Sand County Almanac*, the "bible" of ecology, until after World War II. "That's how new we are at our profession. Geologists have been at it a lot longer and their textbooks can't keep up with the discoveries. We're rethinking some basic concepts too."

We used to believe the balance of nature was right up there with the laws of gravitation. But nature is always more intricate and inventive than we suppose, and ecologists no longer accept the notion that nature exists in a state of equilibrium. Biological diversity is assured not by stability but by disturbances such as weather changes and fire. Without these upheavals the variety and abundance of natural communities would be greatly diminished. Response to the Mount St. Helens volcanic eruption, which seemingly destroyed all living things for miles around, was a gigantic tree-planting effort to prevent erosion and provide habitat for wildlife. Ironically, scientists now conclude nature would have done the job far better.

Most people who come to Yellowstone, Don said, have a basic misconception. They want to see the features they've heard so much about, and when they do they think they have seen Yellowstone. In a talk he had given some years earlier to a group of ranger trainees, which was recorded by Paul Schullery, Don explained that in Yellowstone "the resource is not twenty thousand elk, or a million lodgepole pines, or a grizzly bear. The resource is *wildness*. The interplay of all the parts of the wilderness—weather, animals, plants, earthquakes—acting upon each other to create the wild setting, creates a state of existence, a wildness that is the product and the resource for which Yellowstone is being preserved."

The breezes carry seeds and spores and spiders as wildlife species move opportunistically among habitats. Nothing endures, said Darwin, but change. The processes of nature, everything that exists, everywhere, are too complex to be grasped. They can only be imagined. But our spirits soar to realize that wolves have been officially restored to Yellowstone before the last bounty hunters have gone to their rewards.

The aspen, too, have returned to Yellowstone, to places where they had not been seen for a great many years. They reproduce from suckers, or secondary shoots, genetic clones developing from the lateral root system of the parent tree. The fires seem to have provided optimum conditions for aspen growth by eliminating competing vegetation, supplying large, open spaces and increased sunshine, and by producing fine ash, which increases the ability of the soil to hold moisture. "It is not unreasonable to assume that many of the clones present today started as the glaciers retreated," Don concluded a few years later. "If this is the case, the aspen we see now have lived through a lot of climatic and environmental changes. It is conceivable that the aspen clones being browsed by deer and elk today were once fed upon by mammoths, horses, and camels."

Carl Sandburg said that what a country needs first is a good piece of geography. The roots of America have always been in the land. A young nation unable to match the cathedrals and castles and ancient cities of the Old World has taken pride in its monumental landscapes and made them national parks. Yellowstone is a part of the idea of this country. Wilderness is the American antiquity.

18

Like a Salmon
Swimming Upstream

Washington's Cosmos Club may not have as many quaint old dears as the Athenaeum in London, but it's a sedate place. During a Sunday brunch in the summer of 1993, the sound of chatter and laughter emanating from a circular table in the middle of the dining room was causing a few gray heads to turn. Eight of us were at the table, one active and three retired Park Service employees and our wives: George Hartzog, our host and former director, and wife Helen; the good-natured Bernie Meyer, who had been George's chief counsel and was now head of the White House Historical Association, and wife Audrey; Deny Galvin, the associate director for planning and development, and wife Martha; and Mary and me.

Tall, lean, and blessed with one of the organization's brightest minds— and most eclectic interests, from grand opera to the luckless Boston Red Sox—Deny views his universe with an amused and judicious eye. Coming out of college with an engineering degree and a yen for adventure, he joined the fledgling Peace Corps. That body, like the former Soviet Union's Communist party, numbers its members consecutively. Because the Peace Corps enrolls about twenty-five hundred volunteers annually, low numbers are prized. Deny is the proud holder of number ten, gaining his first park experience by designing a water system for the Ngorongoro Crater in Tanzania.

We were a companionable group, sharing memories of absent friends and keeping the waiter who pours the complimentary champagne busy. Bernie happened to mention that he'd received a call from Tom Flynn, a fixture in the higher levels of the Washington office during the Hartzog era and now retired in Florida. There was an immediate rush to tell Tom Flynn stories.

The one I told happened on a slow day at the office. It must have been around 1970. George was on travel status, and Tom was the acting director. I was reviewing a piece of legislation that would connect the southern boundary of Yellowstone to the northern boundary of Grand Teton by transferring a corridor of land and the enclosed highway from the Forest Service to the Park Service. In honor of the man whose generosity led to the establishment of the Grand Teton park, the new addition to the park system was to be called the John D. Rockefeller, Jr., Memorial Parkway.

Studying the lengthy title of the bill, I was reminded of one of the rascally mayors in Edwin O'Connor's classic, *The Last Hurrah*. Naming a new highway for himself, he had unintentionally supplied a hilarious title: "The Phil T. Rooney Memorial Macadam Parkway." Perhaps because I felt the office was in need of levity, and knowing that Tom, a lawyer and a stickler for detail, would give the package a close scrutiny, I had a secretary make a slight alteration. Then I sent the legislation creating the John D. Rockefeller, Jr., Memorial Macadam Parkway to the next reviewer and awaited developments.

No one else noticed the change, and the new name might have been immortalized had it not been for Tom. He lectured me sternly, and not for the first time, when he called. The Park Service expected prudence and restraint from me, not practical jokes. A little later he was back on the telephone, this time in a boisterous mood. George had just called to see if anything needed his attention. "You know what he said when I told him what you tried to do?" he asked. "He told me to call the Park Police and have you shot on sight." Breaking into his trademark cackle, he hung up.

If you worked for George, you knew he would be on your case instantly should you fail to treat the Congress with deference. I was a little worried that he might be aroused enough to load me down with someone else's work, a favorite Hartzog corrective for bungling. But I also knew Tom didn't lack a sense of humor. I had my secretary drop around his office and casually ask his secretary whether George had called in recently. He hadn't.

∪ ∪

After we toasted Tom, Deny remarked, "The difference between the old and new Park Service is that we have so little to laugh about now." Deny was right. There is a consensus that George Hartzog presided over the last—and some might say the best—years of the old Park Service and that the old Park Service came to an end when he was dismissed by Richard Nixon in 1972. His firing began the politicizing of the Park Service and broke a tradition as old as the agency.

Following the swearing-in of the first director, Steve Mather, the interior secretary had remarked, "By the way, Steve, I forgot to ask you—what are your politics?" Mather was a well-known Republican, and it was the secretary's way of saying that he could rest easy in the Democratic administration of Woodrow Wilson. For more than half a century that custom was respected, and no director was fired or removed for partisan reasons. Incoming presidents rewarding supporters with choice positions kept hands off the Park Service.

Nixon had good cause to mark Hartzog. Victor by a thin margin over Hubert Humphrey in 1968, he hadn't felt secure enough to oust all holdover bureaucrats. Hartzog was spared—the only interior agency chief to survive—after it became apparent that he was highly regarded in Congress. It must not have gone well with Nixon to have in his administration a popular bureaucrat appointed by a Democratic president. H. R. Haldeman, Nixon's chief of staff, described in *The Ends of Power* how Nixon planned to bring all government agencies under his personal control, placing White House loyalists in key positions after the 1972 election. The tape from which Haldeman quoted reveals the petty vindictiveness of Richard Nixon. "Knock them the hell out of there . . . any Goddam thing. Clean the bastards out. . . . Take that Park Service, they've been screwing us for years."

Nixon personally gave the order to fire Hartzog, provoked in part by a trivial incident. It involved his long-time companion Bebe Rebozo, Rebozo's brother-in-law, and a boat dock at Biscayne National Park off the south coast of Florida that Rebozo and Nixon considered their private property until George ordered it opened to the public. "I was told the only thing Rebozo asked of Nixon in 1972 was that I be fired," George has said.

Nixon replaced him with a thirty-four-year-old underling, Ronald Walker, a White House advance man deemed qualified for the position because he had visited several parks. From the White House, the office of Vice-President Spiro Agnew, and the Committee to Re-elect the President the new director recruited an unremarkable staff of a half-dozen administrative assistants, executive assistants, and confidential assistants who conveyed his orders and were soon referred to as "the family." His imprudent actions quickly became a liability to the administration. Immediately after his patron resigned the presidency, he was invited by the interior secretary to do the same.

There had been only seven directors in the first fifty-six years of the Park Service. Capable men who were fierce defenders of the parks and undaunted by bureaucratic restraints, they were highly respected by employees who looked to them for leadership and a sense of purpose. In the eight years from 1972 to 1980, counting Hartzog, there were five directors, and four were fired. Because political parties now regarded the position as a political plum, park people knew what to expect after Ronald Reagan's victory in 1980. Having campaigned against the federal government and those who composed it, he appointed as his interior secretary James Watt, who had been a leader of the "Sagebrush Rebellion" and advocated opposition to federal regulation of public land use in the West. Watt was right out of a conservationist's nightmare. He promised to reopen sensitive offshore areas to oil drilling and to greatly expand oil and gas exploration in proposed wilderness areas adjacent to national parks—and he wasn't subtle about it. Critics of his proposal were termed "enemies of the American way."

In fairness to Watt, so far as the Park Service was concerned, he did retain the director, Russ Dickenson, the only interior agency chief he didn't fire. He instituted a Park Restoration and Improvement Program that provided a billion dollars to correct health and safety hazards and repair roads and buildings. But he also stocked the high offices of interior with modern-day buffalo hunters. A brazen example was the man appointed to be the assistant secretary in charge of the Park Service, G. Ray Arnett. An oil company executive, he shared Watt's declared bias for private enterprise over preservation. Whenever we want to do something for America, Arnett complained—drill a well or mine some ore near the parks, for example—conservationists and Park Service officials say it's too close because they want buffer zones from the Atlantic to the Pacific.

He preferred hunting to all other pursuits, arranging official travel so he could always get away to do a little shooting. The time a couple of mountain lions strayed out of Guadalupe Mountains National Park in Texas and killed sheep, the rancher asked the assistant secretary for authorization to take a pack of hounds into the park and kill the mountain lions. Arnett agreed until a game superintendent, Bill Dunmire, said, "Over my dead body." Arnett's next assignment reveals his true nature. He became head of the National Rifle Association, from which post he was fired after "serious charges of mismanagement."

The target of many Alaskans was the Park Service regional director, John Cook. A standout administrator who never shirked hard decisions, Cook kept a window from his Anchorage office containing five bullet holes as a "keepsake" of the fight over the Alaska lands bill. Cook's planners were evicted from their quarters in one town and refused service in another, and one of their aircraft was destroyed by arsonists.

After passage of the bill, which doubled the size of the national park system, Cook had the unimaginably difficult task of protecting these vast parks with little more than a corporal's guard of rangers. When Alaskans defied Park Service authority, continuing to treat the land as their own, he ordered his rangers to enforce the laws. Angered by his unyielding approach, they took their complaints to Watt. Cook was banished from Alaska and reduced to the rank of superintendent.

It would have been a miracle if Park Service people had not become disillusioned and discouraged during the repressive years under Reagan and Bush. "Career employees manned the bunkers," George Hartzog observes in his engrossing and straight-from-the-shoulder narrative *Battling for the National Parks*. In it he reveals the tawdriness and gall of some of the people who ran the interior department for Reagan and Bush. One episode took place at the beginning of Reagan's second term. He picked Bill Mott, an old friend who had been his state park director in California, to be the director of the Park Service. It was a surprising choice. Mott was a highly respected conservationist. Park Service employees could hardly believe their good fortune. Mott started strongly, selecting Deny Galvin to be his deputy director. Meeting with conservation leaders and Park Service officials, he adopted an impressive list of goals for his administration.

"Rumor had it," George notes, that interior secretary Donald P. Hodel attempted to head off the Mott nomination. He wasn't anxious to have a subordinate who was close to the president and First Lady. Unsuccessful, Hodel countered by naming a former associate, William Horn, to be Mott's boss as the assistant secretary for fish and wildlife and parks. Mott was allowed considerable freedom to support policies publicly that the administration opposed, including wolf reintroduction in Yellowstone, but his action plans ended up in the wastebasket of Assistant Secretary Horn.

Among other failings, Horn was a devious meddler, interfering in operational matters that would normally be settled by a superintendent or regional director. He would pick up the telephone, order a park scientist to report to his office, and ridicule his research findings. He changed the efficiency rating Mott gave regional director Howard Chapman from excellent to marginal until Howard threatened to bring suit in federal court and he backed down. He changed Mott's recommendations for bonus awards to outstanding employees so drastically that an outraged Mott refused to attend the awards ceremony, remaining in his office at the other end of the hall.

A plan submitted by Mott to reorganize his Washington office staff gave Horn what he believed was a rare opportunity. He made revisions, primarily establishing a new associate director in charge of budget, personnel, and policy. On all policy matters, and perhaps others, the incumbent, already selected, would report directly to Horn, by-passing Mott. "It was," George remarks, "a thinly disguised ploy to take over substantive park management."

Mott signed a strong letter of protest to Hodel, written by Deny at his direction. Hodel ignored the appeal, approved the reorganization plan, and the matter appeared to be settled until Robert C. Byrd, the Senate's then powerful majority leader and chair of the subcommittee on interior appropriations, intervened. Disgusted by the clumsy attempt to shove aside the Park Service director, Byrd inserted a provision in the pending Park Service appropriation bill suspending payment of Horn's salary until the reorganization plan was retracted.

Fearful of moving against Mott, who had White House access, the chagrined Hodel took his revenge by handing Deny a letter of censure, a career-damaging stain on Deny's record, for the purported offense of drafting the letter Mott signed. Next, Deny was removed from the post of deputy director, exiled from the interior building, and almost hounded out of the organization. For a time he considered other work. But career bureaucrats have an ace in the hole against the spiteful political variety. They can outlast the bastards.

∪ ∪

"Because I believe so deeply in the Park Service mission and understand the extraordinary pressure which has been placed on the director and his staff," regional director Lorraine Mintzmyer testified before a House committee on September 24, 1992, "I have tried to keep my peace about this matter." Last seen doing a clog dance at a Yellowstone party, Mintzmyer was being punished by the administration for approving a draft document that had aroused immediate controversy when released: "Vision for the Future: A Framework for Coordination in the Greater Yellowstone Area."

The concept of a "Greater Yellowstone" had been talked about almost since the park was set aside. Yellowstone is a rectangle, near enough, about sixty-five miles north to south by fifty-five miles east to west. The original boundaries, intended only to enclose the newly discovered geologic curiosities, were drawn by passing straight lines through four reference points, establishing boundaries that cut across rivers and up the sides of mountains.

You do not have to be a wildlife biologist to understand why the boundaries, as originally drawn, do not protect Yellowstone's wildlife. A map that shows the extent of grizzly habitat would cover an area twice the size of the park. Most grizzly bears cross state, forest, and park boundaries several times a year, the leader of the Interagency Grizzly Bear Study Team has said, making populations within any political jurisdiction meaningless and cooperative management a necessity. Yellowstone's elk range does not constitute an ecological whole in which the elk herds can survive year round. As winter approaches, many thousands migrate out of the park into lower elevations to the north, east, and south.

Gen. Phil Sheridan, a Yellowstone enthusiast, was the first to realize that the park was too small, proposing in 1882 that it be doubled in size. The idea gained a title in 1917 after writer Emerson Hough told the citizens of Wyoming in a *Saturday Evening Post* article, "Give her [Wyoming] Greater Yellowstone and she will inevitably become Greater Wyoming."

A Greater Yellowstone could be accomplished only by carving it out of the Forest Service lands on all sides of the park. Warren G. Harding, who campaigned as a supporter of national parks, appointed a commission to negotiate a Greater Yellowstone. Political opposition locally, from those who wanted no change in the multiple-use management of the affected lands, killed the idea despite the support of the next president, Calvin Coolidge. A few small additions along the north boundary added elk range, and the eastern boundary is now more respectful of contour lines.

In more recent times there has been a refinement of Emerson Hough's concept, a realization that Yellowstone and the federal lands around it, amounting to some fifteen million acres, constitute a unique ecosystem. Spreading into three states and ten counties and administered by the Forest Service, Park Service, and Fish and Wildlife Service, the area is increasingly referred to as the "Greater Yellowstone ecosystem." It is politically fragmented by old rivalries that exist among the agencies and by conflicting land use policies, some of which threaten Yellowstone itself.

On the park's west side, the boundary with Targhee National Forest is so cleanly defined that it might have been marked off with a ruler—unbroken forest on one side, clear-cuts on the other. To the north, the attractive valleys of the Madison, Gallatin, and Yellowstone rivers are sprouting vacation homes and celebrity ranchettes. To the northeast, owners of the New World Gold Mine were ready to begin operations at a site in critical grizzly habitat on the headwaters of three tributaries of the Yellowstone River. An agreement by the company to exchange the mine site for other federal holdings was reached in 1996 and should end the threat.

These and other troubling threats prompted a small band of conservationists in 1983 to form the Greater Yellowstone Coalition, now a union of a hundred member organizations and thousands of individuals. Its statement of purpose is a ringing battle cry: "to ensure preservation of the

Greater Yellowstone Ecosystem, one of the largest essentially intact eco-systems remaining in the temperate zones of the earth."

The Park Service welcomed the creation of the Greater Yellowstone Coalition. The Forest Service was more restrained. In the 1980s this vener-able agency was being pressured to alter its basic philosophy. For nearly a century it had been an organization of foresters devoted primarily to tim-ber production. The public could denounce clear-cuts, but the practice made sense to professional foresters. For the first time the Forest Service was receiving consistently bad press for favoring timber production over environmental goals. Employees formed an association to work for change from within, and a group of forest supervisors signed a letter to the chief of the Forest Service requesting that environmental considerations be taken into account in determining the size and location of the timber cut in the national forests.

It was during these unsettling times that forest supervisors and park superintendents of the Yellowstone region sat down together to consider how they might work together in support of the Greater Yellowstone eco-system. Because of their differing missions, the parks and forests had long been managed as separate entities. Much American wilderness is being pre-served in national forests, yet on other forest lands mining, grazing, and oil and gas extraction are permitted. How these multiple uses could con-tinue within the framework of a protected ecosystem was the fundamental problem facing the working group. My understanding of the rise and fall of the vision plan has been considerably strengthened by the coverage in that estimable conservation newspaper *High Country News*.

"Vision For the Future," soon tagged "The Vision Plan," was introduced as a draft document at public meetings in Wyoming, Montana, and Idaho in 1990. "We were hoping," a forest supervisor said in *High Country News* on June 3, 1991, "that if we could get the public talking about this, we would have found that environmental groups and commodity groups have com-mon goals for this area. It was to give us a common target to shoot for."

The plan was denounced by timber, grazing, and mining interests for going too far and by conservationists for not going far enough. A group formed to oppose the plan warned hunters, fishermen, snowmobilers, and off-road vehicle owners that "you will lose many of your existing rights." The Wyoming legislature predicted economic ruin for the state. Support-ers of the Greater Yellowstone ecosystem, objecting to the vagueness of the language and lack of a time frame for achieving real goals, called the plan weak. "Somewhere along the line something went awry," Bob Barbee said in the same article. "All of a sudden it became an evil on one side and a toothless wonder on the other."

With most of the citizens and almost all of the business people of the northern Rockies resisting the vision plan, politicians in Washington applied pressure where it would do the most good. *High Country News* also reported Alan Simpson's letter to the director, which may have sounded genial but was a warning shot across the bow: "I cannot understand why the Park Service, as an agency, is interested in these matters, as they occur within the greater Yellowstone area on lands that lie outside the park system."

The House Civil Service Committee looked into reports that Park Service and Forest Service officials were being intimidated. Mintzmyer, and regional forester John Mumma, who testified he had been subjected to "undue interference" from politicians demanding he cut more timber in his region than permitted by environmental laws, were the principal witnesses. Mintzmyer testified that she had been called to the office of the deputy assistant secretary, Scott Sewell, who told her "significant political contacts and pressure had been made to the White House and the secretary regarding the vision document by political delegations." In a lapse he was to regret, Sewell failed to notice that Mintzmyer, who began her career as a secretary, was taking down every word: "He then stated that Mr. John Sununu [Bush's chief of staff who was removed the same year for abusing the perquisites of his office] had personally spoken to him about this issue. He stated Mr. Sununu told him that from a political perspective the existing draft of the vision document was a disaster and must be rewritten." Sewell was given the job with instructions "to retain the appearance that the document was the product of professional and scientific efforts by the agencies involved, but that the reality would be that the document would be reviewed based on these political concerns."

Carrying out Sununu's orders to the letter, Sewell reduced the original seventy-page plan to a watered-down, ten-page report that spoke vaguely of cooperation and other good things. The change of heart by the conservationists, who belatedly praised the plan, only weakened their position.

One is tempted to conclude the vision plan did more harm than good, that it served to harden opposition to the Greater Yellowstone ecosystem concept. Although the drafters of the plan were aware of prevailing opinion in the region and were seeking a workable compromise, they obviously had not forseen the intensity of the backlash. Many who condemned the vision plan saw it as a genuine threat to their jobs or life-styles.

Those who love Yellowstone must not lose heart. The vision of a Greater Yellowstone ecosystem is too good an idea to be defeated. The chance of success for the wilderness bill looked no better when it was first introduced by Sen. Hubert Humphrey. Congress reviewed and debated sixty-five versions of the original legislation, and congressional committees held eighteen separate sets of hearings before the bill became law. By then, the nation had taken notice. The assistant superintendent of Grand Teton gave a reminder that these are long roads: "A few of us are a little gun-shy from all this now. But we hope this can be a blueprint of what Greater Yellowstone should be for future generations. Maybe they can solve the conflicts and carry this forward."

By means of a "directed reassignment," the interior department forced Mintzmyer to accept a transfer to the position of regional director in Philadelphia, presiding over the battlefields and historic buildings of the mid-Atlantic region where she would cause the merchants and lumberjacks of the northern Rockies no further anxiety. Disheartened by the bickering and the duplicity, she soon retired. A previous interior secretary had granted her the department's highest honor, the Distinguished Service Award, for rising through the ranks to become the agency's first woman regional director. This loyal and talented civil servant did not go quietly. Her suit against the interior department in federal court, charging that the accusations used to justify her transfer were invented for the purpose, was settled in her favor.

◡ ◡

Robert Cahn, a staff writer for the *Christian Science Monitor*, wrote a series of articles for his newspaper in 1969: "Will Success Spoil the National Parks?" A tireless journalist, Bob made the parks his beat and must have talked to hundreds of employees. His accurate and informative series won a Pulitzer Prize, and he has never lost his enthusiasm for the parks. He was a member of the President's Council on Environmental Quality, the Washington editor of *Audubon* magazine, and has been a respected commentator on environmental issues, especially on those affecting the parks.

Cahn returned to the *Monitor* to do another series in 1991, the seventy-fifth anniversary of the Park Service. The title he chose, "Parks under Siege," was a measure of the changes he had observed. In so many places "the aging infrastructure deteriorates and the well-being of its wildlife and natural resources becomes increasingly precarious." Working conditions tested the commitment of employees at all levels. He devoted "Endangered Rangers," a May 30, 1991, article in the series, to the group that may have suffered the most. At Shenandoah, Cahn joined ranger Reed Johnson for a patrol along the Skyline Drive and found Johnson's story typical of many rangers he met. Coming out of college Johnson had fulfilled a "childhood dream" when he signed on with the San Antonio Missions site in Texas.

Taking advantage of all training opportunities, he became a commissioned law enforcement officer and certified as a fire fighter, emergency medical technician, and search and rescue specialist.

He struck Cahn as a skilled ranger on his way to a successful career, but the outlook for rangers had changed completely in the twenty years since Cahn's first series. Much as Johnson loved the work, he couldn't afford to stay. After seven years his salary was $19,200. He and his wife were just getting by, unable to put a penny aside to finance the college educations of their two children. The same month Cahn talked to him Johnson resigned. The Forest Service offered him higher pay and a promise of quick promotions.

His departure, Cahn said, was "part of the growing exodus of skilled rangers who leave the Park Service for better paying salaries and opportunities in other federal and state agencies." In times past, the satisfactions of the job compensated rangers for low entry salaries. Then, government housing in attractive park surroundings was inexpensive and advancement reasonably swift. But rents had skyrocketed following an Office of Management and Budget decree that the cost of government quarters must be comparable to prices charged in neighboring communities. Employees now pay the inflated rates of tourist towns, and park housing is no longer attractive. A study ordered by Congress found much of it "degrading." Of five thousand employee housing units, half were in "fair to poor to obsolete condition."

The bare-bones appropriations and rigid personnel ceiling have substantially reduced promotions and transfers. Half of the ranger force is caught in a logjam at the entry-level grades. Budget restrictions gave superintendents no other option but to cut back on maintenance and seasonal employees. Pressed by the Reagan administration, the Park Service for the first time in its history placed receptacles in the visitor centers asking for donations. "Poor boxes!" George Hartzog called them and worse. Parks began to use more and more Volunteers in Parks (VIPs), who do almost all jobs except the risky ones. Volunteers in Parks was a Hartzog innovation, the legislation permitting the Park Service to reimburse volunteers for incidental expenses. The program started with a thousand. Currently, they number seventy thousand, two hundred for every park in the system. The year 1991 was supposed to be a banner anniversary year, Cahn noted, "but among Park Service managers and rangers there is little celebration. Instead it is a time for hunkering down."

The only conservation organization primarily interested in the parks, the National Park and Conservation Association, also took a look at the state of the park system in 1991, publishing a grim report, *National Parks in*

Crisis. An update to the report, published in 1993, contained "snapshots" of existing conditions in fourteen selected parks based on information submitted by the superintendents. The examples were new, the problems familiar. Great Smoky Mountains, for example, is one of the most popular parks in the system, recording nine million visits annually. "Each year more than half-a-million hikers and eighty thousand equestrians use park trails, shelters, and other resources the park cannot afford to regularly maintain and repair. Thirty percent of the park's 975-mile trail system is in poor condition. With repairs costing $1 per foot, it will require more than 1.5 million dollars to bring trails up to park standards. About 52 miles, or 15 percent, of park roads need repair at an estimated cost of more than $13.7 million. An estimated $800,000 is needed to repair 50 buildings, including 30 comfort stations."

Next to the Canadian border, North Cascades is a mountain wilderness where I was perched in a helicopter one day beside Ted Swem, who inveigled me into so many great adventures. As we viewed the snowy peaks and veered close to glaciers hanging from lofty cirques, we knew we were richer than kings. "In the summer of 1992, the park had a total of 120 staff members. This summer, budget shortfalls caused the number to drop to a total of 87 staff. . . . The number of walks, talks, guided tours, and evening campfire programs dropped sharply this summer. In June and July of 1992, 342 programs were offered; during the same months this year, only 99 were given. A large number of those were given only because park employees volunteered to do them on their own time."

Shenandoah is the national park nearest to the heavily congested eastern corridor. "More than 313,000 people visited the park this July—10 percent more than in July of 1992. There are also 35 fewer seasonal rangers—70 percent less than a year ago! . . . . Interpretation, down 50 percent from last summer, has 'gone by the wayside' so that we could make it through the summer. . . . Shenandoah faces a $12-million backlog in repair and maintenance of water lines, trails, vehicles, and buildings. The Dickey Ridge visitor center needs total rehabilitation. . . . Ranger housing at Shenandoah is dismal, but goes unattended, along with a majority of operations needs."

The NPCA survey showed every park in the system was being run on a shoestring. There wasn't much disagreement that the organization had lost its momentum. One regional office veteran told Bob Cahn, "In my twenty-six years as a ranger I've seen the Park Service go through some bad times, but never as bad as this." That's why the election of Bill Clinton in 1992 and appointment of Bruce Babbitt to interior were received with wary optimism rather than wild enthusiasm.

John Cook and Deny Galvin, for example, would have been worthy candidates for Park Service director. If Babbitt thought seriously of making his selection from within the agency, it wasn't apparent. After Tom Brokaw turned him down, he settled on Roger Kennedy, whose background an associate described as "a restless career of radio and television, government positions, finance, the study and criticism of architecture, a dabbling in history and science." After law school, Kennedy ran for Congress, unsuccessfully, against Eugene McCarthy, and he also headed the Smithsonian's National Museum of American History. Despite his unfamiliarity with national parks, Kennedy was initially well received, but it takes time to catch up if you start from scratch. Why new administrations believe that a person with no previous experience would make a better director is not clear.

Babbitt seemed to be a secretary in the mold of fellow Arizonian Stewart Udall. Author of a book on Grand Canyon, where his family operated a park concession, he lifted the hearts of all Park Service people with his early pledge of support for the parks. But Babbitt's performance mystified and often dismayed the conservationists. His hand was undoubtedly weakened by an administration that soon backed away from promised reforms of logging, grazing, and mining practices. He spoke in defense of park protection and publicized park needs, but it was difficult to gauge his influence on the Clinton White House or to identify his contributions, although the Park Service budget and personnel ceilings fared better than those of most agencies.

Confidence in Kennedy ebbed after several of his early memorandums containing advice on proper employee behavior found their way into the *Washington Post*, creating vast amusement and strengthening general belief that Washington bureaucrats are seldom in touch with reality. Although he delighted in wearing the ranger uniform on all occasions, he would have been more popular with the rank and file had he not spoken dismissively of Park Service traditions and if he hadn't gone out of his way to avoid contact with staff members on his visits to the parks. Employees had trouble relating to him or detecting an orderly pattern to his leadership.

A generation ago, the authority of a park superintendent was compared to that of a ship's captain. Over time the size of the organization reflected the growth of the park system. The annual budget, a little over twenty million dollars when I joined, was by the end of the 1990s approaching two billion dollars, the number of park visits increasing from forty million to three hundred and fifty million. Regrettably, the Park Service was transformed into a bureaucracy, or nearly so. References to the captain of a ship were seldom heard because the outfit was so well supplied with admirals, but in times of stress the good ones took charge, as Bob Barbee did during the fires of 1988.

Bill Wade, superintendent of Shenandoah, put his career on the line in late 1992 when he decided to close portions of the Skyline Drive, the park's major attraction. He had trimmed expenditures every year for so long that there was no other choice. He had also managed to strengthen the park's research program and the monitoring of its biological health. He announced that the northern and southern ends of the road would be closed through the winter and spring. It wasn't the same as shutting the park down, but close.

The citizens of Front Royal, the gateway community at the northern entrance to the Skyline Drive, were incensed by the announcement, and the executive director of the town's Chamber of Commerce quickly organized resistance. When Wade walked into a meeting room on Capitol Hill he faced a group of businessmen from Front Royal and the Shenandoah Valley, several Virginia members of the House of Representatives, and the two Virginia senators often in the news, John Warner and Charles Robb. The sides, however, were not as lopsided as they seemed.

Wade is a big, bearded, earnest man who, on matters of principle, is on the likable side of obstinacy. If given a chance to explain his action he might have said that roads and trails in Shenandoah badly needed repairs, buildings and equipment were wearing out, utility pipes were leaking, and radio equipment was undependable. Dozens of staff positions couldn't be filled for lack of funds, leaving him without an assistant superintendent and a chief of maintenance. Two of the park's five campgrounds were closed indefinitely. The road closings would save $200,000. The money was desperately needed.

Wade could also have repeated what he'd often said before, that the park was literally dying. Vegetation is being attacked by acid rain carried from power plants and factories in the Ohio Valley and by tail-pipe emissions. Concentration of pollutants in summer are high enough to constitute a health hazard, frequently at a level the American Lung Association rates dangerous to people with heart and lung problems.

Sparkling clear views of distant Blue Ridge peaks are rare. Statistics kept by the Federal Aviation Administration show haze has reduced visibility by 80 percent since record-keeping began after World War II to an average of twelve miles on hot summer days. When the Skyline Drive was built in the 1930s, visitors could frequently see the Washington Monument seventy miles away.

The drive was constructed, Wade told a *Washington Post Magazine* reporter who, on October 31, 1993, did a story on his bold action, "as an elevated viewing platform. That's why they put it right down the backbone of the ridge. That's why they built seventy-eight overlooks; so people could pull off and look on either side and get those magnificent views. We have the worst air quality of any national park. And it's our job as protector of the resources to do something about it."

I'm just guessing what Wade might have said in the meeting. According to the Chamber of Commerce representative, his explanations were brushed aside. "We were saying, 'We don't care what you cut, but that road has to stay open.'" In a situation calling for finesse, or maybe capitulation, Wade was as inelastic as rawhide, drawing a line in the sand and refusing to retreat, even after the proceedings "got a little ugly."

I was astounded to hear of the stand-off. Not within living memory had that much congressional firepower been leveled at a field employee of the Park Service. The thought of those bigwigs stalking out of the room livid, bested, if you will, by a ship's captain, was intensely pleasurable. Of course Wade was overruled almost immediately by the director when the firepower was turned his way. But his colleagues must have gotten quite a lift out of his act of defiance, saying to themselves, as I did, "Way to go Bill!"

U U

In this book I have endeavored to express my esteem for the people who work in the national parks. This admiration is shared, I think, by most visitors who have encountered the friendly hospitality and dependable competence of the men and women who wear the green uniforms and Smokey Bear hats. On March 27, 1990, the *Washington Post* reported that the Roper organization had found that "at the top of the list" of a poll of how Americans view their federal agencies "was the Interior Department's National Park Service."

The growth of the national park idea from a single tract of frontier wilderness to a nationwide system preserving the best of what we have been given and what we have tried to be is such an undeviating success story that it seems almost to have been inevitable. On the whole, Congress has acted wisely and generously. Credit should fairly go also to the organization that scouted for new parks, displayed commendable prudence in balancing preservation with use, and served as the model for the other park agencies of the world.

The strength of the Park Service has derived from its ability to attract able people, beginning with the charismatic Steve Mather. There is always an outpouring of affection and emotion at the retirement of one of the organization's great old characters. Someone inevitably asks, "Will we ever see anyone that special again?" The answer in the 1990s is the same as it was in the 1920s when Mather stepped down. "We always have."

By the end of the 1990s the Park Service was in trouble, as it has been in the past and will be again. "How do you feel?" I asked an employee, an old friend. "Like a salmon swimming upstream," he replied, but with a smile. As we talked it was evident that he'd lost none of his relish for the work. He couldn't wait, he said, until they got it all going again. So the Mather tradition lives on: "Men and women are working, planning maneuvering, doing everything humanly possible to save and protect America's great natural wonders. It is a grinding and often heartbreaking job, but few jobs are worthier."

Afterword

Park geologist Rick Hutchinson, who received only a brief mention in this book, assuredly deserved more.

Rick's degree in earth sciences from the University of Iowa had brought him to Yellowstone as a seasonal naturalist in 1970. Stationed at Norris Geyser Basin, he was awakened one night by a slight but unmistakable earthquake. By daylight he had counted fifty-five more and knew what he wanted to do with his life. "The more things shake," he told me, "the better I feel." Small of frame and meticulous in speech, with a welcoming grin and a ginger beard that covered his throat like a ruff, Rick was totally unselfconscious. You could depend on a quip or a bit of Hutchinson down-to-earth philosophy, yet he was so absorbed in his work he often neglected to use his annual leave. "What I do is better than a vacation," he would say.

His endless study and observation of Yellowstone's array of thermal phenomena earned him world renown. He facilitated the research being done by outside scientists and was invited to inspect the extensive thermal fields in the other three places on earth where the interior fires are so close to the surface: in Iceland and New Zealand and on Russia's Kamchatka Peninsula.

Not totally immersed in his scientific investigations, he married the park botanist. It was a union of equals. His wife Jennifer knew as much about plants as Rick knew about geysers and hot springs. He would often collect a crowd as he walked through the geyser basins, stopping to answer questions and explain the mysterious workings of the thermal features.

The story is told that one day, as he was explaining to a group of visitors that he needed a portable computer to record field data, a young woman slipped one out of her pack and went to work. Diane Dustman, a computer whiz with an interest in geology, soon became a Park Service volunteer and assisted Rick on many studies.

Rick roamed through Yellowstone for twenty-seven years, indifferent to grizzlies or the many other dangers present in the backcountry. His luck ran out on March 3, 1997, when he and Diane were killed by an avalanche while monitoring thermal features on Factory Hill, a peak of nearly ten thousand feet in the Heart Lake region of the park.

Yellowstone normally doesn't clear its roads of snow until May 1. Because of Rick's fondness for Yellowstone, however, it was decided to hold his memorial service in the park interior. A gigantic effort by the maintenance division and the park concessioner was required to plow a route through the deepest snowpack in forty years from the residential area at Mammoth to Madison Junction, a distance of thirty-five miles, where people boarded snow coaches from West Yellowstone for the final sixteen miles to Old Faithful.

Wearing parkas and daypacks, three hundred of Rick's friends gathered in the unheated lobby of the Old Faithful Lodge on March 14. A dozen speakers told anecdotes and recalled the qualities that made Rick such a beloved character. There was more laughter than tears. Food contributed by participants featured chocolate, Rick's special weakness.

In a moving tribute written for the Park Service *Newsletter*, superintendent Mike Finley caught the spirit of this kindly, generous, funny, warm-hearted man:

> For more than a quarter of a century Rick Hutchinson has been a Yellowstone institution, one of those rare, authentic experts who can be counted on to help the many people, visitors and researchers alike, who come and go in a place like Yellowstone. It was almost as if he was a part of the park itself, a gentle presence that had always been here and would go on forever. Nobody loved Yellowstone more, or was more wholly devoted to embracing its spirit and caring for its wonders. Rick touched many lives here, and will not be forgotten.

Notes

ix   "He recalls going": W. C. Storrick, *The Battle of Gettysburg* (Harrisburg: Mount Pleasant Press, 1969), p. 5.

xiii   "The chief aim": Freeman Tilden, *Interpreting Our Heritage* (Chapel Hill: University of North Carolina Press, 1977), p. 9.

xiv   "Let's close": Bernard DeVoto, "The Easy Chair," *Harpers*, Oct. 1953.

xv   "Dear Steve": Robert Shankland, *Steve Mather of the National Parks* (New York: Alfred A. Knopf, 1970), p. 7.

xviii   "There was": George B. Hartzog, Jr., *Battling for the National Parks* (Mt. Kisco: Moyer Bell, 1988), p. xii.

xviii   "George Hartzog proved": Hartzog, Jr., *Battling for the National Parks*, dust-jacket blurb.

xxi   "I don't have to see": Ken Ashley, National Park Service History Collection, Harpers Ferry Center, Harpers Ferry, W. Va.

xxii   "Interpretation is": Freeman Tilden, *Interpreting Our History*, 3d ed. (Chapel Hill: University of North Carolina Press, 1977), p. 9.

7   "The secret of snow": Henry Beston, *Northern Farm* (New York: Ballantine Books, 1976), p. 19.

20   "Roger Rudolph": Logbooks have been kept at all patrol cabins since army days. In them, travelers record observations worthy of noting or passing thoughts. When filled, the logs are placed in the Yellowstone Archives at Mammoth.

24   "beyond the reach": Aubrey Haines, *The Yellowstone Story* (Boulder: Colorado Associated University Press, 1977), vol. 1, p. 146.

27   "I regarded the National Park Service": National Park Service History Collection, Harpers Ferry Center, Harpers Ferry, W. Va.

38   "They lurked": Shankland, *Steve Mather*, p. 122.

39   "A travel writer": Haines, *The Yellowstone Story*, vol. 2, p. 160.

40   "Their carcasses": Gen. W. E. Strong, *A Trip to the Yellowstone National Park in July, August, and September, 1875* (Norman: University of Oklahoma Press, 1968), p. 105.

40   "Nature, abandoning": Kenneth H. Baldwin, *Enchanted Enclosure* (Washington, D.C.: Office of the Chief of Engineers, U.S. Army, 1976), p. 67.

40   "with tucked-up skirts": Baldwin, *Enchanted Enclosure*, p. 80.

40   "If authorized to do so": H. Duane Hampton, *How the U.S. Cavalry Saved Our National Parks* (Bloomington: Indiana University Press, 1971), p. 55.

40   "He went upon": Hiram M. Chittenden, *Yellowstone National Park* (Stanford: Stanford University Press, 1954), p. 109.

41   "and the 'go-fever' ": Rudyard Kipling, *Old Yellowstone Days*, ed. Paul Schullery (Boulder: Associated University Press, 1979), pp. 92–93.

42   "There is a photograph": Haines, *The Yellowstone Story*, vol. 2, p. 173.

42   "A photograph of the park's finest": Ibid., p. 292.

52   "the lumbering Yellowstone Wagons": Ibid., p. 107.

69   "We would be sitting": Kipling, *Old Yellowstone Days*, p. 72.

71   "a big feller": Larry Bausness, "The Bison in Art and History," *American West Magazine* (March–April 1977): 11.

71   "This should provide": James B. Trefethen, *Crusade for Wildlife* (Harrisburg: Stackpole, 1961), p. 85.

72   "For six days": Trefethen, *Crusade for Wildlife*, p. 86.

72   "It would be difficult": Ibid., p. 89.

72   "On the floor": Ibid., pp. 89–90.

74   "His arms and outfit": Ibid., p. 39.

75   "The bison of Yellowstone": Mary Meagher, *The Bison of Yellowstone National Park* (Washington, D.C.: U.S. Government Printing Office, 1973), p. 1.

76   "and thanked his god": Bernard DeVoto, *The Journals of Lewis and Clark* (Boston: Houghton Mifflin, 1953), p. 189.

76   "Encamped opposit": DeVoto, *Journals*, p. 239.

77   "calling this western tour": Wallace Stegner, *The Uneasy Chair* (Garden City: Doubleday, 1974), p. 293.

77   "used to sit": Stegner, *Uneasy Chair*, p. 382.

77   "tourists who": Ibid., p. 383.

79   "Thar was old grit": Bernard DeVoto, *Across the Wide Missouri* (Boston: Houghton Mifflin, 1947), p. 46.

79   "that if I am": DeVoto, *Across the Wide Missouri*, pp. 361–62.

80   "Something moves": Ibid., p. 362.

82   "I remember Harry": Haines, *The Yellowstone Story*, vol. 2, p. 198.

90   "For black Americans": Benjamin Hooks, *Amsterdam News*, Dec. 30, 1978.

113   "When you were up there": Haines, *The Yellowstone Story*, vol. 2, p. 295.

115   "The superintendent said": National Park Service History Collection, Harpers Ferry Center, Harpers Ferry, W. Va.

119   "notably enriched": DeVoto, *Across the Wide Missouri*, p. 306.

121   "His wound": Jim Bishop, *The Day Lincoln Was Shot* (New York: Harper and Bros., 1955), p. 216.

123   "a very attractive gateway town": Sam Eagle and Ed Eagle, *West Yellowstone's Seventieth Anniversary* (West Yellowstone: Eagle Company, 1978), p. 17.

124   "We have tried": Eagle and Eagle, *West Yellowstone's Seventieth Anniversary*, p. 17.

130   "In honor of": Luke Dalton, "Decker Geyser," p. 5. Typescript report in Geothermal Files, Yellowstone National Park.

137   "I'd fought fire": Steve Smith, *Fly the Biggest Piece Back* (Missoula: Mountain Press, 1979), p. 162.

145   "through all future time": Chittenden, *Yellowstone National Park*, p. 181.

146   "an exceptionally difficult": Ibid., p. 249.

150   "that chaotic wilderness": Haines, *The Yellowstone Story*, vol. 2, p. 218.

155   "too little mail": Ibid., vol. 2, p. 191.

175   "Not because of good service": *Yellowstone National Park Concessions Management Review*, Yellowstone Concessions Study Team, 1976, pp. 11–12.

179   "I have a smoke": Jim Carrier, *Summer of Fire* (Salt Lake City: Peregrine Smith Books, 1989), p. 10. This is the most complete and dependable of the several illustrated booklets on the fires. Carrier was a roving correspondent for the *Denver Post*, well acquainted with Yellowstone. Dan Sholly's adventure, which follows, comes from this source.

182   "In my mind": Carrier, *Summer of Fire*, p. 24.

182   "on July 21": Paul Schullery, "Yellowstone Fires: A Preliminary Report," *Northwest Science* 63, no. 1 (1989): 48.

183   "That kind": Alan Carey and Sandy Carey, *Yellowstone's Red Summer* (Flagstaff: Northland, 1989), p. 40.

184   "The end result": Ross Simpson, *The Fires of '88* (Helena: American Geographic, 1989), p. 25.

184   "strike and move": A good description of this technique is in Simpson, *Fires of '88*, p. 44.

185   "a mere scratch": Thomas Hackett, "Fire," *New Yorker*, Oct. 2, 1989, p. 53.

185   "Bump up!": Hackett, "Fire," p. 26.

185   "The smoke seared and scalded": Ibid., p. 53.

185   "to contain": Ibid., p. 54.

185   "slipped through the fire": Ibid., p. 54.

185   "At one time": Carey and Carey, *Yellowstone's Red Summer*, p. 75.

186   "We began flying": Ibid., p. 78.

186   "The heat of the fire": Ibid., p. 79.

186   "The probability of ignition": Ibid., p. 44.

187   "the inaccurate impression": Conrad Smith, "Flames, Firefighters and Moonscapes: Network Television Pictures of the Yellowstone Fires." Paper presented at the Third Annual Visual Communications Conference, Park City, Utah, June 26, 1989, p. 1.

187   "the fires that will not die": Smith, "Flames, Firefighters," p. 10.

190   "Oh, God!": Hackett, "Fire," p. 71.

190   "Trees blew down": George Wuerther, *Yellowstone and the Fires of Change* (Salt Lake City: Haggis House Publications, 1988), p. 50.

193   "We expect it": David Jeffery, "Yellowstone: The Great Fires of 1988," *National Geographic*, Feb. 1989, p. 261.

193   "4:04 wind": Jeffery, "Yellowstone," p. 263.

194   "Come down now": Carey and Carey, *Yellowstone's Red Summer*, p. 1194

194   "No amount": Robert Ekey, *Yellowstone on Fire!* (Billings: Billings Gazette, 1989), p. 75.

194   "a natural force": Peter Mattheissen, "Our National Parks: The Case for Burning," *New York Times Magazine*, Dec. 11, 1988, p. 128.

194   "Today, if we get": Jeffery, "Yellowstone," p. 268.

194   "Rain fell": Carrier, *Summer of Fire*, p. 90.

195   "All we ask for": Hackett, "Fire," p. 51.

195   "The station was fogged": Carrier, *Summer of Fire*, p. 90.

196   "The ecology is sitting under the ground": Ibid., p. 88.

196   "There is a widespread if informal feeling": Susan M. Mills, ed., *The Greater Yellowstone Postfire Assessment* (Washington, D.C.: National Park Service/ U.S. Forest Service, 1989), p. 4.

199   "would put pressure": Greater Yellowstone Postfire Ecological Assessment Workshop, *Ecological Consequences*, p. 36.

200   "Barbee is": Matthiessen, "Our National Parks," p. 123.

204   "Chase's work": Holmes Rolston III, "Biology and Philosophy in Yellowstone," *Biology and Philosophy* 4 (1989): 14.

206   "My legs were weak": Richard Conniff, "Yellowstone's 'Rebirth' amid the Ashes Is Not Neat or Simple, but It's Real," *Smithsonian* (Sept. 1989): 41.

206   "Three pairs of grizzlies": Coniff, "Yellowstone's 'Rebirth.' "

207   "the fires of 1988 represented": William H. Romme and Don G. Despain, "In the Long History of Fire in the Greater Yellowstone Ecosystem," *Western Wildlands* 15 (Summer 1989): 17.

208   "the resource is not": Paul Schullery, *Mountain Time* (New York: Nick Lyons Books, 1984), p. 71.

209   "It is not unreasonable": *High Country News*, Oct. 7, 1994.

212   "By the way Steve": Shankland, *Steve Mather*, p. 10.

212   "Knock them": H. R. Haldeman with Joseph D. Mona, *The Ends of Power* (New York: Times Books, 1978), p. 172.

214   "Career employees": Hartzog, Jr., *Battling for the National Parks*, p. 269.

214   "Rumor had it": Ibid., p. 270.

215   "It was": Ibid., pp. 271–72.

215   "Because I believe": Lorraine Mintzmyer, regional director, testifying before the House Subcommittee on Civil Service, Sept. 24, 1991, reported in *High Country News*, Oct. 7, 1991. This issue contains the testimony of Mintz-

myer and regional director, Forest Service, and a detailed account of the rise and fall of the "vision plan" for the Greater Yellowstone Area.

216   "Give her": Haines, *The Yellowstone Story*, vol. 2, p. 320.

218   "significant political": *High Country News*, Oct. 7, 1991.

219   "A few of us": *High Country News*, June 3, 1991.

219   "the aging infrastructure": "New Trails, New Travels," pt. 1, *Christian Science Monitor*, May 28, 1991.

221   "snapshots": *National Parks in Crisis: A Summer 1993 Update on Threats Endangering America's National Parks* (Washington, D.C.: National Park and Conservation Association), 1993.

222   "a restless career": Edwards Park, "Around the Mall and Beyond," *Smithsonian* (Feb. 1993): 16.

225   "Men and women": Shankland, *Steve Mather*, p. 346.

Index

BILL EVERHART earned a bachelor's degree from Gettysburg College and after serving in the Infantry in World War II received master's degrees from Columbia University and Penn State. He began his twenty-seven-year tenure with the National Park Service as a park historian at Gettysburg and served in several other parks and on surveys to identify historic landmarks and national seashores. As assistant director for interpretation, he oversaw construction and was first director of an interpretive design center at Harpers Ferry that designs all NPS museums and produces its films and publications. Retired from the NPS in 1977, he was a visiting professor at Clemson University and a resident consultant to the Desert Museum in Tucson. He is the author of *The National Park Service* (1972; revised, 1983).